Legal Certainty in a Contemporary Context

Mark Fenwick • Stefan Wrbka
Editors

Legal Certainty in a Contemporary Context

Private and Criminal Law Perspectives

Springer

Editors
Mark Fenwick
Faculty of Law
Kyushu University
Fukuoka, Fukuoka
Japan

Stefan Wrbka
Faculty of Law
Kyushu University
Fukuoka, Fukuoka
Japan

ISBN 978-981-10-0112-3 ISBN 978-981-10-0114-7 (eBook)
DOI 10.1007/978-981-10-0114-7

Library of Congress Control Number: 2016934311

Printed on acid-free paper

This Springer imprint is published by Springer Nature
The registered company is Springer Science+Business Media Singapore Pte Ltd

Contents

List of Contributors

Mark Fenwick Faculty of Law, Kyushu University, Fukuoka, Japan

Branislav Hazucha Graduate School of Law, Hokkaido University, Sapporo, Japan

Jakob Søren Hedegaard Assistant Attorney, Lassen Ricard, Copenhagen, Denmark

Jason D. Hitch Lawyer, Sydney, NSW, Australia

Katrin Höffler Faculty of Law, Goettingen University, Goettingen, Germany

Georg C. Langheld Noerr LLP, Munich, Germany

Zhen Meng Nanjing University of Science and Technology, School of Public Affairs, Department of Law, Nanjing, China

Sebastian Stehle Faculty of Law, Munich University (LMU), Munich, Germany

Andreas Werkmeister Faculty of Law, Munich University, Munich, Germany

Stefan Wrbka Faculty of Law, Kyushu University, Fukuoka, Japan

The Shifting Meaning of Legal Certainty

Mark Fenwick and Stefan Wrbka

Contents

Abstract In the context of legal modernity, the principle of legal certainty – the idea that the law must be sufficiently clear to provide those subject to legal norms with the means to regulate their own conduct and to protect against the arbitrary exercise of public power – has operated as a foundational rule of law value. As such, legal certainty has played a vital role in determining the space of individual freedom and the scope of state power. In this way, the ideal of legal certainty has been central in stabilizing normative expectations and in providing a framework for social interaction, as well as defining individual freedom and political power in modern societies. Legal certainty has been pivotal to the project of political liberalism and the ideals and aspirations of political modernity. This chapter introduces the concept of legal certainty and introduces the idea that the meaning of legal certainty has shifted.

Keywords Legal certainty • Legal theory • Legal modernity

1 The Shifting Meaning of Legal Certainty

In the context of legal modernity, the principle of legal certainty—the idea that the law must be sufficiently clear to provide those subject to legal norms with the means to regulate their own conduct and to protect against the arbitrary exercise of public power—has operated as a foundational rule of law value. As such, legal certainty has played a vital role in determining the space of individual freedom and the scope

M. Fenwick • S. Wrbka (✉)
Faculty of Law, Kyushu University, Fukuoka, Japan
e-mail: stefan.wrbka@law.kyushu-u.ac.jp

M. Fenwick, S. Wrbka (eds.), *Legal Certainty in a Contemporary Context*,
DOI 10.1007/978-981-10-0114-7_1

of state power. In this way, the ideal of legal certainty has been central in stabilizing normative expectations and in providing a framework for social interaction, as well as defining individual freedom and political power in modern societies. Legal certainty has been pivotal to the project of political liberalism and the ideals and aspirations of political modernity.

Of course, this demand for clarity and predictability can come into conflict with other important principles, such as public policy and, on occasion, substantive justice. And yet, in spite of these conflicts and the empirical fact that certainty cannot always be fully realized, the ideal of legal certainty has functioned as a core value and aspiration that has structured normative debates both at a national, regional and international level. The requirement of certainty is an explicit constitutional principle in most domestic constitutions. It also functions as a core principle in many regional organizations; both the European Union and the European Court of Human Rights recognize legal certainty as one of a small number of such general or fundamental principles. As some of the chapters in this volume attest, certainty also functions as an important constraint at the level of contemporary public international law.

Nevertheless, in spite of its central role in the development of modern legal order, there have been a number of academic critiques of law's aspirations to legal certainty. Starting with American Realism in the 1930s and culminating with more recent work in Critical Legal Studies, successive generations of scholars have questioned the prevailing formalism of modern law and this pursuit of certainty. One significant effect of such critiques has been the introduction of a "counter-concept" to that of certainty, namely that of legal indeterminacy. The indeterminacy thesis, in its most radical articulation suggests that law is always indefinite and that *any* outcome decision can be justified by reference to a particular norm. Even in its softer versions, advocates of indeterminacy suggest that while the law constrains actors within the legal system, it cannot uniquely determine outcomes. According to either account, law is just politics in disguise.

Although this type of critique has not had a profound impact on legal practice—at least, in terms of the commitment to legal certainty—it does articulate the broader shift, which this book wishes to explore, namely a recent shift in the meaning of legal certainty.

Over recent decades, legal certainty has come under increasing pressure from a number of competing demands that are made of contemporary law, in particular the demand that the law be more flexible and responsive to a social environment characterized by rapid economic, social and technological change. In particular, the expectation that the law operates in new transnational contexts and regulates ever-widening spheres of social life has created a new degree of uncertainty about legal certainty. These social and economic transformations raise difficult questions regarding both the meaning of legal certainty, as well as its possibility and desirability.

This book aims to address these issues by bringing together scholars from various fields of legal debate to examine the shifting contemporary meaning of legal certainty. In particular, the book focuses on exploring the emerging tensions that exist between the demand for legal certainty and the challenges of regulating complex, late modern societies. The book is divided into two parts; the first part focusing on debates around legal certainty in a private law (broadly defined) context and the second part focuses on debates in a criminal law context.

2 Chapters

The discussion is divided into two main parts: legal certainty in the context of private law, on the one hand, and in the context of criminal law, on the other.

Stefan Wrbka opens the private law discussion with comments on the certainty concept in three different jurisdictions: the EU, Austria and Japan. Using a range of recent private law examples from these regions, he explains that legal certainty can be understood in a variety of sometimes closely related, sometimes opposing ideas, including key challenges for private law such as legal clarity, legal stability and legal peace. Depending on the social, economic and cultural circumstances the respective legislator may put the emphasis on different certainty notions. In the later part of his analysis the author explains that the wish for legal flexibility (to accompany special scenarios) might have an impact on the level of legislative activity and clarity. The three jurisdictions chosen for the analysis exemplify these trends, which lead to interesting conclusions from a comparative law perspective.

Branislav Hazucha adds insights from the viewpoint of intellectual property. In this context he discusses the interplay of legal certainty with private ordering. In doing so he takes a different approach than the one chosen by Wrbka and puts the emphasis on *non*-legislative trends and consequences for legal certainty. Hazucha argues that the area of intellectual property enjoys a special treatment (different from the conventional rule-standard dichotomy) that is caused by the rapid development of intellectual property-related technologies and globalisation. An increasing number of private players enter the market and aim to create their own legal rules and settings under the guise of increasing the certainty level. The author critically examines the consequences of this development and points out that in various cases such efforts are—despite several positive examples—not unproblematic and could actually put a risk to maintaining a high level of legal certainty. He also concludes that courts enjoy an important role in this respect, because ultimately it is for them to determine the authority of private ordering for the sake of safeguarding legal certainty.

Jason Hitch switches from intellectual property to international commercial arbitration as seen from the perspective of transnationality. Like Hazucha he puts the emphasis on certainty trends that do not—at least not directly—stem from a certain state power, but are rather detached from any national legal system. In this context Hitch focuses on the term 'anational' and examines the conditions under which international commercial arbitral awards may be considered as not 'belonging' to a certain jurisdiction. The author points out that classifying international commercial arbitral awards as transnational and anational decisions might—despite international mechanisms (such as the New York Convention)—create some interesting questions of legitimacy, validity and recognition. He argues that from the viewpoint of state power the increasing significance of international commercial arbitral awards might lead to non-negligible challenges for legal certainty.

Jakob Hedegaard and Stefan Wrbka return to more conventional forms of rule-creating by taking a look at legal certainty from the perspective of EU lawmaking and EU case law. More precisely, the authors discuss the certainty concept in the context of the consumer notion. Hedegaard and Wrbka examine different consumer definitions found at the EU level and argue that the existence of different definitions might cause some problems from the viewpoint of enhancing clarity and transparency. At the same time they point out that the vagueness of the consumer notions found in several legislative instruments might be explained with the wish to accommodate the wish for legal flexibility that can be exercised whenever special scenarios ask for special treatment. In the later part of their analysis the authors explain that—unlike the EU legislator—EU case law has taken a stricter approach and has been aiming to standardise the consumer concepts by introducing a unitary consumer definition. This might remedy the uncertainty caused by EU legislation, but at the same time raises certain questions of individual appropriateness.

Zhen Meng concludes the private law part by commenting on the Chinese Trust Law enacted 2001. She points out that this law creates some considerable challenges from the viewpoint of safeguarding legal certainty, which is mainly due to the vagueness of the instrument. In particular the question of locating the ownership of trust property has remained widely unsolved under the Chinese Trust Law. The author shows that various different interpretations exist to remedy this shortcoming. Although one might expect that the unsolved ownership dimension would be detrimental to the success of trusts, Meng explains that the Chinese trust business is a flourishing economy. She concludes her analysis with the prediction that the legal landscape nevertheless might change in the nearer future to satisfy the call for a clearer legislative framework to compete with foreign trust systems.

Georg Langheld opens the criminal law part of this book by examining EU criminal law from a linguistic perspective. He focuses on the fact that the equal authenticity of 24 different languages poses difficulties for upholding a high level of legal certainty. In case different language versions (of EU laws) lead to different legal consequences EU case law would have to clarify which language version enjoys authority. Although the existence of 24 authentic versions aims to simplify the determination of rights and wrongs for EU citizens by providing them with a translation into their respective mother tongue, certain predictability and transparency concerns clearly exist. Langheld tries to look for a fair solution for affected citizens by differentiating between legal norms and sanctions. He concludes that uniform interpretation efforts of the ECJ should play a stronger role with respect to sanctions and less in the context of legal norms in the sense of overriding the authenticity of linguistic nuances of norms.

Sebastian Stehle discusses the significance of empirical judgements in criminal proceedings and their interrelationship with legal certainty. The author begins his analysis with explaining different forms of empirical judgements. In doing this he puts an emphasis on the degree of objectivity that can (or cannot) be achieved by applying empirical judgements in court decision-making. Although empirical judgements could close argumentative gaps, they might—depending on their universality and accuracy—create certain threats for unbiased court decisions. In the second part of his analysis Stehle more closely looks at the situation of Germany and possible negative implications of an overuse of empirical judgements for objectivity and legal certainty. He concludes his contribution by arguing that a good balance must be found between applying empirical judgements and guaranteeing a high level of objectivity for the sake of predictability, fairness and clarity.

Mark Fenwick examines the issue of legal certainty from the perspective of contemporary business regulation, with specific reference to corporate criminal law. This refers to the body of legal norms that imposes criminal liability on the corporation, rather than individual members of the corporation, such as directors, officers, managers or employees. This chapter suggests that the reach of corporate criminal law has greatly expanded over the last three decades. In addition, criminal law in this field is often plagued by a lack of legal certainty as to the scope of the offence. Examples of legal "uncertainty" are introduced from various offences. The chapter goes on to argue that the legal basis for the new corporate criminal law—the doctrine of corporate legal liability—is similarly characterized by uncertainties of various kinds. The discussion highlights how a concern with legal certainty seems to run up against other policy considerations, notably the pragmatic need to take meaningful action against corporate wrongdoing. The chapter concludes with the suggestion that in the context of contemporary corporate criminal law, the meaning of legal certainty has been transformed from a fundamental principle of criminal justice to one of a number of competing policy considerations that have to be resolved in responding to socially undesirable corporate behaviour. The combined effect of this net-widening and legal "uncertainty" has been to greatly increase legal risk for companies and to provide a strong incentive to invest in internal governance mechanisms aimed at social enforcement, i.e. corporate compliance.

Kathrin Höffler examines the issue of certainty in the context of classifying offenders in criminal law. There is a long tradition of classifying offenders based on certain attributions and, in recent years, it is generally considered as a negative approach, as it carries the risk of excluding certain categories of offender by labeling. But a closer look reveals that classifications of this type are still routinely occurring within criminal justice and that such classification often takes place without becoming fully conscious. As a result neither the benefits nor the potential risks of this classifying approach is sufficiently taken into consideration. The chapter argues that systematic analysis of the historical contexts of existing types of offenders will help to answer the question if classifying delinquent behavior is an appropriate way to deal with offenders and the consequences of criminal behavior.

Andreas Werkmeister, who takes a look at International Criminal Law, completes the elaborations in this book. In this context the author discusses the tension between two different approaches: Liberal Criminal Law and Enemy Criminal Law. He argues that the trend at the international level differs from the prevailing trend found nationally in the sense that within International Criminal Law one can find a stronger reliance on the Enemy Criminal Law concept. Explaining that International Criminal Law has its roots in some of the darkest ages in modern history, Werkmeister defines the approach taken at the international level as a fight against the enemy of all mankind. In the later part of his analysis he discusses the consequences of this trend for the dignity of the offender and from the perspective of legal certainty.

Part I
Perspectives from Private Law

Comments on Legal Certainty from the Perspective of European, Austrian and Japanese Private Law

Stefan Wrbka

Contents

Abstract On occasion, lawmakers justify their moves with the argument of enhanced legal certainty. But what does 'legal certainty' mean? This chapter explains the certainty concept by taking a look at some more recent European (Union), Austrian and Japanese private law issues. In doing so, it argues that the certainty concept shows various facets that address different legal issues, comprising ideas of *inter alia* legal clarity, legal stability and legal peace.

Although improved legal certainty should generally be welcome, the chapter indicates that an overemphasis of this concept might create some tension with other arguably important considerations – most notably with legal flexibility. The examples given in this analysis illustrate how policy makers try to react to this. Although the strategies taken in the discussed jurisdictions might differ, they all aim to reconcile the interests of natural and legal persons affected by lawmaking.

Keywords Legal certainty • Private law • European Union • Austria • Japan • Law of Obligations • Law reform

S. Wrbka (✉)
Faculty of Law, Kyushu University, Fukuoka, Japan
e-mail: stefan.wrbka@law.kyushu-u.ac.jp

M. Fenwick, S. Wrbka (eds.), *Legal Certainty in a Contemporary Context*,
DOI 10.1007/978-981-10-0114-7_2

1 Introduction

Legal certainty is undeniably one of the 'fundamental principles'[1] or 'highest values'[2] of every modern legal system. With respect to European Private Law, for example, the Draft Common Frame of Reference (hereinafter, *DCFR*)[3] is a good case to exemplify this. It considers legal certainty as being an expression of (contractual) security,[4] one of the four key private law principles identified by the DCFR.[5] In the accompanying general comments on the DCFR, Christian von Bar, Hugh Beale, Eric Clive and Hans Schulte-Nölke, four members of the research group consortium that drafted the DCFR, list legal certainty as one of 15 key elements of European and domestic private law.[6]

The aim of this contribution is to highlight different notions of legal certainty in private law with the example of three jurisdictions – the European Union (*hereinafter*, EU), Austria and Japan. Although one might expect that the perceptions of the certainty concept are quite similar in these jurisdictions – with Austrian private law to a certain extent influenced by EU law and Japanese private law (at least) basically belonging to the same legal family as Austrian private law, i.e., to the group of civil law countries – the analysis shall illustrate that legal certainty can be interpreted in different ways, even with respect to the same umbrella area – in our case private law – and more than that: even within one and the same jurisdiction. The examples used in this analysis shall further show the challenges these three jurisdictions face when aiming to improve legal certainty.

The contribution will start by taking a brief, more general look at the legal certainty concept before looking slightly closer at key issues of legal certainty at the EU, Austrian and Japanese private law levels. In this respect I will not only define the notion of legal certainty in the area of private law, but aim to highlight certain possible tensions and challenges that the respective understanding can cause or lead to. The contribution concludes with comments on the steps taken thus far in the respective legal certainty context(s) and general remarks on the possible future of the concept(s) in the three jurisdictions.

---

[1] See, e.g., Bydlinski F (1988), p. 173, where the author refers to legal certainty as a 'fundamental principle' (*Fundamentalprinzip*).

[2] See, e.g., Canaris (1969), p. 17, where Canaris refers to legal certainty as a 'highest value' (*oberster Wert*).

[3] The DCFR, published in 2009, is the result of extensive research on European private law rules primarily (but not only) focusing on contract law. For details on the DCFR see, e.g., Wrbka (2015a, pp. 195–208, 2014b), pp. 159–160; von Bar et al. (2009); von Bar and Clive (2009).

[4] See Recital 22 of the DCFR Principles. Rule I. – I:102 DCFR (Interpretation and development) lists – in its third paragraph – legal certainty as one of the parameters that need to be taken into consideration in the 'interpretation and development' of private law rules (falling under the DCFR) – see Rule I. – I:102(2)(c) DCFR.

[5] The other three are: freedom, justice and efficiency.

[6] von Bar et al. (2009), p. 10.

2 The Notion of Legal Certainty in General and in Private Law in Particular

At first sight, the term 'legal certainty' might seem unambiguous. However, when taking a closer look, one will realise that the certainty concept shows several, sometimes closely related, sometimes opposing facets. As, for example, Franz Bydlinski, points out in a broader context, one has to understand the concept as an umbrella term that can be subdivided into certain categories. According to Bydlinski, one should differentiate between the following certainty notion layers: legal clarity (*Rechtsklarheit*), legal stability (*Rechtsstabilität*), legal accessibility (*Rechtszugänglichkeit*), legal peace (*Rechtsfriede*) and legal enforcement (*Rechtsdurchsetzung*).[7] In a comparable vein is Claus-Wilhelm Canaris' model. Canaris explains that legal certainty could embody any of the following, narrower concepts: legal firmness and predictability (*Bestimmtheit* and *Vorhersehbarkeit*), legislative and judicial stability and continuity (*Stabilität* and *Kontinuität*) and practicability of the application of law (*Praktikabilität der Rechtsanwendung*).[8]

Several authors have sought to define the meaning of legal certainty with respect to their respective research fields. Some of these elaborations – at least to a certain degree – touch upon questions linked (also) to private law issues. Jaap Hage, for example, looks at the certainty concept primarily from the viewpoint of how to create legal norms in civil law countries. He emphasises the importance of legal certainty understood as legal predictability and stability from the user's point of view and explains that these goals are best achieved by reserving lawmaking competences to the legislator, who anchors legal norms into statutory law. The positive consequence from a clear allocation of legislative competences and the written compilation/codification of rights and duties is that 'the rules only need to be looked up'.[9] This should guarantee a solid legislative procedure and simplify the finding of what – from a legislative perspective – is to be considered as right and wrong.[10]

On the same two subpillars of legal certainty – legal predictability and stability – rests Reza Banakar's explanation of the certainty concept in the context of the rule of law. Banakar argues that both principles – legal certainty and the rule of law – are immanently interlinked with the question of legitimacy and that it is the duty of the legislator to prevent arbitrariness that could impair legal stability and predictability.[11]

---

[7] For details, see Bydlinski F (1988, p. 293, 2011), p. 325.

[8] For details, see Canaris (1969), p. 17.

[9] Hage (2014a), p. 4.

[10] At a different occasion Hage comments on legal certainty from the viewpoint of legal philosophy. He (once again) links the discussion to the concept of legal positivism – in the context of normative legal positivism – and refers to Thomas Hobbes. Hage explains that Hobbes can be considered as a prime advocate of 'an effective state authority' to achieve legal peace and clarity with the help of a set of precise and comprehensive rules. For details see Hage (2014b), p. 331 with reference to Hobbes' 'Leviathan'.

[11] Banakar (1998), pp. 353 et seq.

Andreas Petzold, Jürgen Neyer and (again) Banakar discuss the certainty concept in the context of cross-border transactions. The authors explain that the existence of diverse legal regimes could impair legal predictability and lead to negative economic consequences. This would be the consequence of difficulties in determining the applicable law, in particular in absence of a contractual agreement. Such confusion could result from both the parallel existence of state-made statutory laws and private ordering or from the availability of conceptually different national laws.[12] I will return to this issue briefly in the context of EU law.

Bram Akkermans comments on legal certainty in the context of property law. He points out that the concept can be used to explain the idea behind the prescription of property rights. In particular for the sake of satisfying the wish for enhanced (external) clarity it could – under certain circumstances – be desirable to take stronger account of fairness considerations and grant property rights to people who exercise rights-like control over property. The prime example for this can be seen in acquiring property in good faith.[13]

Looking at legal certainty from a civil procedural perspective, Fokke Fernhout and Remco van Rhee focus on the legal stability dimension of legal certainty. Fernhout and van Rhee argue that fixed periods for taking legal actions must be welcome from the viewpoint of realising legal peace and clarity. Only under certain, limited conditions fairness considerations could enjoy preference over legal certainty. The reinstatement in a case of procedural default can be considered as a prime example.[14]

[12] For further details, see Petzold (1998), p. 283; Neyer (1998), pp. 403 and 416; Banakar (1998), p. 385.

[13] Akkermans (2014), p. 93.

[14] Fernhout and van Rhee (2014), p. 295. The legal certainty concept is, of course, also discussed in other areas than within private law. One such example is, e.g., found in the field of criminal law. Johannes Keiler, Michele Panzavolta and David Roes discuss legal certainty in that context and by doing this stress the legal predictability aspect of legal certainty and explain that criminal law must meet a very high standard of unambiguousness to meet this demand. This is the consequence of the informative side of criminal law, i.e., of the idea that everybody should be able to predict the possible (il)legality of actions and the respective legal consequences thereof – see Keiler et al. (2014), p. 134. Aalt Willem Heringa adds that criminal law (as viewed from the state power or execution side) is characterised by the wish to accomplish legal peace. He further explains that the ultimate source for legal certainty should be seen in constitutions, because they allocate legal and legislative competences and powers among different stakeholders to accommodate different expressions of legal certainty – see Heringa (2014), p. 157. Another example of a non-private law area, where one can find discussions of legal certainty is administrative law. Chris Backes and Mariolina Eliantonio emphasise the practicability of the application of law and legal accessibility side of legal certainty in that area. They list legal certainty as one of eight key principles of administrative law in Europe, with some other more prominent principles being the right to be heard, the equality principle and the principle of impartiality – for details see Backes and Eliantonio (2014), p. 197.

These elaborations show us that legal certainty can be understood in several ways. It is the concrete circumstance that defines the certainty concept.[15] When discussing it in the context of private law, one will usually approach it in one of the two following ways. First (and arguably more often), the focus can be put on legal clarity, stability, predictability or transparency. We could refer to this first group of legal certainty considerations as the group of 'legal clarification'. Here the question arises either whether rules exist at all or – if they exist – to which extent legal norms should (or actually do) leave room for interpretation. Put differently (with respect to the latter): How precise are legal provisions? How precise should they be? The clearer the wording and the legislator's intention, the less ambiguity and confusion exist for those who apply or are subject to relevant provisions.

Second, legal certainty could be understood in a more 'value-oriented justice'[16] way. One might argue that legal certainty and value-oriented justice ideas are two opposing – or at least different – considerations that cannot be reconciled, mainly because the latter one would require a certain degree of flexibility to adjust to special situations and thus could be seen as being detrimental to legal clarity, stability and predictability.[17] However, the earlier mentioned certainty expressions of legal accessibility, legal enforcement and the practicability of the application of law can be considered as adding a certain fairness dimension to the overall legal certainty concept. For the sake of simplification this second bigger subpillar of legal certainty could be titled as 'legal rationalisation'. In this sense one can, for example, understand Bydlinski when he argues as follows: 'The deliberate creation and application of guiding ethnic-juristic principles is necessary especially to provide or maintain practical jurisprudence the fundaments for methodical procedures. Practical jurisprudence has to apply them as deliberatively, thoroughly and reflectively as possible to improve the rational quality of legal working. This is – above all – true for the case of rational legal drafting.'[18] Lawmakers have to create rational legal fundaments and procedures to allow for a 'suitable' application of rules. Since language is, however, limited legal rules – via their wording – can only very rarely accommodate every thinkable scenario.[19] Legal interpretation and a certain degree of flexibility (in legal application) are needed to satisfy the call for a properly working legal framework that takes account of the afore-mentioned certainty layers of legal accessibility, legal enforcement and practicability of the application of law.

---

[15] In a similar way, e.g., Volkmar Gessner, who – when discussing the certainty principle in the context of globalisation – states as follows: 'The term 'legal certainty' needs some explanations before we examine what psychological and economic approaches contribute to our understanding of the dilemma of legal (un)certainty in the context of global legal interaction' – see Gessner (1998), p. 428.

[16] For a definition of this term from the perspective of justice, see Wrbka (2015a), pp. 6 et seq.

[17] See, e.g., Canaris (1969), p. 83, where Canaris explains that 'in addition to the value of legal certainty it is the concept of fairness that could contradict a flexible system' (translation mine).

[18] Bydlinski F (1990), p. 87 (translation mine).

[19] In a similar vein Peter Bydlinski, who argues that 'legal norms are only rarely totally unambiguous' (translation mine) – see Bydlinski P (2014), § 6 Recital 1.

Striking an appropriate balance between legal clarity, stability and predictability on the one hand and the possibility to take account of special circumstances on the other is one of the key challenges for those who create legal rules. I already commented on the value-oriented justice notion of legal certainty at a different occasion[20] and will thus focus more on the first bigger subcategory of legal certainty, i.e., the certainty group of what I called legal clarity. We will see, however, that the certainty sublayers cannot always be easily divided. Hence, some of the examples below will take account of a variety of different certainty perceptions.

3 Legal Certainty Discussed with the Example of EU Private Law

The certainty notion of EU private law is a unique example of legal certainty. Unique, because EU private law approaches the certainty concept from a different perspective than domestic private law.[21] While domestic laws usually address (at least) one of the two private law expressions of legal certainty discussed at the end of the previous chapter, EU private law principally – or at least primarily – deals with a different issue. The main emphasis is neither put on what I defined as legal clarification – at least not in a narrow sense – nor on a more flexible application of law, i.e., on legal rationalisation. The focus is rather put on a defragmentation of national private laws for the sake of enhancing the Internal Market.

The main driving force behind this approach is the (at the EU level often found) assumption that differences in national private laws are counterproductive from the viewpoint of simplifying cross-border trade.[22] Against this background, it does not come as a surprise that the European Commission (*hereinafter* Commission) commonly brings this legal certainty argument when trying to justify the need for EU legislation in trade-related situations. Two examples of this can be seen in the new Timeshare Directive[23] (*hereinafter* 2009 Timeshare Directive) and the

[20] For a discussion of the interplay between the flexibility and certainty of law in the context of the Austrian warranty regime see Wrbka (2015b).

[21] For some comments on EU law from the perspective of legal certainty, see Petzold (1998); Neyer (1998); Banakar (1998).

[22] For examples of this assumption, see, e.g., Wrbka (2015a), pp. 217–221 with further references.

[23] Directive 2008/122/EC of the European Parliament and of the Council on the protection of consumers in respect of certain aspects of timeshare, long-term holiday product, resale and exchange contracts, 14 January 2009, OJ 2009 No. L33/10. The 2009 Timeshare Directive replaced the minimum harmonised 1994 Timeshare Directive (Directive 94/47/EC of the European Parliament and of the Council on the protection of purchasers in respect of certain aspects of contracts relating to the purchase of a right to use immovable properties on a timeshare basis, 26 October 1994, OJ 1994 No. L280/83).

Proposal for a Regulation on a Common European Sales Law (*hereinafter* CESL Regulation Proposal[24]).[25]

Unlike its predecessor, the Timeshare Directive of 1994, the 2009 Timeshare Directive is based on full harmonisation. Recital 3 2009 Timeshare Directive explains the legislative choice of full harmonisation as follows: 'In order *to enhance legal certainty* and fully achieve the benefits of the internal market for consumers and businesses, the relevant laws of the Member States need to be approximated further. Therefore, certain aspects of the marketing, sale and resale of timeshares ... should be *fully harmonised*' (emphasis added).

Enhanced legal certainty, understood in the context of EU private lawmaking as the result of standardising national rules to the highest possible extent, is also one of the arguments the Commission used for its CESL Regulation Proposal. In the view of the Commission, the interests of both sides of relevant cross-border contracts are impaired by the existence of diverse national sales law. With respect to the sellers' side, the Commission is convinced that the CESL would convince more sellers to offer their products across borders, because sellers could more easily contract with foreign buyers if they could offer their products under one and the same legal framework regardless of where the (European) buyer shops from.[26] As for the buyers' side, the Commission assumes that consumers are deterred from shopping across border mainly because they are confused by the existence of different national sales laws. Introducing a commonly applicable, fully harmonised set of

---

[24] For details on the CESL Regulation Proposal, see, e.g., Wrbka (2012a, b, 2014b, 2015a), pp. 190 et seq. (all with further references).

[25] The list is not exhaustive. Most pieces of (at least partial) fully harmonised EU law can be used to explain the Commission's wish to align domestic law for the sake of 'legal certainty' – see, e.g., Recital 5 of the Proposal for a (new) Directive on Package Travel (*hereinafter* 2013 Package Travel Proposal): 'The [full] harmonisation of certain aspects of package contracts and assisted travel arrangements is necessary for the creation of a real consumer internal market'. Unlike the old Package Travel Directive of 1990 (Council Directive 90/314/EEC on package travel, package holidays and package tours, 13 June 1990, OJ 1990 No. L 158/59), the 2013 Package Travel Proposal partially rests on full harmonisation – for details see Proposal for a Directive of the European Parliament and of the Council on package travel and assisted travel arrangements, amending Regulation (EC) No 2006/2004, Directive 2011/83/EU and repealing Council Directive 90/314/EEC, 9 July 2013, COM(2013) 512 final.

[26] See CESL Explanatory Memorandum (i.e., the explanatory memorandum that accompanies the CESL Regulation Proposal; *hereinafter* CESL Explanatory Memorandum), p. 11: '[F]or traders ... [the CESL] would eliminate the need for research of different national laws' – for details see Proposal for a Regulation of the European Parliament and of the Council on a Common European Sales Law, 11 October 2011, COM(2011) 635 final. As already explained at a different occasion, the Commission is convinced that traders consider contract law-related issues as among the biggest barriers to entering the cross-border market. Two of the three most often mentioned disincentives for trading across borders identified in a study of 2011 were the '[d]ifficulty in finding out about the provisions of a foreign contract law' (ranked first with a total of 40 % of respondents considering this issue to have at least some practical impact) and '[t]he need to adapt and comply with different consumer protection rules in ... foreign contract laws' (ranked third with a total of 38 %) – for details see The Gallup Organization Hungary, 'European Contract Law in Consumer Transactions. Analytical Report', Flash Eurobarometer 321 (2011), p. 19, available at http://ec.europa.eu/public_opinion/flash/fl_321_en.pdf and Wrbka (2015a), p. 225.

sales law would, so the Commission believes, ensure that consumers would not be distracted by diverse national rules anymore.[27]

Not everybody shares the positive view of the Commission, however. Stefan Grundmann, for example, explains as follows: 'The more broadly the full harmonization mode is used, the more frustrated become the advantages that the national systems of law have achieved because of centuries of scholarship and practice – advantages in substantive justice and in legal certainty'.[28] It is noteworthy that not only the Commission, but also sceptical authors like Grundmann, use the legal certainty argument in the context of the harmonisation debate. They do so, however, to *criticise* full harmonisation by stressing a different notion of legal certainty. For them the afore-mentioned subpillars of legal stability and continuity would be put at risk if EU legislation forced national legislators to give up their (not rarely) well established national concepts. On top of that, examples like the CESL show that it can also be legal clarity (in the Bydlinski sense) that suffers. This is the case, if (full) harmonisation leads to the establishment of a two-tiered regime – rules that are different at a purely domestic and cross-border level. Regardless of which view one follows, the increased shift from minimum to full harmonisation in the field of EU private law shows that EU policy-makers believe that legal certainty is best achieved by comprehensive legal standardisation.

The following chapters will explain that legal certainty challenges for national legislators look slightly different. The first of the two jurisdictions discussed below – Austria – will additionally show how the legal certainty efforts at the EU level can complicate the certainty debate at the national, EU Member State (*hereinafter* Member State) level.

4 Legal Certainty Discussed with the Example of Austrian Private Law

At a national level legal certainty debates usually revolve around the earlier discussed subcategories of legal clarity (in a broader sense) and legal rationality. The discussions in this context are generally multidimensional in a sense that they are linked to a balancing of different certainty notions. For Member States, the process is intensified by supranational legislation, i.e., by 'superior' EU legislation that is either directly applicable in the Member States[29] or that needs to be implemented into domestic law,[30] because it adds an outside perspective or parameter to national legislative considerations. Hence, some of the following examples will take account of the latter issue one as well.

---

[27] See, e.g., CESL Explanatory Memorandum, p. 4: '[Consumers] would also enjoy more certainty about their rights when shopping cross-border on the basis of a single set of mandatory rules'.

[28] Grundmann (2013), p. 126.

[29] This refers to EU regulations.

[30] This refers to EU directives.

Our first example shows a potential clash between transparency, on the one hand, and continuity, on the other. In this context, we will further see that attempts to clarify the legal situation can – despite some clarification – actually cause a shift in uncertainty.

Although it could be assumed that most observers would not hesitate to opt for enhanced understandability, legislators – for whatever reason – do not always choose this option, but in several cases remain passive. § 429 ABGB deals with property law consequences with respect to sale by dispatch contract (and via § 1064 ABGB was and further via § 905(3) now is also decisive for the question of the passing of risk in a sale by dispatch contract scenario).[31] For a long time, the provision stated as follows: 'In principle, sent goods are deemed to be passed, when the transferee receives them; unless the transferee determines or agrees on the method of sending' (translation mine).

Looking at this provision from a purely linguistic perspective, one might get the impression that the default rule under § 429 ABGB-old was that the receipt of a sent good by the transferee (and not its handing over to a carrier) should have been the decisive factor for declaring the good to be passed to the transferee. Case-law played an important role, because it introduced the necessity to distinguish between common and uncommon methods of sending goods and by doing this altered the default rule (or at least reinterpreted it). Courts arrived at the conclusion that *common* methods of sending goods – sending goods by post arguably is the prime example of a common method[32] – have to be considered as having been agreed upon by the parties. This basically meant that goods that are, e.g., sent by post fall under the exemption clause of being considered as being passed to the transferee at an earlier stage than their receipt by the transferee, namely with the handing over to the carrier.

From the perspective of clarity, one might have justifiably questioned whether this understanding (that was not explicitly reflected by the wording of § 429 ABGB-old) served the wish for legal certainty. Without knowledge of pertinent case-law it was undeniably difficult to understand the true meaning of § 429. Unfortunately, the legislator had – for a long time – not found it necessary to bring the provision in line with case-law, but instead opted for legal continuity (understood here as not changing the wording of written rules).

With the adoption of the Directive on Consumer Rights (hereinafter *Consumer Rights Directive* or *CRD*)[33] the Austrian legislator had to react, because the CRD introduced – with respect to business-to-consumer (*hereinafter* B2C) situations – a

[31] For details on this issue, see Wrbka (2014c), pp. 35 and 45.

[32] For this and some further examples of common methods of sending, see, e.g., Rabl (2002), p. 148; Eccher and Riss (2014b), § 429 Recital 2. For a comment on uncommon methods of sending see, e.g., Rabl (2002), pp. 137–138.

[33] Directive 2011/83/EU of the European Parliament and of the Council on consumer rights, amending Council Directive 93/13/EEC and Directive 1999/44/EC of the European Parliament and of the Council and repealing Council Directive 85/577/EEC and Directive 97/7/EC of the European Parliament and of the Council, 25 October 2011, OJ 2011 No. L 304/260.

sale by dispatch contract concept that differed from the Austrian approach. The pertinent provision of the CRD, its Article 20, reads as follows:

> In contracts where the trader dispatches the goods to the consumer, the risk of loss of or damage to the goods shall pass to the consumer when he or a third party indicated by the consumer and other than the carrier has acquired the physical possession of the goods. However, the risk shall pass to the consumer upon delivery to the carrier if the carrier was commissioned by the consumer to carry the goods and that choice was not offered by the trader, without prejudice to the rights of the consumer against the carrier.

Austria more or less copied the provision and inserted a new § 7b into its Consumer Protection Act (KSchG). § 7b KSchG reads as follows:

> In contracts where the trader dispatches the good to the consumer, the risk of loss of or damage to the good shall pass to the consumer only if and at the moment that he or a third party indicated by him and other than the carrier has received the good. If, however, the consumer concluded the transportation contract by himself, without having been offered this transportation method as an option by the trader, the risk shall pass to the consumer already upon delivery to the carrier if the carrier was commissioned by the consumer to carry the goods (translation mine).

The Austrian legislator did not stop at this point. In the course of implementing Article 20 CRD one took the opportunity to clarify the passing of risk concept applicable to non-B2C sale by dispatch contracts as well. This affected §§ 429 and 905 ABGB-old.[34] § 429 and (the relevant part of) § 905 ABGB-new read as follows:

> § 429 ABGB-new: If the good—with the transferee's [note: i.e., the creditor's] consent—is dispatched to a different place than the place of performance, then the good is deemed to be transferred [to the transferee] the moment it is transferred to the person who is mandated with the transfer [note, i.e., the carrier], if the method of transfer corresponds the agreed—or in its absence: a commonly accepted—method of transportation (translation mine).
>
> § 905(3) ABGB-new: The risk with respect to goods that are—with the transferee's [note: i.e., the creditor's] consent—dispatched to a different place than the place of performance is passed to the creditor at the moment of transfer (§ 429) (translation mine).

From a legal certainty perspective these steps led to an interesting consequence. Undeniably the obligation to implement Article 20 CRD meant that – with respect to B2C sale by dispatch contracts – one had to sacrifice the wish for continuity. (Note: This was done via the insertion of § 7b KSchG, which introduced a new concept in this respect.) At the same time, one took the chance to clarify the general sale by dispatch contract concept by improving the understandability of the underlying transfer rule(s). However, when taking a closer look at the decision to install a two-tiered system with different rules for B2C and non-B2C contracts, one will see that the Austrian implementation of Article 20 CRD led to a shift into uncertainty.[35] While the basic legal situation for B2C and non-B2C contracts seems to be transparent now, the introduction of different legal consequences can arguably cause confusion.

---

[34] For details on these two see Wrbka (2014c), pp. 32–37.

[35] For both negative *and* positive remarks on the two-tiered regime see Wrbka (2014c), pp. 46–49.

Two issues should be stressed in this respect. First, classifying a contract as a B2C or non-B2C contract might not always be that easy. This is, in particular, true in cases of so-called "mixed-purpose" contracts. Although there is some case law on the question on when to qualify a contract as a B2C contract if the contract is partially concluded for private, partially for business purposes,[36] the correct classification might prove difficult, especially for legally less experienced parties. Since the legal consequences under the new concept differ (§ 7b KSchG vs. §§ 429 and 905(3) ABGB-new), determining a scenario correctly is now of utmost importance.

Second, even in cases where there is no mixed-purpose situation, the two-tiered system might cause some predictability issues. Since the application of § 7b KSchG necessitates that the good in question is sold by a trader to a consumer, situations might occur where the parties to a contract do not possess sufficient proof of the other party's status. How can, for example, a consumer who buys a good via an online portal know for sure that the seller is a professional seller and not a private seller? (Only in the first case the more favourable § 7b KSchG would apply.) Vice versa, a trader might want to know beforehand which pertinent concept – § 7b KSchG or §§ 429 in combination with 905(3) ABGB-new – would be basically applicable. Again, without clear evidence it might be tricky to make the correct predetermination. If a problem arises, courts would be able to clarify the situation, but from the perspective of foreseeability the two-tiered regime might cause some headache. The example of § 7b KSchG and the revision of §§ 429 and 905 ABGB clearly show that there can be a certain tension between the different layers of legal certainty. Let us move on to another certainty example.

This second example shows the transparency or understandability challenges in the context of legal revision. § 903 ABGB deals with the calculation of time-limitation periods. In addition to regulating the commencement day of said periods, it contains – in its third sentence – a provision on the suspension of expiry. If the last day of a period falls on either a Sunday or an official holiday, the period would not end on that day, but on the following weekday. Special statutory laws added that the expiry of a period was further suspended if the last day were a Saturday, Good Friday[37] or 31 December.[38] A similar regulation can be found in the directly applicable European Convention on the Calculation of Time-Limits.[39] In 2011 the Austrian legislator decided to get rid of the special laws.[40] Their repeal meant that the underlying provisions are now split in between (only) two legal sources – § 903 ABGB and the European Convention on the Calculation of Time-Limits. From a substantive point this did not lead to a change, because the provisions enshrined in the special laws were also contained in the European Convention on the Calculation

[36] For details see, e.g., Stuyck (2010), pp. 50–54.

[37] BGBl 1961/37.

[38] BGBl 1999/186.

[39] Note that Austria is a Contracting Party to this Convention. For details see, e.g., Kietaibl (2012), § 903 Recitals 7–12; Bollenberger (2014), § 903 Recital 3; Binder and Kolmasch (2014), § 903 Recitals 18–21 (each with further references).

[40] BGBl 2011/100.

of Time-Limits.[41] Although this obviously led to a change of the legal framework, the legislator did not find it necessary to merge the two sources into one. From a legal certainty perspective – with certainty understood in its transparency or understandability notion – this inactivity is arguably regrettable, because the new scheme failed to provide a *really* transparent concept.

Our next example discusses the tension between legal stability on the one hand and legal rationalisation on the other. With respect to time-limitations of warranty claims the ABGB has traditionally been differentiating between material defects and rights-related effects. (I will not comment on the additional differentiation between defects in movables and immovables here).[42] Pursuant to § 933(1) ABGB the basic rule is that in the first case the relevant commencement event for the warranty period is the day of delivery, while in the case of rights-related defects it should be the day the transferee becomes aware of the defect. With respect to material defects legal academia and case law have allowed for a narrow deviation from the default rule. If the parties agree on certain, special characteristics of a good that cannot be proven existing or non-existing at the time of transfer, then one should assume that they mutually agree on shifting the commencement-relevant event from the day of delivery to the day of verifiability.[43] From a dogmatic point of view this was explained with a tacit agreement pursuant to § 863 ABGB. This view has been widely appreciated by legal academia.[44]

Several commentators have argued that from a rationality perspective one further exception needs to be acknowledged. In the case of hidden material defects a commencement solution similar to the afore-mentioned default deviation should be declared permissible, if the hidden defect were a 'typical' one, i.e., a hidden defect that *objectively* could not be discovered at the time of delivery. As shown at a different context,[45] this additional deviation would – under certain, strict preconditions – indeed make sense, but unfortunately case law has not yet taken this view. The basic argument used in this respect is that the wording of § 933(1) ABGB would be too clear to allow for any flexible application. More than that: Although there are good arguments in favour of a more fairness-oriented approach, the legislator seems to give preference to legal stability over transferee-friendlier legal rationalisation considerations.

The last example in the context of Austrian private law somehow relates to what Akkermans argued with respect to property law. § 297a ABGB deals with the legal situation regarding movable machines that are brought into connection with immovable property (without becoming its component part). A (*bona fide*) acquirer of an immovable property might expect that machines that are in connection with

[41] See Article 5 European Convention on the Calculation of Time-Limits.

[42] For this differentiation see, e.g., § 933(1) ABGB and Wrbka (2015c), p. 18.

[43] For case-law examples, see, in particular, the following judgments of the Austrian Supreme Court: 2 Ob 535/90; 7 Ob 506/91; 5 Ob 504/96 (5 Ob 505/96); 1 Ob 41/03 s; 7 Ob 32/04 p; 1 Ob 138/05 h; 5 Ob 53/12 y.

[44] See, e.g., Kurschel (1989), pp. 97 et seq.; Wrbka (2015c), p. 37 with further references.

[45] Wrbka (2015c), pp. 45–52.

the property belong to the owner of the immovable property. If such machines belong to a third party – the prime example would be a reservation of ownership – the acquirer's expectation might be impaired. To protect his interests, a partial amendment of the ABGB[46] led to the insertion of § 297a. Pursuant to this rule, machines connected to immovable objects are deemed to share the ownership of the immovable property unless their ownership by a third party is registered in the land register (*Grundbuch*). § 297a ABGB does not change the concept of acquiring ownership *per se*, but it leads to the protection of *bona fide* acquirers.[47] This example shows how the Austrian legislator has tried to serve interests in enhanced (external) clarity or rationality to enhance overall legal certainty.

5 Legal Certainty Discussed with the Example of Japanese Private Law

Compared to the ABGB, its Japanese equivalent – the Japanese Civil Code (民法; *minpō*; *hereinafter* JCC) is of more recent origin, but nevertheless relatively old. Influenced largely by the French Civil Code (*Code civil des Français*; *hereinafter*, CC) and drafts of the German Civil Code (*Bürgerliches Gesetzbuch*; *hereinafter*, BGB) while (originally) reflecting traditional, Japanese ideas in the areas of Family and Inheritance Law, the JCC was enacted in 1896 (Books I-III) and 1898 (Books IV-V on Family and Inheritance Law) respectively.[48] The influences by different legal and cultural ideas undeniably gave it a unique look. After World War II, Books IV-V on Family and Inheritance Law were modernised, or rather 'Westernised', primarily to take greater account of conceptions of gender equality.[49] Several partial amendments (also) to the other three JCC books have followed since then. However – unlike Family and Inheritance Law – Books I-III have conceptually more or less been left untouched since the enactment of the JCC.[50]

Although the Japanese legislator has, for a very long time, shown little interest in revising Books I-III, case law has developed private law further. This had several reasons. First, the JCC is quite short and incomplete compared to its European paragons. The number of its provisions is only approximately half the number of the French *Code Civil* or the German BGB provisions, for example. This meant that a

[46] RGBl Nr. 69/1916 (3rd partial amendment of the ABGB, which came into effect on 1 January 1917).

[47] For details on § 297a ABGB, see, e.g., Eccher and Riss (2014a), § 297a; Helmich (2012), § 297a; Homann (2012), § 297a (each with further references).

[48] On the history of the JCC, see, e.g., Sokolowski (2010); Oda (2009), pp. 113–117; Marutschke (2009), pp. 85–97; Igarashi (1990), pp. 2–6; Haley (1991), pp. 75–77.

[49] See, e.g., Wrbka (2014a), p. 1 with further references.

[50] For details, see, e.g., Wrbka (2014a); Kano (2013), pp. 251–252 with further references. For additional, general comments on the development of Japanese Private Law see further, e g., Okuda (1985), pp. 1–22; Ishikawa (2013), pp. 267–285; Kitagawa (1990), pp. 125–141; Stoll(1990), pp. 151–175; Müller-Freinfels (1990), pp. 177–202; Minear (1970).

considerable number of possible legal questions were not addressed by the JCC. Second, many of the provisions of the JCC were quite vaguely formulated, which meant that the exact meaning of several provisions was not entirely clear. Third (but only rarely), some JCC provisions went too far and introduced a very complicated framework.[51]

For observers of Japanese Law, in general, and Japanese Private, in particular, the short and vagueness of the JCC does not come as a major surprise. Marc Dernauer, for example, points out that the perception among the Japanese society of what is right and wrong might be one explanation why the JCC has not experienced a standing comparable to (continental) European civil codes. With reference to Japanese commentators, Dernauer notes as follows: 'When a Japanese makes an agreement with another person, the goodwill and friendship that gave rise to the agreement is [sic!] more important to him than the agreement itself'.[52] Could this be understood in a way that means that written law does not play a comparably important role? Put differently, can the 'special' look of the JCC (understood as differing vastly from its two model codes, the *Code Civil* and the BGB) be explained with the argument that legal issues are primarily solved without the influence of legal norms? The – from a Western perspective – very low number of court cases could be seen as an indicator to prove this. Some commentators seem to support this view,[53] while others explain that the JCC is just not Japanese enough and that there is the need for a 'truly' Japanese Civil Code.[54]

Be that as it may, over the years criticism has risen – especially from within legal academia. In particular Book III JCC, the JCC's Law of Obligations (that has been among the least updated fields of the JCC) was at the centre of calls for reform. From the standpoint of legal certainty the just mentioned deficiencies of the JCC showed the need to improve various certainty facets, most notably the transparency, completeness and understandability of the JCC. Several academic groups had

[51] Kano (2013), p. 256. For general comments on the perceived problem of the JCC as being incomplete, outdated and imprecise see, e.g., Uchida (2011), pp. 707–708; Kano (2013), pp. 252–253; Nakata (2013), p. 205; Wrbka (2014a), p. 4.

[52] Dernauer (2013) with reference to Kawashima Takeyoshi, a Japanese private law scholar who lived in the twentieth century, and Hattori Shirō, a Japanese linguist.

[53] See, e.g., Ramseyer and Nakazato (1999), pp. 6–21; Haley (1998), pp. 156–176; Haley (1991), pp. 169–200; Upham (1978), pp. 205–221. For more recent comments on this topic see, e.g., the contributions in Vanoverbeke et al. (2014), in particular Takahashi (2014); Vande Walle (2014); Ozaki (2014); Hamano (2014).

[54] Dernauer refers to Takashi Uchida, one of the most influential figures in the JCC debate. Just like Kawashima and Hattori, Uchida is of the opinion that the Japanese society, in particular the way social interactions take place, asks for an independent or special civil code. Nevertheless, the discussions within the JCC Reform Commission show that strong account is taken of developments in other parts of the world. In particular, developments in the EU, such as the Principles of European Contract Law (PECL) and the Draft Common Frame of Reference (DCFR), but also at a bigger stage, such as UNIDROIT Principles of International Commercial Contracts, the UN Convention on Contracts for the Sale of Goods (CISG), have influenced the discussion. For details see, e.g., Uchida (2011) and Nakata (2013), pp. 208–214.

initiated attempts to draft revision proposals.[55] After years of refusal, the Japanese Ministry of Justice finally launched its own initiative in 2009 by installing an official working group.[56] The 'Working Group on the Civil Code (Law of Obligations)' (法制審議会民法 (債権関係); *hōsei shingikai minpō (saiken kankei)*) (*hereinafter* Civil Code Working Group) had the mandate to review Book III JCC and – if found necessary – draft a reform proposal.[57]

The Civil Code Working Group has – especially for Japanese standards – proceeded quite quickly. In 2013 it published its Interim Draft Proposal on the Reform of the Civil Code (law of obligations) (民法 (債権関係)の改正に関する中間試案; *minpō (saiken kankei) no kaisei ni kan suru chūkan shian*)[58] (*hereinafter* Interim Draft Proposal)[59] and roughly 2 years later, in early 2015, it presented its final proposal, the民法 (債権関係)の改正に関する要綱案 (*minpō (saiken kankei) no kaisei ni kansuru yōkōan*; *hereinafter* Final Draft Proposal).[60] In March 2015 the Japanese government announced that it planned to implement the proposal as soon as possible. Concrete results are, however, still pending (at the time of writing this contribution).[61]

One of the areas that have been heavily debated in the course of the reform discussion is the field of standard business terms, in particular, the questions of the legal requirements that need to be fulfilled to declare them as forming a part of a concrete contract as well as of the consequences of an inclusion of legally impermissible clauses into standard business terms. To date concrete rules on these issues are still missing in Japanese statutory law. Case law deals with the question on a

---

[55] See, e.g., the works of the Japanese Civil Code (Law of Obligations) Reform Commission ('民法 (債権法) 改正検討委員会'; *minpō (saikenhō) kaisei kentō iinkai*; hereinafter *JCC Reform Commission*) (for details see http://www.shojihomu.or.jp/saikenhou/English/index_e.html; Accessed 31 August 2015) or the Research Group on the Civil Code Reform (民法改正研究会; *minpō kaisei kenkyūkai*). Both groups focused on the law of obligations. Several other groups added narrower or sectoral research output. The Research Group on the Prescription Rules (時効研究会; *jikō kenkyūkai*) can be considered as one such example – for details on these see Kano (2013), p. 253 at note 11.

[56] Some authors argue that the Japanese Ministry of Justice was not able to withstand the pressure for reform by legal academia – see, e.g., Nakata (2013), p. 207, where the author in this context uses the term 'strong driving force' (*starke Antriebskraft*) of the academic groups; Kamo (2010), p. 171, where also this author refers to the academic working groups as a 'driving force'.

[57] For details, see the classification by Kozuka and Nottage (2014), p. 239. For a members' list see, e.g., http://www.moj.go.jp/content/000068987.pdf.

[58] The text of the Interim Draft Proposal is available at, e.g., http://www.moj.go.jp/content/000112242.pdf. Commented versions are available at, e.g., http://www.moj.go.jp/content/000112244.pdf and http://www.moj.go.jp/content/000112247.pdf (all in Japanese) (Accessed 31 August 2015).

[59] For comments on the Interim Draft Proposal, see, e.g., Nakata (2013).

[60] Die Ergebnisse liegen derzeit nur in japanischer Sprache vor und sind unter http://www.moj.go.jp/shingi1/shingikai_saiken.html abrufbar. Der JBGB-AG-Reformvorschlag ist unter http://www.moj.go.jp/content/001136445.pdf erhältlich.

[61] Für eine kurze, englischsprachige Zusammenfassung der Regierungsentscheidung s Jiji Press (2015).

case-by-case basis, but applies relatively flexible conditions. From a viewpoint of legal certainty, in particular, predictability and stability, this fact is undeniably regrettable. Another heavily-discussed issue in the context of standard business terms revolved around the question whether or not one should introduce more concrete rules for – or better: examples of – business terms that should be considered as impermissible. To date Japanese law does not know any comparable rules (although it should be noted that the area of unfair business *practices* has enjoyed clarification in the Japanese Consumer Contract Act (消費者契約法; *shōhisha-keiyakuhō*; JCCA)).[62]

In the early stages, i.e., before the installation of the Civil Code Working Group, proposals pointed into a quite progressive direction regarding the just mentioned standard business terms issues. The Japanese Civil Code (Law of Obligations) Reform Commission, for example, – arguably the most influential, at least most comprehensive private initiative – devoted relatively broad space to those questions. In its Civil Code reform draft ('Basic Policy of the Reform of the Law of Obligations'; 債権法改正の基本方針 *saikenhō kaisei no kihon hōshin*; hereinafter *JCC Reform Commission Draft*)[63] it regulated them in Articles 3.1.1.A-3.1.1.C and 3.1.25–3.1.26. The core message of these provisions was the wish to establish both a black list and grey list of (in certain situations) unfair terms (Articles 3.1.1.A-3.1.1.C) and quite precise rules on the questions of the necessary requirements to incorporate business terms into contracts as well as the consequence of unfair or surprise business terms (Articles 3.1.25–3.1.26).[64]

---

[62] On this issue in the context of unfair standard business terms, see, e.g., Kano (2013), p. 258. For details on the JCCA see, e.g., Dernauer (2006), pp. 245–268.

[63] An English language-version is available at http://www.shojihomu.or.jp/saikenhou/English/index_e.html (Accessed 31 August 2015).

[64] Article 3.1.25(1) JCC Reform Commission Draft titled defines general conditions, i.e., business terms as 'the aggregate of contract terms which are formulated in advance for use in multiple contracts'. Article 3.1.26 JCC Reform Commission Draft ('requirements of incorporation of the general conditions') adds the following conditions for their contractual inclusion:

(1) The person supplying the general conditions shall present (hereinafter referred to as 'disclose') the general conditions to the other party by the time of conclusion of the contract, and when both parties agree to using such general conditions in the contract, the general conditions shall become the contents of the contract; provided, however, that in cases where, owing to the nature of the contract, it is extremely difficult to disclose the general conditions at the time of conclusion of the contract, the person supplying the general conditions shall indicate to the other party to the effect that the general conditions will be used at the time of conclusion of the contract, and when the other party was placed in a position of being able to know the general conditions by the time of conclusion of the contract, the general conditions shall be deemed to have been disclosed at the time of conclusion of the contract.

(2) Notwithstanding the provision of (1), with regard to contents of terms which the other party to the person supplying the general conditions knew of at the time of conclusion of the contract, it may not assert that those terms should not be the contents of the contract on the grounds that the general conditions were not disclosed.

Translation taken from http://www.shojihomu.or.jp/saikenhou/English/index_e.html.

In contrast, the Civil Code Working Group, however, decided to take a more traditional approach and abandoned the idea to include any lists of declared or deemed unfair business terms. At the same time, however, the Civil Code Working Group stressed the need for clear(er) rules on the incorporation of standard business terms into contractual relationships and the consequences of unfair business terms by addressing these questions in Article 30 Interim Draft Proposal. As for the question of unfairness itself, the working group did not alter the current situation and proposed 'only' a general definition of the unfairness parameter.[65] Anyway, the idea to include standard business terms related solutions into the JCC would clearly mean a step forward in terms of enhanced legal transparency and understandability. The more recently published Final Draft Proposal of the Civil Code Working Group confirms the chosen path and suggests a regulation similar to the Interim Draft Proposal (Article 28 Final Draft Proposal).

A few shorter examples shall explain how the Civil Code Working Group has been trying to answer to the perceived incompleteness of the JCC. First, the areas of warranty rights is statutorily (at best) only very rudimentarily regulated. In absence of clear rules both the notion and the legal nature of the Japanese warranty regime, for example, have been heavily discussed in legal academia.[66] Both the Interim Draft Proposal and the Final Draft Proposal aim to end the discussion and to introduce a clearer framework by proposing relatively detailed rules, including a revised scheme of remedies and a definition of the term 'defect'.[67]

Second, also the issue of mental capacity is only partially regulated by the JCC. Although the JCC contains certain provisions on the commencement of guardianship, curatorship and assistance for people (constantly) lacking mental capacity[68] as well as on legal acts by people declared as lacking mental capacity by the family court,[69] it does not contain any broader or comprehensive rules on legal acts by people with a lack of sufficient mental capacity. Put differently, for cases of a lack of mental capacity where a court decision does not exist yet or the lack is only temporary, clear rules are missing. Case law developed the solution that legal acts by such people should be considered as voidable.[70] To fill the lacuna, both the Interim Draft Proposal and the Final Draft Proposal aim to complete the mental capacity regime in line with case law via Article 2 Interim Draft Proposal and Article 2 Final Draft Proposal respectively.

Third, to date precise, statutory rules on the legal consequences of what is considered as constituting usury are missing. Article 90 JCC deals with juristic acts that are incompatible with public policy considerations and declares them void.

---

[65] Article 30(5) Interim Draft Proposal.

[66] See, e.g., Kano (2013), p. 258–259.

[67] See, in particular, Article 35(3) and (4) Interim Draft Proposal and Article 30(2) and (3) Final Draft Proposal.

[68] Articles 7, 11 and 15 JCC respectively.

[69] Articles 9, 13 and 17 JCC respectively.

[70] See, e.g., Kano (2013), p. 255; Oda (2009), p. 123.

But unlike, e.g., § 879(2)lit 4 of the Austrian Civil Code (ABGB) that declares usury as inacceptable *ex lege*, the JCC does not list any concrete examples. Hence, in the Japanese context the question arises how the term 'public policy' is to be understood and whether usury constitutes a breach thereof. In Japan, it was again case law that developed supporting rules and in that context declared usury as one expression of violating public policy. To improve legal clarity and transparency, the Interim Draft Proposal suggested the inclusion of an explicit usury clause (Article 1 (2)(2) Interim Draft Proposal). However, unlike in the first two mentioned cases (i.e., warranty law and legal acts by people lacking sufficient mental capacity), the Civil Code Working Group decided to change the direction and removed usury from the Final Draft Proposal. Parallels to the afore-mentioned grey/black list can be drawn. It can be argued that – despite certain, basic enhancements in legal clarity – the policy-makers thought that it was not (yet) the time for any more precise regulation. Examples of how to define terms in the JCC might have led to the consequence that legal practice would have drawn wrong conclusions, i.e., that cases not explicitly mentioned in the revised text of the JCC would have to be considered as legally permissible.

One issue that has been widely discussed in attempts to revise the Law of Obligations was whether one should follow the German example and merge consumer contract law with relating general provision of the JCC, i.e., whether consumer contract law should be incorporated in the JCC. Adopted in 2000 the JCCA[71] was an attempt to clarify consumer rights by answering to the growing number of complaints resulting from B2C transactions. To achieve this, the JCCA introduced *inter alia* rules for impermissible B2C contract clauses[72] and the enforcement of breaches (incl rules on injunctive relief and the enforcement by consumer organizations).[73] Commentators influenced by German developments have tried to push for an inclusion of (in particular these) consumer contract issues into the JCC, mainly with the argument to improve the transparency and coherence of the affected rules.[74] In the early deliberative stages it indeed seemed that this approach would enjoy the majority support. This is best exemplified with the JCC Reform Commission Draft that incorporated consumer contract topics into the general framework. However – and in contrast to the purely academic JCC Reform Commission Draft – both the Interim Draft Proposal and the Final Draft Proposal of the Civil Code Working Group again opted for a more reserved approach. Like Austria and its division between the ABGB and the Consumer Act (*Konsumentenschutzgesetz*; *KSchG*), Japan would – if a potential revision of the Law of Obligations followed the basic structure of the Interim and Final Draft Proposals –

[71] For a translation of the JCCA, see, e.g., http://www.consumer.go.jp/english/cca/index.html or http://www.japaneselawtranslation.go.jp/law/detail/?id=108&vm=04&re=02 (both last accessed 31 August 2015).

[72] For details, see Chap. 2 JCCA.

[73] For details, see Chap. 3 Sects. 1 and 2 JCCA.

[74] See, e.g., Kano (2013), pp. 259–260.

still distinguish between a general civil code (the JCC) and additional norms in a separate text (the JCCA). Also, in this case, legal stability (understood as retaining the status quo) was given preference over a broadened JCC, although this situation – if looked at from a legal certainty perspective –looks slightly different than the afore-discussed grey/black list and usury issues. In the present case, one can argue that upholding the status quo actually serves transparency and understandability wishes more than an integrative approach would/could, because – unlike in the other cases – clear statutory law already exists (in the form of the JCCA).

Although most of the efforts to improve legal certainty have been revolving around the question of how to enhance legal clarity, transparency and understandability by adding provisions to the JCC (or at least by completing existing rules), one last example shall show that the debate has *not absolutely* focused on broadening the text. While many legal concepts are only rudimentarily or vaguely covered by the JCC, the prescription regime went off the rails. The basic rule under the JCC is quite simple and introduces a general limitation period of 10 years (Article 167(1)).[75] Looking at the prescription period regime of Articles 166 et seq. JCC more closely, one will, however, see that the Japanese legislator decided to add numerous exceptions in the form of special, shorter periods that apply in (sometimes very) narrow scenarios.[76] Many stakeholders have – in particular from the perspective of reasonableness, understandability and transparency – been strongly questioning the necessity to maintain this remarkably broad catalogue of exceptions.[77] The Interim Draft Proposal answered with two alternative approaches that both seek to standardise the prescription period regime. One idea was to introduce a general, absolute 5 year-prescription period that would commence at an objective point of time. The second idea was to maintain the longer, objective 10 year-period and to combine it with a subjective period of 3 or 5 years.[78] In its Final Draft Proposal the Civil Code Working Group chose the second approach and proposed the introduction of a subjective 5-year-period combined with an absolute, objective 10-year-period (Article 7(1) Final Draft Proposal).[79] The underlying reason was again the same. A revised JCC should primarily reflect the wish for more clarity, transparency and understandability.

---

[75] Article 167(1) JCC. For comments on the Japanese system of prescription periods, see, e.g., Nagata (2006).

[76] See, e.g., the special prescription periods for claims relating to services provided by lawyers (Articles 171 and 172 JCC; 2, 3 or 5 years), certain medical services (Article 170(i) JCC; 3 years) or services in the context of construction works (Article Article 170(ii) JCC; 3 years).

[77] In this sense, see also Kano (2013), p. 256.

[78] See Article 7(2) Interim Draft Proposal.

[79] For parallels to European discussions, see, e.g., the DCFR, more precisely III. – 7:201 DCFR (general rule of 3 years) and III. – 7:307 DCFR (absolute rule of 10 years in general and 30 years for claims for damages for personal injury) and the Part VIII CESL Proposal (Article 179 to be exact). The latter one proposes a general, short/objective period of 2 years and a long or absolute period of 10 years (30 years in case of personal injury).

6 Concluding Remarks

The examples garnered in this contribution have shown that the legal certainty concept is not as one-dimensional as one might think. Depending on the jurisdiction and the issue at stake, different understandings of legal certainty might apply to explain the legislator's activity or passivity.

The example of the EU illustrated the (perceived) need to standardise legal regulations at an international (or supranational) level to simplify legal transactions that cross borders. In the case of the EU this is usually done by harmonising national rules to the fullest possible extent.

The Austrian example showed that this, i.e., EU legislation does (from a domestic point of view) not necessarily lead to a clarification of rights and obligations, but that – on the contrary – implementing steps taken at the national level could lead to a (sometimes complicated) multi-tiered regime at the domestic level. Some other Austrian examples were used to discuss the tensions that the different certainty notions can cause. In this context the Austrian warranty rules, for example, highlighted the tension between legal stability on the one side and legal rationalisation on the other.

The Japanese examples, finally, illustrated that Japan faces a more fundamental question. Because of the incompleteness and vagueness of the JCC the discussions here revolve around the question to what extent statutory law should be 'completed' to strike a balance between clarity, transparency and understandability on the one hand and flexibility to adjust to special circumstances.

From these observations one can conclude that discussions on legal certainty need to take proper account of the conditions and the environment that particular legal issues are embedded in. One should further note that not only the 'special' characteristics of a legal system, but also the broader context (that involves cultural and social perspectives) can impact those questions. In any event, carrying out research in a multitude of different legal settings undeniably poses challenges to anybody who aims to truly understand the respective legal certainty issues at hand.

References

Akkermans B (2014) Property law. In: Hage J, Akkermans B (eds) Introduction to law. Springer, Heidelberg, pp 71–99

Backes C, Eliantonio M (2014) Administrative law. In: Hage J, Akkermans B (eds) Introduction to law. Springer, Heidelberg, pp 189–209

Banakar R (1998) Reflexive legitimacy in international arbitration. In: Gessner V, Budak AC (eds) Emerging legal certainty. Ashgate, Aldershot, pp 347–398

Binder M, Kolmasch W (2014) § 903. In: Schwimann M, Kodek G (eds) ABGB Praxiskommentar Band IV, 4th edn. LexisNexis, Vienna

Bollenberger R (2014) § 903. In: Koziol H, Bydlinski P, Bollenberger R (eds) ABGB Kurzkommentar, 4th edn. Verlag Österreich, Vienna

Bydlinski F (1988) Fundamentale Rechtsgrundsätze. Springer, Vienna

Bydlinski F (1990) Die praktische Bedeutung der Rechtsethik und die Möglichkeiten ihrer Vermittlung. In: Bydlinski F, Mayer-Maly T (eds) Rechtsethik und Rechtspraxis. Tyrolia-Verlag, Innsbruck, pp 11–96
Bydlinski F (2011) Juristische Methodenlehre und Rechtsbegriff, 2nd edn. Springer, Vienna
Bydlinski P (2014) § 6. In: Koziol H, Bydlinski P, Bollenberger R (eds) ABGB Kurzkommentar, 4th edn. Verlag Österreich, Vienna
Canaris C-W (1969) Systemdenken und Systembegriff in der Jurisprudenz. Duncker & Humblot, Berlin
Dernauer M (2006) Verbraucherschutz und Vertragsfreiheit im japanischen Recht Tübingen. Mohr Siebeck, Tübingen
Dernauer M (2013) Japanese contract law from a European perspective. Yomiuri Shimbun, http://www.yomiuri.co.jp/adv/chuo/dy/research/20131128.html. Accessed 31 Aug 2015
Eccher B, Riss O (2014a) § 297a. In: Koziol H, Bydlinski P, Bollenberger R (eds) ABGB Kurzkommentar, 4th edn. Verlag Österreich, Vienna
Eccher B, Riss O (2014b) § 429. In: Koziol H, Bydlinski P, Bollenberger R (eds) ABGB Kurzkommentar, 4th edn. Verlag Österreich, Vienna
Fernhout F, van Rhee R (2014) Elements of procedural law. In: Hage J, Akkermans B (eds) Introduction to law. Springer, Heidelberg, pp 287–311
Gessner V (1998) Globalization and legal certainty. In: Gessner V, Budak AC (eds) Emerging legal certainty. Ashgate, Aldershot, pp 427–450
Grundmann S (2013) The EU consumer rights directive: optimizing, creating alternatives, or a dead end? Uniform Law Rev 18(1):98–127
Hage J (2014a) Foundations. In: Hage J, Akkermans B (eds) Introduction to law. Springer, Heidelberg, pp 1–22
Hage J (2014b) Philosophy of law. In: Hage J, Akkermans B (eds) Introduction to law. Springer, Heidelberg, pp 313–335
Haley JO (1991) Authority without power. Oxford University Press, Oxford
Haley JO (1998) The spirit of Japanese law. University of Georgia Press, Athens
Hamano R (2014) Access to attorneys in Japan and judicial reform. In: Vanoverbeke D, Maesschalck J, Nelken D, Parmentier S (eds) The changing role of law in Japan – empirical studies in culture, society and policy making. Edward Elgar, Cheltenham, pp 157–172
Helmich E (2012) § 297a. In: Kletečka A, Schauer M (eds), ABGB-ON, rdb.at, Vienna
Heringa AW (2014) Consitutional law. In: Hage J, Akkermans B (eds) Introduction to law. Springer, Heidelberg, pp 157–188
Homann N (2012) § 297a. In: Schwimann M, Kodek G (eds) ABGB Praxiskommentar Band II, 4th edn. LexisNexis, Vienna
Igarashi K (1990) Einführung in das japanische Recht. Wissenschaftliche Buchgesellschaft, Darmstadt
Ishikawa H (2013) Codification, decodification, and recodification of the Japanese civil code. In: Rivera JC (ed) The scope and structures of civil codes. Springer, Heidelberg, pp 267–285
Jiji Press (2015) Administration to push major revision to civil code. The Japan Times online. http://www.japantimes.co.jp/news/2015/03/31/national/crime-legal/administration-to-push-major-revisions-to-civil-code. Accessed 31 Aug 2015
Kamo A (2010) Crystallization, unification, or differentiation? The Japanese civil code (law of obligations) reform commission and basic reform policy (draft proposals). Columbia Journal of Asian Law 24:171–212
Kano N (2013) Reform of the Japanese civil code – the interim draft proposal of 2013. ZJapanR/JJapanL 18:249–261
Keiler J, Panzavolta M, Roes D (2014) Criminal law. In: Hage J, Akkermans B (eds) Introduction to law. Springer, Heidelberg, pp 121–156
Kietaibl C (2012) § 903. In: Kletečka A, Schauer M (eds), ABGB-ON, rdb.at, Vienna

Kitagawa Z (1990) Drei Entwicklungsphasen im japanischen Zivilrecht. In: Coing H, Hirano R, Kitagawa Z, Murakami J, Nörr KW, Oppermann T, Shiono H (eds) Die Japanisierung des westlichen Rechts. J.C.B. Mohr, Tübingen, pp 125–141
Kozuka S, Nottage L (2014) Policy and politics in contract law reform in Japan. In: Adams M, Heirbaut D (eds) The method and culture of comparative law: essays in honour of Mark Van Hoecke. Hart, Oxford, pp 235–253
Kurschel I (1989) Die Gewährleistung beim Werkvertrag. Manz, Vienna
Marutschke H-P (2009) Einführung in das japanische Recht, 2nd edn. C.H. Beck, Munich
Minear RH (1970) Japanese tradition and western law. Harvard University Press, Cambridge, MA
Müller-Freinfels W (1990) Japanisierung westlichen Rechts oder Verwestlichung japanischen Rechts? In: Coing H, Hirano R, Kitagawa Z, Murakami J, Nörr KW, Oppermann T, Shiono H (eds) Die Japanisierung des westlichen Rechts. J.C.B. Mohr, Tübingen, pp 177–202
Nagata M (2006) Das Verjährungsrecht in Japan – Entstehungsgeschichte, objektive und subjektive Elemente. In: Kunig P, Nagata M (eds) Deutschland und Japan im rechtswissenschaftlichen Dialog. Carl Heymans, Cologne, pp 71–90
Nakata K (2013) Die Internationalisierung des Vertragsrechts und das japanische Recht. ZJapanR/JJapanL 18:165–201
Neyer J (1998) Binding territoriality and functionality? Globalization meets the law. In: Gessner V, Budak AC (eds) Emerging legal certainty. Ashgate, Aldershot, pp 401–426
Oda H (2009) Japanese law, 3rd edn. Oxford University Press, Oxford
Okuda M (1985) Zivilrecht und Zivilrechtswissenschaften in Japan seit der Rezeption europäischer Rechte im 19. Jahrhundert. In: Gottfried Baumgärtel (ed) Grundprobleme des Privatrechts. Carl Heymanns, Cologne, pp 1–22
Ozaki I (2014) Law, culture and society in modernizing Japan. In: Vanoverbeke D, Maesschalck J, Nelken D, Parmentier S (eds) The changing role of law in Japan – empirical studies in culture, society and policy making. Edward Elgar, Cheltenham, pp 50–65
Petzold A (1998) Obtaining information on foreign legal systems. In: Gessner V, Budak AC (eds) Emerging legal certainty. Ashgate, Aldershot, pp 283–321
Rabl C (2002) Die Gefahrtragung beim Kauf. Manz, Vienna
Ramseyer JM, Nakazato M (1999) Japanese law – an economic approach. University of Chicago Press, Chicago
Sokolowski C (2010) Der so genannte Kodifikationenstreit in Japan. Iudicium, Munich
Stoll H (1990) Zur neueren Entwicklung des japanischen Zivilrechts in rechtsvergleichender Sicht. In: Coing H, Hirano R, Kitagawa Z, Murakami J, Nörr KW, Oppermann T, Shiono H (eds) Die Japanisierung des westlichen Rechts. J.C.B. Mohr, Tübingen, pp 151–175
Stuyck J (2010) Setting the scene, in cases, materials and text on consumer law. In: Micklitz H-W, Stuyck J, Terryn E (eds) Cases, materials and text on consumer law. Hart, Oxford, pp 1–69
Takahashi H (2014) Towards an understanding of the 'Japanese' way of dispute resolution: how is it different from the west. In: Vanoverbeke D, Maesschalck J, Nelken D, Parmentier S (eds) The changing role of law in Japan – empirical studies in culture, society and policy making. Edward Elgar, Cheltenham, pp 95–110
Uchida T (2011) Contract law reform in Japan and the UNIDROIT principles. Uniform Law Rev XVI:705–717
Upham FK (1978) Law and social change in postwar Japan. Harvard University Press, Cambridge, MA
Vande Walle S (2014) What keeps plaintiffs away from the court? An analysis of antitrust in Japan, Europe and the US. In: Vanoverbeke D, Maesschalck J, Nelken D, Parmentier S (eds) The changing role of law in Japan – empirical studies in culture, society and policy making. Edward Elgar, Cheltenham, pp 209–228
Vanoverbeke D, Maesschalck J, Nelken D, Parmentier S (eds) (2014) The changing role of law in Japan – empirical studies in culture, society and policy making. Edward Elgar, Cheltenham
von Bar C, Clive E (eds) (2009) Principles, definitions and model rules of European private law: draft common frame of reference (DCFR), Full Editionth edn. Sellier, Munich

von Bar C, Clive E, Schulte-Nölke H (eds) (2009) Principles, definitions and model rules of European private law – draft common frame of reference (DCFR) outline edition. Sellier, Munich

Wrbka S (2012a) Consumers and the proposal for an optional common European sales law – no roads lead to Rome? Kyushu University Legal Research Bulletin. http://www.law.kyushu-u.ac.jp/programsinenglish/kulrb/stefan.pdf. Accessed 31 Aug 2015

Wrbka S (2012b) The proposal for an optional common European sales law – a step in the right direction for consumer protection? EUIJ-Kyushu Rev 2:1–26

Wrbka S (2014a) Japan's civil code reform plan – seen from a western perspective. Kyushu University Legal Research Bulletin. http://www.law.kyushu-u.ac.jp/programsinenglish/kulrb/stefan2.pdf. Accessed 31 Aug 2015

Wrbka S (2014b) The dilemma of European consumer representation in deliberative networks – the democratic deficit in the context of the drafting of the common European sales law. In: Fenwick M, Van Uytsel S, Wrbka S (eds) Networked governance, transnational business & the law. Springer, Heidelberg

Wrbka S (2014c) The (paritally) revised Austrian passing of risk regime: an example of fragmentation of domestic law as a consequence of EU harmonisation. EUIJ-Kyushu Rev 3 and 4:29–52

Wrbka S (2015a) European consumer access to justice revisited. Cambridge University Press, Cambridge

Wrbka S (2015b) The potential and limits of teleological reduction shown with the example of the Austrian warranty regime. In: Fenwick M, Wrbka S (eds) Flexibility in modern business law: a comparative assessment. Springer, Heidelberg

Wrbka S (2015c) Geplante Obsoleszenz aus Sicht des Gewährleistungsrechts. Expert Opinion for the Vienna Chamber of Labour, Vienna

Intellectual Property, Private Ordering and Legal Certainty

Branislav Hazucha

Contents

Abstract The issues related to legal certainty are conventionally discussed in scholarly writings through the rule-standard dichotomy. However, the problems brought by new technologies and globalization have a significant impact on legal certainty in the present societies and are more complex than the standard analysis is able to cope with. This Chapter scrutinizes the controversies of this kind, brought by diverse private ordering regimes employed by the intellectual property right holders worldwide nowadays. It points out that these endeavours to increase legal certainty and protection for the right holders have their limits and are doomed to fail, unless they take into account the legitimate interests of all the concerned stakeholders.

Keywords Legal certainty • Copyright • Patent • Private ordering • Technological protection measures • Digital rights management • Standard essential patent

B. Hazucha (✉)
Graduate School of Law, Hokkaido University, Sapporo, Japan
e-mail: bhazucha@juris.hokudai.ac.jp

M. Fenwick, S. Wrbka (eds.), *Legal Certainty in a Contemporary Context*,
DOI 10.1007/978-981-10-0114-7_3

1 Introduction

The last few decades in the field of intellectual property law are characterized by growing use of private ordering through various forms of licensing agreements.[1] Private ordering is seen as a mechanism which allows the parties to adjust legal rules so that they better fit to a particular legal relationship. Private entities can create their own rules in order to substitute the default rules provided by statutory provisions or case law. In this way, the individual parties can achieve higher legal certainty which is beneficial to both of them.

However, if the bargaining power of contracting parties is not equal or at least comparable, private ordering can lead to a completely reverse outcome. In such a case, it can bring more legal uncertainty not only to the weaker party, but to both of them at the end. A good example is presented by the use of technological protection measures and digital right management systems with regard to certain types of copyrighted works, such as sound recordings, movies, computer programs or videogames.[2] These technological measures allow the copyright holders to set up the rules of how individuals are permitted to use the right holders' copyrighted works. The restriction can affect the users' possibility to make copies of copyrighted works for private non-commercial purposes, the number of how many times the users may watch, listen to or play them, or the territory where the works can be marketed and used.[3]

At the same time, the users have no option of any bargaining on those restrictions. They can only take them or leave them. A person who downloads a sound recording, movie or computer application is not able to reach any alteration in the terms and conditions of that online service. She can then unpleasantly find out that she will have to purchase it again, if her player, cell phone or computer upon which it is saved breaks down. This outcome is commonly brought by non-negotiable terms and conditions which are buttressed and implemented by special technological measures.

Similarly, anyone, who purchases a pre-recorded movie medium, such as a movie DVD or Blu-ray Disc, during her foreign trip or who orders it online from overseas, can be equally surprised when she discovers that she is unable to watch it on her player at home due to the regional zoning of movie DVDs and Blu-ray Discs guarded by another technological measure.[4]

Although those copies of copyrighted work are authorized and the concerned copyright holders have already been remunerated for them, their users are technologically restricted by the copyright holders beyond the scope of many national copyright laws in using them. In this way, the right holders attempt to avoid the

---

[1] See, e.g., Bell (1998); Elkin-Koren (1998); Benkler (2000); Efroni (2011).

[2] See, e.g., Dam (1999); Becker et al. (2003).

[3] See, e.g., Neuwirth (2009), pp. 415–418; Yu (2012), pp. 193–199; Trimble (2012), pp. 586–599.

[4] See, e.g., Neuwirth (2009), p. 414.

application of the exhaustion of rights or first sale doctrine[5] and of fair use,[6] fair dealing[7] or private copying[8] exception by setting up worldwide their own uniform rules of using the copies of their copyrighted works.

Likewise, many newcomers in the field of information and communication technologies can find themselves in the situation where they have to comply with a technical standard developed by a consortium of private entities and where at the same time they have no other option than to transfer a considerable portion of their revenues to the private entities holding patents which are essential for the implementation of that standard.[9] Many can deem such a situation as paying a sort of "private tax" or levy for complying with the mandatory rules governing the manufacture of specific products.

This situation was partially caused by imposing upon the World Trade Organization (WTO) members the obligation to use the international technical standards as a basis of their national technical regulations[10] and technical standards.[11] At first glance, such a solution seems beneficial for the liberalization of international trade and free movement of goods.[12] Nonetheless, many international technical standards, especially those in the field of information and communication technologies, have incorporated proprietary technologies which tend to be controlled by major multinational corporations.[13] The manufacturers of affected technologies in countries with emerging economies can then often do nothing else than to transfer a considerable portion of their revenues to the major multinational corporations established in a few developed countries.[14]

The aim of this Chapter is to scrutinize the abovementioned controversies brought by the private ordering regimes in the field of intellectual property law. Although private ordering is normally seen as a form of increasing legal certainty between the contracting parties, the Chapter shows that private ordering can increase legal certainty only when the legitimate interests of all the concerned stakeholders, and not only of entities with a stronger bargaining power, are taken into account. As a result, any attempt to impose privately created rules on those with weaker power merely leads to more legal uncertainty, because such rules will

[5] See, e.g., Goldstein and Hugenholtz (2010), pp. 305–307; Bently and Sherman (2014), pp. 151–152.

[6] See, e.g., Patry (1985); Goldstein and Hugenholtz (2010), pp. 362 and 372–373.

[7] See, e.g., Goldstein and Hugenholtz (2010), pp. 362–363 and 370–371; Bently and Sherman (2014), pp. 223–230.

[8] See, e.g., Davies (1984); Goldstein and Hugenholtz (2010), pp. 363 and 370–372.

[9] See, e.g., Li and An (2009), p. 22; An (2010).

[10] Agreement on Technical Barriers to Trade, Article 2.4, 15 April 1994, Marrakesh Agreement Establishing the World Trade Organization, Annex 1A, Agreements on Trade in Goods, 1186 UNTS 276 [hereinafter TBT Agreement].

[11] TBT Agreement, Annex 3 F.

[12] See, e.g., Sykes (1995), pp. 13–15.

[13] See, e.g., Blind et al. (2011); Maskus and Merrill (2013).

[14] See, e.g., Li and An (2009), p. 22.

be considered as unjust and unfair by the weaker parties which will tend to search for the ways of avoiding their application.

The Chapter is divided into two sections. Section 2 outlines possible views on the concept of legal certainty in the field of intellectual property law. Section 3 then scrutinizes several variants of private ordering and their impacts on legal certainty in intellectual property law. At the end, I make a few conclusions and observations on the limits of private ordering in increasing legal certainty.

2 Several Views on the Concept of Legal Certainty

A human is a social being[15] and life in a human society brings an array of social interactions with its other members. Some of those human conducts are advantageous for both interacting entities or entire society and are therefore encouraged by society; the others are either restricted or completely prohibited. This is accomplished through social or legal norms which role is to regulate human behaviour in a socially beneficial way.[16] Social and legal norms thus create and maintain certainty and stability in interpersonal interactions amongst the strangers by setting up the standard of recognized, restricted or completely prohibited human conduct.[17]

Nevertheless, the creation of norms requires certain level of abstraction which allows to broaden the scope of their application and then to cover a wider group of social interactions. Any abstraction, however, causes uncertainty in the application of those norms to the facts of a particular case. Hence, certainty is a cognitive phenomenon which is closely related to the ability to predict a specific outcome or consequence of certain human conduct in the form of social or legal sanctions for deviating from the pattern required by the norm in question.[18] The higher the predictability of an outcome there is, the higher the degree of certainty.

Accordingly, in the academic literature the scholarly discussions about legal certainty employ the terms such as "expectation",[19] "probability"[20] and "determinacy".[21] The discussion then focuses on the expectations of an individual as to the legal consequences of her conduct expressed in the degree of probability that a court will decide any dispute in a specific way. There are, therefore, several aspects which are crucial with regard to legal certainty. They concern the certainty in interpreting a norm and the impact of an authority which has the power to settle

[15] See, e.g., Aristotle, p. 5.

[16] See, e.g., Lessig (2006), p. 124.

[17] See, e.g., Gessner (1998), pp. 429–430.

[18] See, e.g., Lessig (2006), p. 124.

[19] See, e.g., Gessner (1998), p. 430.

[20] See, e.g., D'Amato (1983).

[21] See, e.g., Maxeiner (2007).

any dispute, of the right holders' attitudes towards the enforcement of their rights and of social changes on that certainty.

Consequently, the first aspect affecting legal certainty is the character of a rule itself which applies to the conduct in question. Individual rules differ in the way of their drafting. They can allow different degrees of freedom during their interpretation.[22] It can even happen that several competing rules can apply to a particular human conduct, be they within the same branch of law or belonging to different branches.[23] In cross-border cases, the situation is even more complicated due to the conflict between the rules from more than one legal system.[24]

For a better comprehension of legal certainty and its role in a contemporary context, it is important to understand that legal certainty is a relative concept. There are no cases where everything is legally certain. A certain degree of legal uncertainty which always exists provides the courts with necessary breathing space for applying generally stipulated legal norms to specific facts in individual cases. In addition, this permits to balance competing interests of concerned stakeholders, what is frequently the case in the field of intellectual property law.

There are numerous examples of legal certainty or uncertainty in the area of intellectual property law. We can take, as an example, a case where a mother records the first shaky movements of her beloved child when the baby listens to music on the radio. Nowadays, in the age of social media everyone wants to share everything with others. Therefore, she uploads that short video on the Facebook or Youtube website in order to share her baby's first dancing movements with her friends, but also millions of strangers. As the background music coming from the radio is copyrighted, it may easily happen that she will receive a cease and decease letter from the concerned copyright holder.[25] The point is that such a use of copyrighted work interferes with the copyright holder's exclusive rights. At the same time, there is no question that the mother in this scenario has no intention to commercially exploit that background music in her video and she does not obtain any financial benefit from its use. For cases of this sort, many national copyright laws provide for certain exceptions or defences.[26]

The question thus arises how the conflict between the competing legitimate interests of different entities should be settled down by a broad or narrow interpretation of a particular norm. In the academic literature, this is conventionally discussed as the difference between crystals and mud[27] or between rules and

[22] See Maxeiner (2007), p. 561.

[23] For diverse interactions between intellectual property law and the other branches of law, see Dinwoodie (2015).

[24] For details on the conflicts of laws in the field of intellectual property law, see van Eechoud (2003); Fawcett and Torremans (2011), pp. 665–940.

[25] See, e.g., Lenz v. Universal Music Corp., 572 F. Supp. 2d 1150 (N.D. Cal., 2008).

[26] See, e.g., Goldstein and Hugenholtz (2010), pp. 362–363 and 370–373.

[27] See, e.g., Rose (1988).

standards.[28] Rules, in this sense, allow a narrow degree of judge's interpretation or discretion, if any. They are therefore expected to be crystal clear. On the other hand, standards are designed so that they should allow the judges to balance the interests of affected stakeholders and thus they bring murky mud into the law.

In the field of intellectual property law, legal certainty in this sense is usually closely linked with broadening the scope of protecting intellectual property rights or with strengthening or weakening their protection. As a delicate balance between the interests of several stakeholders is struck in intellectual property law, it frequently happens that once legal certainty of protecting the legitimate interests of one stakeholder is increased, legal certainty of protecting the legitimate interests of other stakeholders is reduced. For instance, the broadening of the scope of patent protection to new therapeutic uses of known pharmaceutical drugs (so-called Swiss-type claims)[29] can provide the inventors of such new uses with legal protection. At the same time, it can cause legal uncertainty for other inventors or users of pharmaceutical drug in question, such as doctors, pharmacists as well as manufacturers of generic drugs. Put otherwise, the question arises here, to what extent and under what conditions a manufacturer of a generic drug should be held liable for a patent infringement of Swiss-type claim, when the manufacturer can reasonably foresee that some of doctors or pharmacists can prescribe its generic drug in a dosage having the protected, newly discovered therapeutic effect. In the case of imposing any liability on such a manufacturer, the right holder's interests are strongly protected against diverse ways of circumventing or evading the legal protection of their interests. Simultaneously, potential patent infringers, *i.e.* manufacturers of general drugs, doctors, pharmacists or even patients, are put into the position where it is not so easy for them to clearly predict the legal consequences of their activities.

The second abovementioned aspect affecting legal certainty relates to an entity which has the authority to adjudicate any dispute concerning the application of a particular norm.[30] Some judges or even entire courts are more open to strengthening the protection of intellectual property rights and the others are more pro-defendant. It can make a considerable difference when a lawsuit is initiated in one jurisdiction than the other. For instance, within the European Union certain courts, such as Dutch or German ones, are known as fast and often deciding in favour of right holders.[31] Conversely, certain other courts are notorious for their long proceedings, such as Belgian or Italian courts.[32] Comparable differences between the court's attitudes can also be found amongst the US federal district and circuit courts which proceedings take shorter or longer time or which are pro-plaintiff or pro-defendant.[33]

---

[28] See, e.g., Kennedy (1976).

[29] See, e.g., Scassa (2001).

[30] See, e.g., Moore and Parisi (2002).

[31] See, e.g., Graham and Van Zeebroeck (2014), pp. 669–674.

[32] See, e.g., Straus (2000), p. 414.

[33] See, e.g., Lemley (2010); Allison et al. (2014), p. 1778.

Moreover, we can observe a significant territorial extension of applying national intellectual property laws to acts conducted in other countries and harms suffered therein.[34] The extraterritorial application of domestic law habitually occurs in countries with stronger protection of intellectual property rights and with courts willing to extraterritorially apply their law in order to strengthen the protection of intellectual property right holders. It might then simply happen that an individual who designs her activities in relying on the domestic law of a particular jurisdiction can be found liable for infringing intellectual property law of another jurisdiction. Here, a note should be made that this is not only a case of pirate countries, but it can also take place between two jurisdictions with strong protection of intellectual property rights, but differing in certain aspects of their protection.[35]

Extraterritorial application of law is a quite controversial issue. On the one side, it attempts to prevent the situation where individual entities seek to avoid the application of a specific national law by moving their activities to one country, while targeting the market of another country. Nonetheless, the extraterritorial application has its own drawbacks which occur when it also covers the cases where the concerned entities did not intend to evade the law of another country. Such entities might not even be thinking that they are doing something wrong.

A good example might be the case where an entity exports from one country a particular component, which does not infringe any patent in that country, but the exported component is combined with another component overseas by a third party and the final product is imported back to the country where the exported component was manufactured and the product infringes a patent in that country.[36] The question is whether the component manufacturer can be held liable for a patent infringement. One case is when the manufacturer had actual knowledge of the future use of its component. Extraterritorial application of intellectual property law could then be justified to a certain degree. Would it be so if the manufacturer were assured that the final product would not be exported back to the country where the component was manufactured and would not infringe any patent in the country of producing the final product?

The attitude of right holders towards the enforcement of their rights can also have a considerable impact on legal certainty. When there is a very low or high probability that a right holder will enforce her exclusive rights against a particular alleged infringer, this probability significantly affects the degree of legal certainty under which the latter decides to act in a specific way. When the prospect of being caught and the severity of potential sanctions are low, an individual can easily disregard the rule restricting or prohibiting that conduct, since the probability of suffering any negative legal consequences for her conduct is low.[37]

[34] See, e.g., Bradley (1997).

[35] See, e.g., Decherney (2011), pp. 284–287 and 325.

[36] See, e.g., Peukert (2012), pp. 216–219.

[37] See, e.g., Becker (1968).

This also includes the cases where a gap appears to emerge between what the law requires and what the public considers as normal. For instance, millions of Internet users disregard copyright law on a daily basis. Individuals upload and download music, movies and other copyrighted works to and from a variety of websites and networks. Although making reproductions of copyrighted works without obtaining an authorization from their copyright holders is an act of infringing the copyright holders' exclusive rights to make reproductions, millions of Internet users consider their activities as normal and harmless. They do not even think that they might infringe the exclusive rights of any right holder. As many of those activities are contrary to contemporary copyright law, copyright law is vastly disregarded by the public and has very weak expressive power[38] towards individuals concerning their private non-commercial activities.[39] Moreover, although the copyright holders regularly lament about the current situation of the ignorance of copyright law by the public, they rarely enforce their exclusive rights against individuals who commit acts of copyright infringement during private non-commercial use of copyrighted works in a small scale.[40]

Finally, legal certainty also varies over time. A certain rule can become uncertain due to a change in the pattern of human behaviour, which can be brought about by a political, economic or social change or by the introduction of new technology allowing or making easier certain types of human conduct.[41] In addition, the change in certainty of a rule can also be produced by competing ways of its interpretation by the courts, individuals, lawyers and so on. At the same time, an uncertain rule can become clarified in a similar way over the time.

For example, in the case of Napster peer-to-peer file-sharing network, the founders of Napster approached a lawyer before its founding in order to obtain legal advice on whether their business activities were complying with US copyright law. Their lawyer concluded that the activities of individuals using their network were covered by the fair use doctrine and therefore peer-to-peer file sharing facilitated by the Napster network was seen as not infringing any exclusive right of copyright holders. Though it is possible to discuss whether the lawyer's legal advice was correct and adequate with the hindsight of the rulings of US federal courts in the Napster case[42] and similar later cases,[43] before and also after the ruling in the Napster case many established commentators were of opinion that there was no copyright infringement in that case.[44] The present situation is that many legal

---

[38] See, e.g., Sunstein (1996); Anderson and Pildes (2000).

[39] See, e.g., Hazucha et al. (2012).

[40] See, e.g., Wu (2008).

[41] See, e.g., Depoorter (2009).

[42] A&M Records, Inc. v. Napster, Inc., 114 F. Supp. 2d 896, 2000 U.S. Dist. LEXIS 11862 (N.D. Cal., 2000), aff'd, 239 F.3d 1004, 2001 U.S. Dist. LEXIS 5446 (9th Cir., 2001).

[43] See, e.g., In re Aimster Copyright Litigation, 2002 U.S. Dist. LEXIS 17054 (N.D. Ill., 2002), aff'd, 334 F.3d 643 (8th Cir., 2004).

[44] See, e.g., Yen (2001).

experts consider the Napster case as a clear example of indirect copyright infringement.[45]

To sum up, legal certainty in a contemporary context brings, in the field of intellectual property, several possible dimensions which should be taken into consideration, such as legal certainty from the perspective of intellectual property right holders, users of protected intellectual property and third parties which can encourage, facilitate or otherwise contribute to the infringement of intellectual property rights. In addition, there are also dimensions brought from the perspective of law making and enforcement, *i.e.* who is the authority which can make a new law or can enforce it.

3 Private Ordering and Legal Certainty

During the last few decades intellectual property law has been notably influenced by private ordering. This situation has also had an impact on legal certainty in the field of intellectual property law. Private ordering can be seen as a spectrum to what extent the power to create legally binding rules is transferred from, or recognized by, the respective public authority in a certain way.[46] On the one side of spectrum is the scenario where the lawmaking authority is exercised by one of state authorities, *i.e.* a legislature or courts. In such a case, the private entities can affect the content of legal rules through various lobbying[47] or litigation activities.[48] On the other side is the case where private entities are completely free to create their own law.

3.1 Lobbying and Forum Shopping

Intellectual property right holders frequently argue that their legitimate interests are not sufficiently protected and the scope of protection should be broadened or the enforcement should be made more efficient and severe. These claims are made on the national, regional as well as international level. Moreover, we can observe steady switches between diverse venues and fora, depending upon their openness to the idea of strengthening intellectual property protection.[49] In order to prevent any watering down of their proposals, the advocates of such changes tend to move their lobbying activities from the national level to the regional or international level and from open to more closed policymaking settings.

[45] See, e.g., Ginsburg (2008), p. 582.

[46] See, e.g., Schwarcz (2002), p. 324.

[47] See, e.g., Komesar (1994), pp. 63–64.

[48] See, e.g., Galanter (1974).

[49] See, e.g., Drahos with Braithwaite (2002).

Consequently, the role of individual intellectual property policymaking fora has notably changed over time. For instance, the World Intellectual Property Organization (WIPO) and its predecessor, the United International Bureaux for the Protection of Intellectual Property (BIRPI), was a vehicle of regular updating intellectual property policies on the international level almost for one century up to the late 1960s, when the developing countries acquired the majority of votes in this United Nation specialized organization.[50] In the field of copyright law, this can be seen on the stalemate brought at the Stockholm conference in 1967, which was partially overcome in 1971.[51] In the field of patent law, the final straw for the advocates of strengthening intellectual property protection was the failure to harmonize patent law within the WIPO framework at the beginning of 1980s.[52]

Since the late 1960s the right holders therefore searched for a forum more open to the idea of strengthening intellectual property protection on the international level. It was found within the framework of international trade negotiations, which led to the WTO establishment in 1995 and the introduction of intellectual property protection into the international trade law in the form of the *Agreement on Trade-Related Aspects of Intellectual Property Rights* (TRIPs Agreement).[53] Contrary to preceding negotiations on intellectual property policies, the TRIPs Agreement was a part of package deal. Any country which wanted to benefit from the WTO regime had to agree with the TRIPs Agreement. Many developing countries were therefore put into a take-it-or-leave-it position.

More recently, we can even observe a switch from the WTO framework to special *ad hoc* trade negotiations between selected major developed countries so that the possible input from other stakeholders is minimized as much as possible. In the case of *Anti-Counterfeiting Trade Agreement* (ACTA),[54] the negotiations were so secret that several national public authorities denied any public access to information concerning the negotiations upon the freedom of information legislations.[55] A similar situation of maintaining secrecy about the content of negotiations has reappeared with the negotiation of *Trans-Pacific Partnership* (TPP),[56] although its implementation will require several considerable changes of national intellectual property laws in many negotiating countries. It will not be only the case of developing countries, but it will also affect the laws of several developed countries, such as Japan and New Zealand.[57]

[50] See, e.g., Clift (2010), p. 6; Deere-Birkbeck (2010), pp. 30–38.

[51] See, e.g., Deere-Birkbeck (2010), p. 34.

[52] See, e.g., Clift (2010), pp. 6–7; Deere-Birkbeck (2010), pp. 38–42; Gervais (2008), pp. 8–10.

[53] Agreement on Trade Related Aspects of Intellectual Property Rights, 15 April 1994, Marrakesh Agreement Establishing the World Trade Organization, Annex 1C, Legal Instruments-Results of the Uruguay Round, 1869 UNTS 299.

[54] For more details on the Anti-Counterfeiting Trade Agreement, see, e.g., Roffe and Seuba (2014).

[55] See, e.g., Kravets (2009).

[56] See, e.g., Kaminski (2015).

[57] See, e.g., Yasoshima (2015).

This raises the issue of the lack of democratic process in the case of adopting such intellectual property policies. In the case of involved countries, their national parliaments are completely circumvented and put into the position to take it or leave it without any possibility to mould it so that the legitimate interests of other stakeholders are taken into consideration. Moreover, in the case of ACTA's success amongst the developed countries that standard of intellectual property law enforcement would be exported to other countries via a range of regional and bilateral free trade agreements between one of major economic powers such as US and EU on the one side and individual developing countries on the other.[58]

Despite the fact that the high level of harmonization of intellectual property laws has been achieved on an international and regional level, the intellectual property rights remain territorial rights. No right holder has a global copyright, global patent or global trademark. Each holder has only the exclusive rights granted by individual national laws. This situation has led to the attempts to harmonize a minimal level of protection provided by national laws since the nineteenth century.

Although a lot has been achieved in this regard, it still does not mean that the exclusive rights provided by national law in one country are exactly same to those guaranteed in other countries. There are still significant differences amongst countries. Individual national laws provide different types of exclusive rights, which can vary in their scope, entitled entities or exceptions.[59] While in many countries, such as Germany or Japan, a copyright user can make a copy of an entire copyrighted work for personal use,[60] the same user can make only a copy of a certain part of copyrighted work in several other countries.[61] In UK it is necessary to examine whether it is fair dealing for a specific purpose recognized by the UK copyright law.[62] In US the courts would examine whether copying satisfies the conditions of fair use doctrine.[63]

Similar observations also apply to industrial property rights. Moreover, if the registration is required for obtaining certain types of industrial rights, such as patents, trademarks or industrial designs, an individual has to obtain the registration of its intellectual property, with or without examination, depending upon a particular type of industrial rights, before she can claim any protection of her exclusive rights. The international intellectual property law provides mechanisms for simplifying the filing of applications in multiple jurisdictions via recognizing the priority of filing[64] and creating the international application systems, which allow to file a

[58] See, e.g., Roffe et al. (2010).

[59] For details, see, e.g., Goldstein and Hugenholtz (2010), pp. 297–357.

[60] See, e.g., Article 53 German Copyright Act of 1965; Article 30 Japanese Copyright Act of 1970.

[61] See, e.g., § 43(2) Slovak Copyright Act of 2015.

[62] See, e.g., Goldstein and Hugenholtz (2010), pp. 362–363 and 370–371; Bently and Sherman (2014), pp. 223–230.

[63] See, e.g., Patry (1985); Goldstein and Hugenholtz (2010), pp. 362 and 372–373.

[64] Paris Convention for the Protection of Industrial Property, Article 4, 20 March 1883, 828 UNTS 305.

single application in order to obtain national registrations in several jurisdictions.[65] The outcome often is that the scope of granted industrial rights can slightly differ, although they can cover the same invention, trademark or industrial design. The reason is that, for example, some of the claims in a patent application might not be allowed in individual countries. Therefore, the claims of granted patents stemming from the same international application might differ. Similarly, in some countries, the application can be divided into several, independently processed applications leading to granting several independent patents.

All these things can create a number of problems for the right holders during using and managing their intellectual property rights on the global level. Therefore, intellectual property right holders tend to search for mechanisms of how to level the playground in addition to the abovementioned lobbying on the national, regional and international level of intellectual property policy making. One of such mechanisms is presented by a spectrum of private ordering allowed on a contractual basis through licensing agreements.

3.2 Setting the Rules by Technological Measures

A classical example of private ordering is presented by contractual freedom.[66] Article 1134(1) of French Civil Code stipulates it tersely by pointing out that "[a] greements lawfully entered into take the place of the law for those who have made them."[67] Contractual freedom guarantees that private parties are free to regulate their own mutual relationships contractually. However, this approach has one significant limitation. The contractual rights and obligations are binding only for the contractual parties.

Under certain conditions, the binding power of private ordering can be broadened even beyond the group of contractual parties. In general, the laws are very reluctant to allow the creation of rights and especially obligations beyond the contractual parties to a contract.[68] Exceptions are presented by property rights which are binding against the world (*erga omnes*), but the list of such rights is strictly restricted by the law and the parties are not in principle allowed to create new types of rights and obligations which would be binding other entities than contractual parties.[69] Unsuccessful attempts to impose obligations on third parties

[65] See, e.g., Patent Cooperation Treaty, 19 June 1970, 1160 UNTS 231; Madrid Agreement Concerning the International Registration of Marks, 14 April 1891, 828 UNTS 389; and Protocol Relating to the Madrid Agreement Concerning the International Registration of Marks, 27 June 1989, WIPO Pub. No. 204(E).

[66] See, e.g., Awrey (2014), pp. 190–193.

[67] Translation by G Rouhette and A Rouhette-Berton. http://www.legifrance.gouv.fr/content/download/1950/13681/version/3/file/Code_22.pdf. Accessed 1 September 2015.

[68] See, e.g., Akkermans (2009).

[69] See, e.g., Keppell v. Bailey [1834] 39 ER 1042; Hill v. Tupper [1863] 2 H & C 121.

in the field of intellectual property law are presented by a number of cases where the authorized copies of copyrighted works contained an array of stipulations, which were not legally binding, although they pretended to be so.[70] For instance, books or sound recordings were published for certain territorial markets and expressly stated this condition on their covers or somewhere inside of a book or leaflet accompanying audiocassettes and music CDs. Similarly, they contained statements that any copying of a book or sound recording was prohibited and it infringed the exclusive rights of concerned right holders. As such statements sought to expand the scope of copyright protection and were not included in the purchase contract, they were found by the court as not binding.[71]

Accordingly, anyone could, during her foreign trip, purchase an authorized copy of copyrighted works and could import it into her home country under many national laws.[72] This was recently expressly acknowledged by the US Supreme Court in *Kirtsaeng v. John Wiley & Sons, Inc.*,[73] where a Thai student at a US university set up a profitable business on importing cheap copies of American textbooks from Thailand and selling them on the eBay website in the United States.

Nonetheless, the digital technologies allow the right holders to circumvent the privity of contract[74] and *numerus clausus*[75] doctrines which confine the effects of private contracts beyond the contractual parties. The technologies thus permit the strengthening of the power of licensing agreements in several ways. The users of diverse copyrighted works, such as computer programs, videogames, e-books and downloaded music and videos, are commonly asked to agree with licensing agreements which incorporates a range of restrictions on the use of copyrighted works. As a result, although the statements on the prohibition of copying or selling outside certain specific territory are not binding in the analogue world, unless they are expressly incorporated into the sale of goods contract, they are contractually binding in the digital world, since the users of copyrighted works have no other option than to agree with the restrictions before being able to use the authorized copies of copyrighted works.

In addition, certain types of copyrighted works are marketed with technological protection measures and digital rights management systems which *de facto* implement those restrictions technologically. For instance, videogames and movie DVDs and Blu-ray Discs contain technologies which allow the copyright holders to divide marketing of their copyrighted works into several territorial zones. In practice, movie DVDs or Blu-ray Discs bought in the US or Canada will not be able to be watched on devices set up for the territories of Europe, Australia or China, and *vice*

[70] See, e.g., Straus v. Victor Talking Machine Co., 243 US 490 (US Sup Ct, 1917).

[71] See, e.g., Bobbs-Merrill Co. v. Straus et al. doing business as R.H. Macy & Company, 210 US 339 (US Sup Ct, 1908).

[72] See, e.g., Goldstein and Hugenholtz (2010), pp. 305–307.

[73] 133 S. Ct. 1351 (2013).

[74] See, e.g., Dunlop Pneumatic Tyre Co. Ltd. v. Selfridge & Co. Ltd. [1915] AC 847 (HL).

[75] See, e.g., 39 ER 1042; [1863] 2 H & C 121.

versa. Hence, if a special edition is released only for the US or Canadian market, the European, Australian or Chinese consumers who would be able to purchase it online or overseas would not be able to play them on their devices set up for their territorial zone. Similarly, the territorial restrictions are available in the case of videogames for videogame consoles. Likewise, comparable restrictions apply to certain music portable players and e-book readers.

The technological protection measures and digital rights management systems thus allow the copyright holders to set up the rules of using the copies of their copyrighted works beyond the scope of present copyright laws. Historically, the so-called first sale or exhaustion of rights doctrine has developed in copyright law in order to strike a balance between the legitimate interests of copyright holders and owners of the authorized copies of copyrighted works. Once an authorized copy of copyrighted work has been lawfully acquired by its first purchaser, she could freely deal with that copy without the need to obtain any additional authorization from the copyright holder. She could keep that copy, could sell it to a third party or could even destroy it.

The first sale doctrine is the expression of fundamental values brought about by the political, economic and social change from feudalism to capitalism. While the feudal regimes were based on an array of restrictions which presented the barriers to free traffic in immovables, one of key features of changing from feudalism and capitalism was the abolition of the types of rights which created the regimes of split ownership or control over lands and other resources. The free movement or traffic in immovables and chattels was considered as vital for capitalist regimes. The courts have therefore been very hostile towards the attempts to create contractually new types of rights and obligations which would be binding towards individuals who were not contractual parties to such a contract.[76] Accordingly, the courts have struck down a number of endeavours to set up the minimal price for the resale of goods which incorporated copyrighted works or patented inventions, or even to restrict any future resale of such goods.[77]

The technological protection measures and digital right management systems have reopened this controversy. As the copyright holders have achieved the adoption of legal protection for technological protection measures and digital rights management systems against their circumvention,[78] they have tried to freely set up restrictions on the use of their copyrighted works through technological measures. The courts in many jurisdictions have been quite open to sustain such technological restrictions imposed by the copyright holders.[79] The only condition which is

[76] See, e.g., [1834] 39 ER 1042; [1863] 2 H & C 121.

[77] See, e.g., 210 US 339; 243 US 490; [1915] AC 847.

[78] WIPO Copyright Treaty, Arts 11 and 12 , 20 December 1996, 2186 UNTS 152; WIPO Performances and Phonograms Treaty, Arts 18 and 19, 20 December 1996, 2186 UNTS 245; Beijing Treaty on Audiovisual Performances, Arts 15 and 16, 24 June 2012.

[79] See, e.g., Sony Computer Entertainment America, Inc. v. GameMasters, Inc., 87 F. Supp. 2d 976 (ND Cal, 1999); Sony Computer Entertainment v. Paul Owen and Others [2002] EWHC 45 (Ch); Kabushiki Kaisha Sony Computer Entertainment Inc. & Others v. Ball & Others [2004] EWHC 1738 (Ch); Stevens v. Kabushiki Kaisha Sony Computer Entertainment [2005] HCA 58, (2005) 221 ALR 448, (2005) 79 ALJR 1850.

required from the copyright holders is to inform the purchasers on the restrictions[80] or at least to return the payment of price for the copy of a copyrighted work back, when its purchaser finds out a particular restriction only after purchasing it and does not agree with the restriction.[81]

In addition, many recent licensing agreements expressly stipulate that the user is not any owner of a copy of copyrighted work, but only a licensee who has the right to use that copy, while the title to it is retained by the copyright holder.[82] As there is freedom of contract in many advanced legal regimes, the contractual parties can freely agree on terms and conditions. The problem is that the consumers rarely have any other option. They can only take it or leave it. There is no bargaining on particular terms of licensing agreements between the parties. In many cases, licensing agreements are quite complex and long for reading and understanding all their nuances by the general public.[83]

Although it might seem that the current regime, which combines the legal protection with private ordering, enhances legal certainty, since the copyright holders can set up the rules of using their copyrighted works and the same standard is applicable worldwide, the actual outcome is completely opposite in many cases. The public disagreement with the current situation of using technological restrictions can be observed on vast disregard and circumvention of technological measures, especially, in the case of movie DVDs and Blu-ray Discs. Despite the fact that the copyright holders have vigorously fought worldwide to prevent the distribution of circumvention applications for movie DVDs and Blu-ray Discs,[84] the necessary computer applications can be easily found in a few minutes through a common search engine. Surveys on consumers' conduct confirm that a significant number of users habitually circumvent the technological protection measures in order to make private or back-up copies of movie DVDs or Blu-ray Discs.[85] Hence, although the existing law has been designed in order to increase legal protection and certainty for the copyright holders, the actual outcome is that it has only brought more legal uncertainty not only for the copyright users, but also for the copyright holders due to vast disregard and circumvention of used technological protection measures by the public.

The technological restrictions have seldom any significant impact on frequent copyright infringers, but they can have considerable negative impact on those who normally comply with copyright law. Those who purchase movie media from other

---

[80] See, e.g., Studio Canal, Soc. Universal Pictures vidéo France and SEV v. S Perquin, UFC Que choisir, Judgment No 549 FS-P + B + R + I (Sup Ct of France, 2006).

[81] See, e.g., ProCD, Inc. v. Zeidenberg, 86 F.3d 1447 (7th Cir., 1996).

[82] See, e.g., Vernor v. Autodesk, Inc., 621 F.3d 1103 (9th Cir., 2010).

[83] See, e.g., Chen-Wishart (2014).

[84] See, e.g., Universal City Studios, Inc. v. Reimerdes, 111 F. Supp. 2d 294 (S.D.N.Y., 2000), aff'd sub nom. Universal City Studios, Inc. v. Corley, 273 F.3d 429 (2d Cir., 2001); and 321 Studios v. Metro Goldwyn Mayer Studios, Inc., 307 F. Supp. 2d 1085 (N.D. Cal., 2004).

[85] See, e.g., Hazucha et al. (2014), p. 154.

geographical regions can be very frustrated after learning that they cannot watch them, although the copies of copyrighted works are authorized and the copyright holders are properly remunerated for them. It can only encourage them to circumvent the used technological restrictions despite their willingness to pay for the authorized copies. This is particularly the case of special regional editions of movies not available to aficionados in the other DVD or Blu-ray Disc regions.

The copyright holders regularly support their practice by several arguments. In the case of restricting making of fair-use or private copies, the right holders habitually argue that it is very difficult to implement those exceptions into technological protection measures. They claim that any exception to such measures can open floodgates of mass unauthorized copying. In addition, although they do not express it vocally, many of them question the appropriateness and adequacy of those exceptions in the digital age. They put forward that those exceptions could be justified in an analogue world, but have no place in the digital age where the copyright holders and the users can agree on diverse variations of their mutual relationships with regard to using copyrighted works. This logic has been rejected by the Canadian Supreme Court which is of opinion that the copyright users should be allowed to do the same things in the digital world as they are allowed to do in the analogue world.[86] This view is shared by many intellectual property scholars worldwide,[87] but not many national courts in other jurisdictions came to a comparable conclusion.[88]

The use of geographical restrictions is often explained by referring to the certain specific features of movie distribution. First, movies are released in individual territorial markets at different time.[89] Movie distribution is thus characterized by certain timing order of releasing movies in different regions. For instance, the US blockbusters are commonly released to movie theatres first on the US and Canadian markets. If they are commercially successful on this primary market, they are also released to movie theatres on other overseas markets.[90]

After a certain period of time from the movie theatre release, the movies are released also on DVDs and Blu-ray Discs.[91] It habitually happens that a movie is released on DVDs and Blu-ray Discs on one market, even though it has not been still released to movie theatres in another territorial market. It is normally argued that if the distribution of movie tangible media were not territorially restricted, it would considerably undermine the entire organization of movie industry and distribution.[92] The reasons for time division between individual venues of movie

[86] See CCH Canadian Ltd. v. Law Society of Upper Canada [2004] 1 SCR 339 (Sup Ct of Canada, 2004).

[87] See, e.g., Geiger et al. (2014); Samuelson (2015), pp. 859–862.

[88] See, e.g., [2002] EWHC 45.

[89] See, e.g., Neuwirth (2009), p. 421; Yu (2012), p. 200.

[90] See, e.g., Neuwirth (2009), p. 421.

[91] See, e.g., Waterman and Weiss (2010).

[92] See, e.g., Neuwirth (2009), pp. 421–422; Yu (2012), p. 200.

distribution, such as movie theatres, DVDs and Blu-ray Discs, and premium subscription and free-to-air TV channels, is to achieve price discrimination which is supposed to allow the copyright holders to maximize their revenues from consumers differing in their willingness to pay for the access to copyrighted movies.[93]

Several objections to this justification can be made. Language is, in many cases, a sufficient barrier for preventing mass distribution of pre-recorded movie media from one country to another. It is also questionable to what extent the delays in releasing movies on different markets are justifiable. The delays in releasing movies on different markets are often explained by the need to prepare local dubbing or subtitles. However, there are countries, such as Australia or New Zealand, where there is no need to make any adjustment to the original versions of US movies, but the movies are habitually released on those market with considerable delays from their initial releases on the US and Canadian markets. Even when the local adjustment of foreign movies is necessary, there is usually time period between the final production of a movie and its release. During this period of time, the local versions for several markets can be prepared. There have been cases where the movies were released almost around the same time on major markets[94] or where the traditional time order in releasing movies on different media was not followed.[95]

Second, the movie distribution is geographically divided.[96] Different entities have exclusive licenses to distribute individual copyrighted movies in different territories. An entity licensed to distribute a movie on the US or Canadian markets can be completely different from the one licensed to do so on the European, Japanese or Australian market. The distribution of movie DVDs and Blu-ray Discs marketed for one region in another one can therefore be considered as an interference with her legitimate interest by the entity having the exclusive license for the latter region. The geographical division allowed by DVD and Blu-ray Disc technology is thus deemed as preventing such interference with the distribution and licensing regime.

Nonetheless, one might argue that the strict geographical division of global market can go against the idea of liberalizing the international trade and competition between the producers of same or similar products.[97] Moreover, in many cases the entities having exclusive licenses for different regions belong to the same multinational groups. Furthermore, some regions are quite broad and cover countries from several continents.[98] It is then impossible that the same entity will have the license to distribute a particular movie within the entire DVD or Blu-ray Disc geographical region. There is therefore a possibility of the movement of movie

[93] See. e.g., Boyle (2000); Landes and Posner (2003), pp. 39–40.

[94] See, e.g., Yu (2012), pp. 204–205.

[95] See, e.g., Eller (2006).

[96] See, e.g., Yu (2012), pp. 209–213.

[97] See, e.g., Neuwirth (2009), pp. 454–458.

[98] See Neuwirth (2009), pp. 416–417; Yu (2012), p. 194.

DVDs and Blu-ray Discs within that region, although it might significantly interfere with the geographical division of markets by licensing agreements.

Finally, some might argue that the geographical division allows the copyright holders to charge more in the developed countries and less in the developing countries.[99] Then, if there were a possibility to export the movie DVDs and Blu-ray Discs from the markets where they were marketed with discount to the premium markets, it would undermine the entire system of price discrimination. However, the problem with this argument is that in many cases the prices are almost same, if not even higher in the developing countries than in the developed ones. In addition, many regions defined by the DVD as well as Blu-ray Disc technologies contain diverse groups of countries from the developed countries to the developing and even the least developed ones.[100] Therefore, this argument does not make much sense, although there are advocates who argue that separating the products aimed to the developed countries from those produced for the developed ones can allow charging less the people with lower incomes.

3.3 *Proprietarization of Technical Standards*

Another form of private ordering on the abovementioned spectrum is when a public authority transfers certain powers to private entities or their associations.[101] One such situation is presented by the case of technical standardization in many developed countries, where drafting of technical standards is left upon private standard setting organizations or even consortia of entities manufacturing a particular product.[102] The technical standardization by private entities has been seen as a form of deregulation and self-regulation, but at the same time it has raised several antitrust issues.

From the perspective of international trade, the national technical standards have been traditionally used as a way of protecting local industries against foreign competition.[103] This is also one of reasons, why two special agreements dealing with diverse types of standards imposed on various products have been incorporated into the WTO regime. The *Agreement on the Application of Sanitary and Phytosanitary Measures* (SPS Agreement)[104] deals with special sanitary and phytosanitary measures adopted in order to achieve food safety and animal and

[99] See, e.g., Yu (2012), pp. 206–207.

[100] See Yu (2012), pp. 208–209; Neuwirth (2009), p. 423.

[101] See, e.g., Schwarcz (2002), pp. 324.

[102] See, e.g., Cargill (1989), pp. 155–195; Krislov (1997), pp. 104–133 and 137–160; Tate (2001), pp. 446–459 and 463–468; Gibson (2007), pp. 1413–1417; Jakobs (2009), pp. 177–179.

[103] See, e.g., Sykes (1995), pp. 13–15.

[104] Agreement on the Application of Sanitary and Phytosanitary Measures, Annex A(3), 15 April 1994, Marrakesh Agreement Establishing the World Trade Organization, Annex 1A, Agreements on Trade in Goods, 1867 UNTS 493.

plant health, and the *Agreement on Technical Barriers to Trade* (TBT Agreement) with other technical standards which can create a technical barrier to trade.

To prevent the creation of a technical barrier to trade, the TBT Agreement requires the WTO members to rely on the international standards[105] in drafting their national technical regulations[106] and technical standards.[107] In this way, the international trade is expected to be liberalized, because it prevents individual WTO members to create an obstacle to the importation of foreign products due to their failure to comply with specific requirements imposed upon them by national technical regulation or technical standards.[108]

The growth of international trade liberalization has resulted in huge surge of international standardization. Since the 1990s the number of international standards has been exponentially growing.[109] The expansion of technical standards is also related to the changes in the organization of technical standardization. In the late 1980s and early 1990s many stakeholders complained that the technical standardization took long time. It could take for several years to reach the final version of a technical standard.[110] Therefore, many stakeholders were calling for making technical standardization more flexible and less formal.[111] This has led to the growth of so-called standard setting consortia which are special interest-based consortia of major market players in a particular field.[112] At the present many international standards especially in the field of information and communication technologies have been created by standard setting consortia and later approved by a formal standard setting organization.[113]

---

[105] TBT Agreement, Annex 1(2) and (4) (defining the terms "standard" and "international body or system"); World Trade Organization (WTO), Committee on Technical Barriers to Trade (2000) *Second Triennial Review of the Operation and Implementation of the Agreement on Technical Barriers to Trade*, G/TBT/9, 20 and Annex 4 (containing the Decision of the Committee on Principles for the Development of International Standards, Guides and Recommendations with Relation to Articles 2, 5 and Annex 3 of the Agreement).

[106] TBT Agreement, Article 1.6 and Annex 1(1) (defining "technical regulation" as "[d]ocument which lays down product characteristics or their related processes and production methods, including the applicable administrative provisions, with which compliance is *mandatory*" [emphasis added]).

[107] TBT Agreement, Article 1.6 and Annex 1(2) (defining "technical standard" as "[d]ocument approved by a recognized body, that provides, for common and repeated use, rules, guidelines or characteristics for products or related processes and production methods, with which compliance is not *mandatory*" [emphasis added]).

[108] See, e.g., Sykes (1995), pp. 13–15.

[109] See, e.g., Büthe and Mattli (2011), pp. 6–7.

[110] See, e.g., David and Shurmer (1996), p. 795 (stating in the 1990s that "the average time taken to produce a standard varies from 2 1/2 years at the national level, through to 4–5 years regionally, and 7 years or more at the international level").

[111] See, e.g., Besen (1995), pp. 142–143.

[112] See, e.g., Blind and Gauch (2008), pp. 505–506.

[113] See, e.g., Hazucha (2013), p. 539–541 (presenting several examples of international technical standards developed by private consortia and approved by international standard setting organizations).

Some may criticize this process as avoiding open formal standardization. The standards can be drafted in secrecy by one of private consortia. Once a standard is proposed to a formal standard setting organization by a consortium, it is hard to make any substantial change to that standard, since it is already finalized. This status quo is also preserved by the special procedures for approving such standards by standard setting organizations.[114]

On the other hand, it should be taken into account that many standard setting consortia cover major market players. Due to their less formal procedure, the consortia can speed up the entire standard setting procedure. Moreover, the empirical studies observe that they are more compliments than substitutes of standard setting organizations.[115] They are usually created *ad hoc* for a particular purpose. Once that goal is achieved, they are dissolved.[116]

A further problem with this privatization of international regulation and making it binding on national level is that many international standards especially in certain fields of technology, such as information and communication technologies, incorporate proprietary technologies. Hence, anyone who wants to produce a product compatible to such an international standard must pay a considerable amount of her revenues to the holders of patents which are essential for the standard's implementation. This practice has been severely criticized because of its privatization of lawmaking and creation of quasi-private taxes or levies.[117] As the products are required to be compatible with technical standards, the consortia of private entities can acquire the power over those who have to comply with the standards containing proprietary technologies.

The history of incorporating proprietary technologies into technical standards is long and perplexed. At the end of nineteenth century, many industries in developed countries were characterized by cartelization.[118] A similar movement has also appeared in the field of then cutting-edge technologies, such as sound recording, movie camera or sewing machine.[119] The holders of essential patents for those complex technologies created patent pools which allowed them to control and divide the respective markets between themselves.[120] In the first half of twentieth century many patent pools were found to be anticompetitive and were dissolved by the antitrust authorities in the United States.[121] For long time, patent pools were then seen as the violation of antitrust law, but the attitude of antitrust authorities towards patent pools changed again in the later part of the twentieth century.[122]

---

114 See, e.g., ISO/IEC (2012), pp. 23–29.

115 See, e.g., Blind and Gauch (2008), pp. 505 and 511–512.

116 See Blind and Gauch (2008), p. 512.

117 See, e.g., Li and An (2009), p. 22.

118 See, e.g., Freyer (1992), pp. 11–42.

119 See, e.g., Lampe and Moser (2010, forthcoming 2016).

120 See, e.g., Bekkers et al. (2011), p. 910; Lampe and Moser (forthcoming 2016).

121 See, e.g., Gilbert (2004); and Bekkers et al. (2011), p. 910; Lampe and Moser (forthcoming 2016).

122 See, e.g., den Uijl et al. (2013), p. 32.

It should be noted that the standards created by those patent pools were private technical standards drafted by consortia of private entities. The first proprietary technologies were incorporated into the technical standards drafted by open standard setting organizations after the World War II, but still until the 1980s this issue was very sensitive. Accordingly, for instance, the two major technical standards for the first generation of mobile telephony, the US Advanced Mobile Phone System (AMPS) and Nordic Mobile Telephony (NMT) standards, were non-proprietary, although in both cases for different reasons. In the case of AMPS standard, AT&T as the major holder of patents for mobile telephony at that time was for long time under the surveillance of US antitrust authority and therefore opted for allowing the free use of its proprietary technologies incorporated into the AMPS standard.[123] On the other hand, in the case of NMT standard its drafters intentionally designed it in the way that only non-proprietary technologies were incorporated.[124]

However, the non-proprietary approach was not possible anymore with regard to the second generation of mobile technology, globally dominated by the European Global System for Mobile Communications (GSM) standard. It was then recognized that a technical standard for mobile telephony should be build upon the state-of-art technologies, which are usually protected by patents or other forms of intellectual property rights. Although the then European Economic Community (EEC) standard setting organization attempted to require the essential patent holders to freely licence their proprietary technologies for the implementation of its standard, this policy faced severe opposition from the holders of major patent portfolios over the wireless communication technologies, especially the US ones, such as Motorola.[125] After the initiation of European competition investigation, the policy was changed so that the patent holders were required to make a declaration that they will licence their proprietary technologies for the implementation of concerned technical standards under the fair, reasonable and non-discriminatory (FRAND) terms.[126]

The operation of FRAND policy under the GSM standard showed that certain entities could exercise a considerable power over the implementation of such technical standards as well as over the entire market with the products complying with the standards in question.[127] The severe criticism was made against the opportunistic use of its large patent portfolio by Motorola.[128] Motorola was criticized for carefully licensing its patent portfolio so that it could obtain the licences to the proprietary technologies needed by Motorola or the other advantages for Motorola.[129] Consequently, only a handful number of companies were able to

[123] See, e.g., Funk (2002), p. 57.

[124] See, e.g., Haug (2002), pp. 103–104.

[125] See, e.g., Bekkers and Liotard (1999), p. 120; Bekkers et al. (2002), pp. 1146–1147; Bekkers and West (2009), p. 81.

[126] See, e.g., Bekkers and Liotard (1999), pp. 121–122; Bekkers and West (2009), p. 81.

[127] See, e.g., Bekkers and Liotard (1999), p. 123; Bekkers et al. (2002).

[128] See, e.g., Bekkers et al. (2002); Bekkers and West (2009), p. 93.

[129] See, e.g., Bekkers et al. (2002), pp. 1154–1159.

swiftly acquire the necessary licenses from Motorola and the others had to wait prolonged time.[130] Moreover, those fortunate few companies were able to acquire the control over an outstanding portion of entire GSM market.[131]

Although several proposals have been made in order to eliminate the most severe, opportunistic conducts of the major holders of essential patents,[132] the situation with the licensing of essential patents has not considerably changed with regard to the third and fourth generations of mobile telephony.[133] One of proposals has seen the solution in creating patent pools. Patent pools have worked quite efficiently with regard to sound and audiovisual recording and coding technologies, such as CD, DVD and MPEG technologies.[134] Therefore, some scholars and practitioners have suggested that the patent pools could also be a solution for wireless communication technologies.[135]

Nevertheless, the mobile telephony technology differs in several aspects from sound and audiovisual recording and coding technologies. First, the investment in developing the former has been much higher than the latter. Second, there have been several competing proposals or even standards at the time of forming the standards for the latter technologies. Therefore, the supporters and advocates of individual technical solutions were more willing to provide their proprietary technologies as a package deal so that several major manufacturers would adopt the same standard which would then have a higher chance to become the dominant standard on the market.[136] Third, in the case of sound and audiovisual recording the practice of providing the proprietary technologies as package deals was established for many years. Finally, in the case of mobile telephony the holders of major portfolios of essential patents had no interest in acceding to any patent pool. They preferred to negotiate individually amongst themselves. One of the reasons was that a few major holders of essential patents controlled an outstanding portion of essential patents and they were able to gain more in individual negotiations amongst themselves than by entering into a patent pool.[137]

On the other hand, many small holders of essential patents for the third and fourth generation of mobile telephony opted for entering into the patent pools.[138] In this way, the patent pools can be seen as significantly reducing the transactions costs, since it is easier to stop in one shop in order to obtain the necessary license for the larger number of essential patents than to negotiate individual licenses with each holder of a few essential patents. The patent pools have thus worked for

[130] See Bekkers et al. (2002), pp. 1147 and 1158.

[131] See Bekkers et al. (2002), p. 1160.

[132] See, e.g., Bekkers and West (2009), pp. 93–96; Bekkers et al. (2011).

[133] See, e.g., Bekkers and West (2009), pp. 89–92.

[134] See, e.g., Li and An (2009), p. 4; den Uijl et al. (2013).

[135] See, e.g., Bekkers and West (2009), p. 94; Bekkers et al. (2011), p. 912.

[136] See, e.g., den Uijl et al. (2013), p. 45.

[137] See, e.g., Bekkers and West (2009), p. 90.

[138] See, e.g., Bekkers and West (2009), p. 95; Bekkers et al. (2011), pp. 912–914.

mobile telephony, but only to a certain degree. They have been a viable option for small holders of essential patents, but have failed to persuade the major holders to participate.

Another proposed solution relates to one of the key criticisms of FRAND licensing that the total amount paid to all the holders of essential patents presents a considerable share of revenues for the manufacturers of affected technologies. The license fees are habitually charged as percentage from the price of a final product or at least as certain minimal amount per one piece. In total, the license fees for the entire technical standard for any of the last three generations of mobile telephony amounted to a two-digit percentage number.[139] Some critics have therefore advocated to set up a cap for the total amount of license fees paid for all the proprietary technologies incorporated into a technical standard.[140] In addition, they have suggested that it should be a one-digit percentage number.[141] But no such proposal has been adopted yet.

Conversely, the recent movement in this field has ended in the situation where the courts in several jurisdictions reject to grant an injunction in the case of infringing essential patents during the implementation of technical standards.[142] At the same time, the courts are willing to calculate the amount of fair, reasonable and non-discriminatory license fees, which tend to be much lower than those initially requested by the holders of essential patents.[143] In this way, the position of essential patent holders has been considerably lowered comparing to the one of the holders of other patents in which case the courts are commonly prepared to provide strong protection, including granting an injunction and in some countries, such as the United States, even statutory damages up to triple amount of normal damages in the case of wilful infringement.[144] Accordingly, we can observe that the position of essential patent holders has been significantly weakened by the courts' activism. This can affect the willingness of patent holders to declare their patents as essential for the implementation of technical standards in the future, contrary to the past when the patent holders normally overestimated their essential patent portfolios.[145]

With regard to the relationship between developed and developing countries, a note should be made that the incorporation of proprietary technologies into international technical standards should not be seen only as the preservation of the dominant position held by the companies from the developed countries over the manufacturers established in the countries with emerging economies. The incorporation of state-of-art technologies into technical standards also allows the transfer of

---

[139] See, e.g., Bekkers and West (2009), p. 92.

[140] See Bekkers and West (2009), pp. 95–96.

[141] See Bekkers and West (2009), p. 95.

[142] See, e.g., Lim (2014), pp. 54–72; Cotter (2014), pp. 320–325.

[143] See, e.g., Lim (2014), pp. 33–54; Cotter (2014), p. 326.

[144] See, e.g., Seaman (2012).

[145] See, e.g., Goodman and Myers (2005); Bekkers and West (2009), pp. 91–92.

such technologies to the developing countries. This can allow the firms from emerging economies to catch up those from the developed countries in technological development.[146]

A good example is presented by the history of individual generations of mobile telephones. While South Korean and Chinese manufacturers had to import the state-of-art technologies for the first and second generations of mobile telephony, this enabled them to make a considerable technological progress and to become from the followers the leaders of innovation.[147] Major South Korean manufacturers, such as Samsung and LG, and Chinese ones, such Huawei and ZTE, have played an important role in designing the technical standards for the third and fourth generations, and at the moment they control a considerable share of essential patents for those generations.

4 Conclusion

This Chapter showed that there are more dimensions of understanding legal certainty than traditionally presented by the rule-standard dichotomy. It also demonstrated that the attempts to unilaterally set up the rules regulating the behaviour of others rarely bring more legal certainty. They are more likely to cause the consequences other than those originally expected by their drafters and advocates.

The main reason is that those endeavours frequently disregard the legitimate interests of the other side which has a weaker bargaining power. The regulated entities therefore rarely obey such restrictions of their behaviour and tend to search for the ways of circumventing the imposed restrictions. This is the present situation with the vast disregard of technological protection measures and digital right management systems employed with regard to movies. Similar problems with the operation of technological protection measures in the case of sound recordings have even led to their complete abandonment.

Likewise, the attempts to control the implementation of private technical regulations by the holders of intellectual property rights have been considerably hampered by the courts trying to re-establish the adequate and appropriate balance between the interests of concerned stakeholders. As a result, the courts' response has led to increasing legal certainty for a weaker party by lowering the legal protection of the holders of patents essential for the implementation of technical standards.

Acknowledgments The research upon which this Chapter is based was partially supported by JSPS Grant-in-Aid for Young Scientists No. 15K16970.

[146] See, e.g., Odagiri et al. (2012).

[147] See, e.g., Wang and Kim (2007).

References

Akkermans B (2009) The principle of *numerus clausus* in European property law. Intersentia, Antwerp

Allison JR, Lemley MA, Schwartz DL (2014) Understanding the realities of modern patent litigation. Texas Law Rev 92:1769–1801

An B (2010) Institutional governance for ICT standards at the international level: within the WTO and beyond. http://smart.whad.org/institutional-governance-for-ict-standards-at-the-internationa. Accessed 1 Sept 2015

Anderson ES, Pildes RH (2000) Expressive theories of law: a general restatement. Univ Pa Law Rev 148:1503–1575

Aristotle, Politics. English edition: Jowett B (1999) Politics. Batoche Books, Kitchener

Awrey D (2014) The limits of private ordering within modern financial markets. Rev Bank Financ Law 34:183–254

Becker GS (1968) Crime and punishment: an economic approach. J Polit Econ 76:169–217

Becker E, Buhse W, Günnewig D, Rump N (eds) (2003) Digital rights management: technological, economic, legal and political aspects. Springer, Berlin

Bekkers R, Liotard I (1999) European standards for mobile communications: the tense relationship between standards and intellectual property rights. Eur Intellect Prop Rev 1999:110–126

Bekkers R, West J (2009) The limits to IPR standardization policies as evidenced by strategic patenting in UMTS. Telecommun Policy 33:80–97

Bekkers R, Duysters G, Verspagen B (2002) Intellectual property rights, strategic technology agreements and market structure: the case of GSM. Res Policy 31:1141–1161

Bekkers R, Iverson E, Blind K (2011) Emerging ways to address the reemerging conflict between patenting and technological standardization. Ind Corp Chang 21:901–931

Bell TW (1998) Fair vs fared use: the impact of automated rights management on copyright's fair use doctrine. North Carolina Law Rev 76:557–619

Benkler Y (2000) An unhurried view of private ordering in information transactions. Vanderbilt Law Rev 53:2063–2080

Bently L, Sherman B (2014) Intellectual property law, 4th edn. Oxford University Press, Oxford

Besen SM (1995) The standards processes in telecommunication and information technology. In: Hawkins R, Mansell R, Skea J (eds) Standards, innovation and competitiveness: the politics and economics of standards in natural and technical environments. Edward Elgar Publishing, Cheltenham, pp 136–146

Blind K, Gauch S (2008) Trends in ICT standards: the relationship between European standardisation bodies and standards consortia. Telecommun Policy 32:503–513

Blind K, Bekkers R, Dietrich Y, Iversen E, Köhler F, Müller B, Pohlmann T, Smeets S, Verweijen J (2011) Study on the interplay between standards and intellectual property rights (IPRs). European Union, Brussels

Boyle J (2000) Cruel, mean, or lavish? Economic analysis, price discrimination and digital intellectual property. Vanderbilt Law Rev 53:2007–2039

Bradley CA (1997) Territorial intellectual property rights in an age of globalism. Vanderbilt J Int Law 37:505–585

Büthe T, Mattli W (2011) The new global rulers: the privatization of regulation in the world economy. Princeton University Press, Princeton

Cargill CF (1989) Information technology standardization: theory, process, and organizations. Digital Press, Bedford

Chen-Wishart M (2014) Controlling unfair terms. In: Gullifer L, Vogenaur S (eds) English and European perspectives on contract and commercial law: essays in honour of Hugh Beale. Hart Publishing, Oxford, pp 105–130

Clift C (2010) Why IPR issues were brought to GATT: a historical perspective on the origins of TRIPS. In: Correa CM (ed) Research handbook on the protection of intellectual property under

WTO rules: intellectual property in the WTO, vol 1. Edward Elgar Publishing, Cheltenham, pp 3–21
Cotter TF (2014) Comparative law and economics of standard-essential patents and FRAND royalties. Tex Intellect Prop Law J 22:311–363
D'Amato A (1983) Legal uncertainty. Calif Law Rev 71:1–55
Dam KW (1999) Self-help in the digital jungle. J Leg Stud 28:393–412
David PA, Shurmer M (1996) Formal standard-setting for global telecommunications and information services: towards an institutional regime transformation? Telecommun Policy 20:789–815
Davies G (1984) Private copying of sound and audio-visual recordings. ESC Publishing, Oxford
Decherney P (2011) Auteurism on trial: moral rights and films on television. Wisconsin Law Rev 2011:273–330
Deere-Birkbeck C (2010) Developing countries in the global IP system before TRIPS: the political context for the TRIPS negotiations. In: Correa CM (ed) Research handbook on the protection of intellectual property under WTO rules: intellectual property in the WTO, vol 1. Edward Elgar Publishing, Cheltenham, pp 22–51
den Uijl S, Bekkers R, de Vries HJ (2013) Managing intellectual property using patent pools: lessons from three generations of pools in the optical disc industry. Calif Manag Rev 55:31–50
Depoorter B (2009) Technology and uncertainty: the shaping effect on copyright law. Univ Pa Law Rev 157:1831–1868
Dinwoodie GB (ed) (2015) Intellectual property and general legal principles: is IP a *lex specialis*? Edward Elgar Publishing, Cheltenham
Drahos P, Braithwaite J (2002) Information feudalism: who owns the knowledge economy? The New Press, New York
Efroni Z (2011) Access-right: the future of digital copyright law. Oxford University Press, Oxford
Elkin-Koren N (1998) Copyrights in cyberspace: rights without laws? Chicago-Kent Law Rev 73:1155–1201
Eller C (2006) "Bubble" bursts film tradition. Los Angeles Times. http://articles.latimes.com/2006/jan/22/local/me-bubble22. Accessed 1 Sept 2015
Fawcett JJ, Torremans P (2011) Intellectual property and private international law, 2nd edn. Oxford University Press, Oxford
Freyer T (1992) Regulating big business: antitrust in Great Britain and America 1880–1990. Cambridge University Press, Cambridge
Funk JL (2002) Global competition between and within standards: the case of mobile phones. Palgrave, Basingstoke
Galanter M (1974) Why the "haves" come out ahead: speculations on the limits of legal change. Law Soc Rev 9:95–160
Geiger C, Gervais D, Senftleben M (2014) The three-step test revisited: how to use the test's flexibility in national copyright law. Am Univ Int Law Rev 29:581–626
Gervais D (2008) The TRIPS agreement: drafting history and analysis, 3rd edn. Sweet & Maxwell, London
Gessner V (1998) Globalization and legal certainty. In: Gessner V, Budak AC (eds) Emerging legal certainty: empirical studies on the globalization of law. Ashgate, Aldershot, pp 427–450
Gibson CS (2007) Globalization and the technology standards game: balancing concerns of protectionism in international standards. Berkeley Technol Law J 22:1403–1484
Gilbert RJ (2004) Antitrust for patent pools: a century of policy evolution. Stanf Technol Law Rev 2004:3
Ginsburg JC (2008) Separating the Sony sheep from the Grokster goats: reckoning the future business plans of copyright-dependent technology entrepreneurs. Ariz Law Rev 50:577–609
Goldstein P, Hugenholtz B (2010) International copyright: principles, law, and practice, 2nd edn. Oxford University Press, Oxford
Goodman DJ, Myers RA (2005) 3G cellular standards and patents. In: Proceedings of 2005 IEEE wireless communications and networking conference, IEEE, pp 415–420

Graham SJH, Van Zeebroeck N (2014) Comparing patent litigation across Europe: a first look. Stanford Technology Law Rev 17:655–708

Haug T (2002) A commentary on standardization practices: lessons from the NMT and GSM mobile telephone standards histories. Telecommun Policy 26:101–107

Hazucha B (2013) Technical barriers to trade in information and communication technologies. In: Epps T, Trebilcock MJ (eds) Research handbook on the WTO and technical barriers to trade. Edward Elgar Publishing, Cheltenham, pp 525–565

Hazucha B, Liu H-C, Watabe T (2012) Attribution of liability for misappropriation of tangible and intangible things in Japan: to change the law or to change the minds. In: Paper presented at the 2012 International conference on law and society, the Law and Society Association, Honolulu, 5–8 June 2012

Hazucha B, Liu H-C, Watabe T (2014) Private ordering and consumer' rights in copyright law: a view of Japanese consumers. In: Dinwoodie GB (ed) Intellectual property and general legal principles: is IP a *lex specialis*? Edward Elgar Publishing, Cheltenham, pp 119–155

ISO/IEC (2012) ISO/IEC Directives, Part 1: Supplement – procedures specific to JTC 1. https://www.jisc.go.jp/international/pdf/jtc1_supplement_2012.pdf. Accessed 1 Sept 2015

Jakobs K (2009) ICT standardisation in China, the EU, and the US. In: ITU (ed) Proceedings of the 2009 ITU-T Kaleidoscope academic conference: innovations for digital inclusion. ITU, Geneva, pp 177–182

Kaminski ME (2015) Don't keep the trans-Pacific partnership talks secret. The New York Times. http://www.nytimes.com/2015/04/14/opinion/dont-keep-trade-talks-secret.html?_r=0. Accessed 1 Sept 2015

Kennedy D (1976) Form and substance in private law adjudication. Harv Law Rev 89:1685–1778

Komesar NK (1994) Imperfect alternatives: choosing institutions in law, economics, and public policy. The University of Chicago Press, Chicago

Kravets D (2009) Obama administration declares proposed IP treaty a "national security" secret. Wired. http://www.wired.com/2009/03/obama-declares/. Accessed 1 Sept 2015

Krislov S (1997) How nations choose product standards and standards change nations. University of Pittsburgh Press, Pittsburgh

Lampe RL, Moser P (2010) Do patent pools encourage innovation? Evidence from the nineteenth-century sewing machine industry. J Econ Hist 70:898–920

Lampe RL, Moser P (forthcoming 2016) Patent pools, competition, and innovation: evidence from 20 U.S. industries under the New Deal. J Law Econ Organ 32

Landes WM, Posner RA (2003) The economic structure of intellectual property law. The Benlknap Press of Harvard University Press, Cambridge

Lemley MA (2010) Where to file your patent case. AIPLA Q J 38:401–436

Lessig L (2006) Code version 2.0. Basic Books, New York

Li X, An B (2009) IPR misuse: the core issue in standards and patents. South Centre Research paper no 21. http://www.southcentre.int/wp-content/uploads/2013/05/RP21_IPR-misuse_EN.pdf. Accessed 1 Sept 2015

Lim D (2014) Standard essential patents, trolls, and the smartphone wars: triangulating the end game. Penn State Law Rev 119:1–91

Maskus K, Merrill SA (eds) (2013) Patent challenges for standard-setting in the global economy: lessons from information and communication technology. National Academies Press, Washington, DC

Maxeiner JR (2007) Legal certainty: a European alternative to American legal indeterminacy? Tulane J Int Comp Law 15:541–607

Moore KA, Parisi F (2002) Rethinking forum shopping in cyberspace. Chicago-Kent Law Rev 77:1325–1355

Neuwirth RJ (2009) The fragmentation of the global market: the case of digital versatile discs (DVDs). Cardozo Arts Entertain Law J 27:409–458

Odagiri H, Goto A, Sunami A, Nelson RR (2012) Intellectual property rights, development, and catch-up: an international comparative study. Oxford University Press, Oxford

Patry WF (1985) The fair use privilege in copyright law. Bureau of National Affairs, Washington, DC
Peukert A (2012) Territoriality and extra-territoriality in intellectual property law. In: Handl G, Zekoll J, Zumbansen P (eds) Beyond territoriality: transnational legal authority in an age of globalization. Martinus Nijhoff Publishers, Leiden, pp 189–228
Roffe P, Seuba X (2014) The ACTA and the plurilateral enforcement agenda: genesis and aftermath. Cambridge University Press, Cambridge
Roffe P, Spennemann C, von Braun J (2010) Intellectual property rights in free trade agreements: moving beyond TRIPS minimum standards. In: Correa CM (ed) Research handbook on the protection of intellectual property under WTO rules: intellectual property in the WTO, vol 1. Edward Elgar Publishing, Cheltenham, pp 266–316
Rose CM (1988) Crystals and mud in property law. Stanf Law Rev 40:577–610
Samuelson P (2015) Possible futures of fair use. Wash Law Rev 90:815–865
Scassa T (2001) Patents for second medical indications and their potential impact on pharmacare in Canada. Health Law J 9:23–59
Schwarcz SL (2002) Private ordering. Northwest Univ Law Rev 97:319–349
Seaman CB (2012) Willful patent infringement and enhanced damages after In Re Seagate: an empirical study. Iowa Law Rev 97:417–471
Straus J (2000) Patent litigation in Europe: a glimmer of hope? Present status and future perspectives. Wash Univ J Law Policy 2:403–428
Sunstein CR (1996) On the expressive function of law. Univ Pa Law Rev 144:2021–2053
Sykes AO (1995) Product standards for internationally integrated goods markets. The Brookings Institution, Washington, DC
Tate J (2001) National varieties of standardization. In: Hall PA, Soskice D (eds) Varieties of capitalism: the institutional foundations of comparative advantage. Oxford University Press, Oxford, pp 442–473
Trimble M (2012) The future of cybertravel: legal implications of the evasion of geolocation. Fordham Intellect Prop Media Entertain Law J 22:567–657
van Eechoud M (2003) Choice of law in copyright and related rights: alternatives to the *lex protectionis*. Kluwer Law International, The Hague
Wang J, Kim S (2007) Time to get in: the contrasting stories about government interventions in information technology standards (the case of CDMA and IMT-2000 in Korea). Gov Inf Q 24:115–134
Waterman D, Weiss AA (2010) Time consistency and seller commitment in intertemporal movie distribution: an empirical study of the video window. J Ind Econ 58:717–738
Wu T (2008) Tolerated use. Columbia J Law Arts 31:617–635
Yasoshima R (2015) TPP nations near deal on 70-year copyright protection. Nikkei Asian Rev. http://asia.nikkei.com/Politics-Economy/International-Relations/TPP-nations-near-deal-on-70-year-copyright-protection. Accessed 1 Sept 2015
Yen AC (2001) A preliminary economic analysis of Napster: internet technology, copyright liability, and the possibility of Coasean bargaining. Dayton Law Rev 26:247–277
Yu PK (2012) Region codes and the territorial mess. Cardozo Arts Entertain Law J 30:187–264

Considerations on the Transnationality of International Commercial Arbitration Awards in the Context of the Demand for Legal Certainty

Jason D. Hitch

Contents

Abstract This chapter will discuss whether or not an arbitral award in an international commercial arbitration can be considered to be transnational in the sense that it is not controlled by the law of the country where it was given (i.e. it is 'anational', that is, detached from any national legal system).

Keywords Transnationality • Arbitration • Arbitral awards • Delocalisation

1 Introduction

This chapter will proceed by first discussing what is known as the delocalisation debate: whether an arbitral award in an international commercial arbitration is or is not controlled by the law of the country where it was given – in essence whether such an award is 'anational' (i.e. detached from any national legal system)[1] and can

This chapter is dedicated to my late Grandmother Lily who passed away during my time at Oxford University when I was first learning about delocalisation & transnational commercial law and was initially presented as a symposium piece for Kyushu University's 7th Annual International Law Conference.

[1] See generally Rensmann (1998), p. 37.

J.D. Hitch (✉)
Lawyer, Sydney, NSW, Australia

M. Fenwick, S. Wrbka (eds.), *Legal Certainty in a Contemporary Context*,
DOI 10.1007/978-981-10-0114-7_4

accordingly be considered to be purely transnational in its nature.[2] Following on from this general discussion of the nature of the award, the delocalisation debate will be discussed in the context of enforcement to determine whether such an award can ever be considered to be truly 'anational' (i.e. purely transnational) in practice. It will be argued that regardless of the conclusion reached in respect to the possible anational character of awards, the fact that an award which has been set aside by a court at the seat of the arbitration can be enforced in certain countries, and that such setting aside is not a mandatory ground for refusal of enforcement, undermines arguments which attempt to dismiss delocalisation outright. Accordingly, it will be submitted in conclusion that in today's world, the extent to which an international commercial arbitral award will be anational is largely determined by the State in which enforcement is sought and thus while this conclusion is broadly encouraging of transnationality in the international commercial arbitration context, it does reflect the more fundamental problem of transnational law being dependent on State sanctioning/recognition for its validity.[3]

2 The Delocalisation Debate

The question of whether an arbitral award in an international commercial arbitration is, or can ever be, anational (i.e. detached from any national legal system) and thus not controlled by the law of the country where it was given is commonly referred to as the 'delocalisation' debate. The idea of an anational award has found particular support in continental Europe which is largely where the majority of delocalisation proponents reside.[4] Early proponents of the theory argued that international commercial arbitration awards were entirely anational not only in terms of their creation and existence but in terms of their enforcement such that the courts of an enforcing State should not have had a say in respect to the validity of such awards.[5]

One State which initially maintained this view was Belgium. By its law of 27 March 1985, Belgium added a provision to Article 1717 of the *Belgian Code Judiciaire* which held that a losing party was not permitted to challenge in the Belgian courts an award made in an international arbitration held in Belgium, unless at least one of the parties had a place of business or other connection with Belgium (i.e. if the parties were both international then so too would be the award).[6]

[2] For discussion of the concept of transnational law in this context see Goode (2001), p. 19.

[3] A problem which is arguably reflected in other related areas, particularly the *lex mercatoria,* for example. For an introduction to the concept of the *lex mercatoria,* see Mustill (1987), p. 86 before turning to Goode et al. [2007].

[4] Goode et al. (2007), pp. 621–686.

[5] See Collier and Lowe (2002), pp. 232–234 regarding the development of the delocalisation debate; Greenberg et al. (2011), pp. 68–70.

[6] Closer to home, Malaysia's former arbitration law had similar properties. As noted by Greenberg et al., prior to 2005, "where the seat of arbitration was in Malaysia and the parties had chosen to

This law unfortunately had the opposite effect of that desired in that international commercial arbitration avoided Belgium as the seat of arbitration. This example highlights that the majority of international parties that use arbitration to resolve their disputes prefer some form of judicial review and supervision grounded in the laws of the *lex arbitri* (the laws of the seat of arbitration), especially in terms of enforcement and in the form of providing 'legitimacy' to their award.[7]

Today, a more restrained version of delocalisation is touted by its proponents who argue that instead of a dual system of control, first by the *lex arbitri* and then by the courts of the State where enforcement of the award is sought, there should be only one point of control – that of the place of enforcement[8] and accordingly that an international commercial arbitration award is anational (detached from its legal system of origin) in terms of its creation and existence; it is this view of delocalisation which will be adopted for the remainder of this discussion. The reference to 'detachment from any national legal system' is adopted here to refer to the creation and existence of the award, not its enforcement.

This view of delocalisation acknowledges the necessary role that State judiciaries play in the enforcement of awards and argues that such judicial interference is justifiable, provided the award itself is free from the shackles of its curial birthplace (and thus the anational character of the award is not in and of itself compromised). The emphasis in the delocalisation literature is accordingly very much focused on 'the importance of the autonomy of the parties, the private, consensual nature of arbitration and the fact that arbitrators are not judges in State courts and, consequently, have greater flexibility and freedom than their judicial counterparts'.[9] A key reason for such detachment in the view of delocalisationists is that the seat of arbitration (the *lex arbitri*) is of little or no significance because it is chosen for reasons of 'geographic appropriateness' or for reasons of neutrality and not because its law was thought by the parties to be suitable for international commercial arbitrations.[10]

Despite the above, powerful arguments not only of principle but also of policy can be made against delocalisation.[11] It can be argued that 'the freedom to settle disputes by arbitration is a concession, a derogation from the monopoly claimed by

adopt the Arbitration Rules of the Kuala Lumpur Regional Centre for Arbitration, the law did not permit any recourse at all from arbitral awards" (Greenberg et al. [2011], p. 75). This Asia-Pacific form of delocalisation was replaced by the Arbitration Act of 2005 which adopted the Model Law. Further commentary as noted by Greenberg et al. can be found in Arfazadeh (1991), p. 103.

[7] See generally Blackaby et al. (2009), 3.80.

[8] See Greenberg et al. (2011), pp. 68–70.

[9] Paulsson (1983), p. 53.

[10] A view which is in stark contrast to that possessed by traditionalists as explained by Ball who understands Arbitration as "not a separate, free-standing system of justice... [Arbitration] is a system established and regulated pursuant to law, and it necessarily bears a close relationship to a nation's courts and judicial system" (Ball [2006], p. 73 – as cited in Greenberg et al. [2011], p. 67). See further Goode et al. (2007), pp. 621–686.

[11] See McKendrick and Goode (2010), pp. 1317–1320; see also Goode et al. (2007), pp. 621–686.

the State in the administration of justice; and the concession is made subject to such conditions, including the supervision and regulation of arbitral proceedings by the local law, as the State may choose'.[12] Furthermore, as noted by Goode, while it is doubtlessly true that considerations of neutrality and convenience feature prominently in the choice of the place of arbitration, it is difficult to believe that parties to international commercial arbitrations pay no regard at all to the quality of the law administered in the place in which the arbitration is to be held.[13] If this were different, there would be little need for the parties to be able to specify the curial law but still have arbitrations in another location (as is provided for in the *UNCITRAL Model Law on International Commercial Arbitration* 1985 at Article 20(2) for example). The example of the Belgian experience also serves to reinforce the point that parties to international commercial arbitration wish for the *lex arbitri* to play a role not only in validating the authenticity of their arbitration but also in being able to provide support for the arbitration (i.e. by design the parties do not wish for their arbitral award to be entirely 'anational' otherwise such procedures as interim injunctions available through the *lex arbitri* would not be available).

There are also strong policy reasons for disputing the existence of truly anational awards. Delocalisation not only hinders finality but also fails to avoid multiple-jeopardy (in that a party can be subject to the same enforcement dispute in multiple jurisdictions), which undermines what is considered to be the core of international commercial arbitration – economic efficiency. Delocalisation also fails to respect the well-established principle of estoppel and gives rise to the strong possibility of conflicting decisions of different foreign courts (as can be seen in the *Hilmarton*[14] and *Chromalloy*[15] cases – discussed further below). More generally, it has been argued by commentators such as Goode, that the main basis for delocalisation has disappeared in that the hostility formerly present in many local courts to arbitration and the excessive jurisdiction asserted over arbitrations in the past has disappeared as state after state has departed from its traditional arbitration rules and enacted legislation along the lines of the UNCITRAL Model Law which reserves a place for the *lex loci arbitri*.[16]

On the basis of the above, it may be argued that parties may not simply by their own agreement free themselves of the mandatory provisions of the *lex arbitri* and that an award cannot (or more rightly should not) ever be entirely anational. This is argued to be the case even at a fundamental level as for an award to even be recognised as 'anational' (delocalised) it requires the permission (recognition) of

[12] Collier and Lowe (2002), pp. 229–234.

[13] Goode et al. (2007), pp. 621–686.

[14] *Hilmarton Ltd v Omnium de Traitement et de Valorisation* (1995) XX Ybk Comm Arb 663; XXI Ybk Comm Arb 524; (1997) XXII Ybk Comm Arb 696. See generally Blackaby et al. (2009), 11.92.

[15] *Arab Republic of Egypt v Chromalloy Air Services* (1997) XXII Ybk Comm Arb 691. See generally Blackaby et al, *op. cit.*, 3.86.

[16] Goode et al. (2007), pp. 621–686.

the law of the *lex arbitri*. The proper interpretation of the award then, it is argued, is that while an award can never be entirely anational, experience shows that the sphere of influence of the provisions contained in the *lex arbitri* are steadily diminishing in scope.[17] Despite this shrinking of influence however, the debate is likely to continue to rage as to the necessity for State recognition in order for transnational law to be valid (or considered to be law in the traditional sense). A debate which was reflected in the arguments between panellists at the 7th Annual Kyushu University International Law Conference,[18] where assertions for the validity of transnational law in and of itself swung back and forth from requiring the recognition of sovereign States for validity to being *sui generis* and entirely separate from State jurisdiction.

Despite this rather strict conclusion however, reality reveals a more convoluted picture. It is arguable that whether an award will be anational in practice is largely dependent on where the award is sought to be enforced. This point is most clearly highlighted by the fact that an award which has been set aside by a court of the seat of arbitration will not necessarily be a ground for refusing to enforce the award in another country (i.e. some jurisdictions may choose to disregard the *lex loci arbitri*).

3 Enforcement of an Annulled Award

One of the key sources which supports the restrained delocalisation argument discussed above is contained in the Convention on the Recognition and Enforcement of Foreign Arbitral Awards 1958 ('New York Convention')[19] (although this is not by design[20]). Article V(1)(a) allows a court in the Contracting State in which enforcement is sought to refuse enforcement if the award is set aside (annulled) under the law of the country where the award was made. The crucial word here is 'may', which allows a Contracting State's court the discretion of whether to enforce an award which has been set aside at the seat of the arbitration – some jurisdictions such as Italy and the Netherlands will refuse to enforce such an award (recognition of an annulled award is prohibited under their domestic law) whereas jurisdictions like France view awards as stateless and existing independently of the *lex arbitri* and pay no mind to annulment at the seat of arbitration.[21]

---

[17] Collier and Lowe (2002), pp. 229–234.

[18] Kyushu University 7th Annual International Law Conference, *Regulatory Hybridization in the Transnational Sphere* (11 & 12 February 2012) Nishijin Plaza, Fukuoka, Japan.

[19] This is especially so when it is considered that the vast majority of the world's major and minor countries are parties to the Convention. See further Greenberg et al. (2011), pp. 72–78.

[20] Commentators such as Goode have strenuously argued that the New York Convention was not intended to be interpreted to support delocalisation (see McKendrick [2010], pp. 1318–1319; Goode et al. [2007], pp. 621–686).

[21] See Blackaby et al. (2009), 11.92 and onward; Greenberg et al. (2011), pp. 72–78; McKendrick (2010), p. 1319.

This discretion supports the argument that an award may be anational (i.e. the award is not controlled by the law of the country where it was given) and that such a setting aside will not be a ground for refusing to enforce the annulled award. The French Courts are particularly known for this approach. A couple of French cases will serve to illustrate the point.

In the *Hilmarton* case, the Cour de Cassation essentially held that judgments of the court of origin setting aside an arbitral award were of no consequence in France as an international commercial arbitration award, though made in a particular state (in this case Switzerland), was not itself integrated into the legal system of that State. The Cour de Cassation on this basis found such awards to be truly 'international' and thus enforceable in France despite their annulment by the court in the State of the award's origin.[22] The Paris Court of Appeal in *Chromalloy* also held that "the award [in this case is]... by definition an international award... [and] is not integrated into the legal order of that State so that its existence remains established despite it being annulled".[23] In the *Chromalloy* case, the French court was only prepared to refuse enforcement if the award went against international public policy (not the domestic public policy of France or the public policy of the seat of arbitration).[24] This refusal further highlights the French view of the 'anational' character of an international commercial arbitration award. This judicial view is cemented in the amended Article 1514 of the *French Code of Civil Procedure* by Decree No. 2011–48 of 13 January 2011.

4 Conclusion

In conclusion, it is postulated that if an international commercial arbitral award is sought to be enforced in France (or another jurisdiction adopting a similar position), it will be treated as being anational. Accordingly, it can arguably be said that depending on the State where enforcement is sought, an international commercial arbitration award may not be controlled by the law of the country where it was given but is indeed anational and detached from any national legal system which gives birth to its existence – an argument which is supported by the fact that an award which has been set aside by a court at the seat of arbitration is not a ground for refusing to enforce it in another country (as per the New York Convention). This does not however mean that the award is entirely separated from State jurisdiction however and is thus 'purely' transnational as the enforcement on the award will still

[22] Blackaby et al. (2009), 11.92 and onward; Greenberg et al. (2011), pp. 72–78; McKendrick (2010), p. 1319.

[23] *Arab Republic of Egypt v Chromalloy Air Services*, *op. cit.*, 692–693. See generally Blackaby et al. (2009), 11.157.

[24] For further discussions on public policy in this context see Blackaby et al. (2009), 11.103–11.120.

depend on State recognition for its validity, which reflects the broader problem of transnational law being tied to sovereign States for its validity and recognition. As noted, this is a problem which is not easily or readily solvable and is likely to be a continued thorn in the side of the recognition of transnational law as being truly 'anational' not only in the context of international commercial arbitral awards but across all legal spheres where it exists.[25]

References

Arfazadeh H (1991) New perspectives in South East Asia and delocalised arbitration in Kuala Lumpur. J Int Arbitr 8(4):103–121

Ball M (2006) The essential judge: the role of the courts in a system of national and international commercial arbitration. Arbitr Int 22:73–93

Blackaby N, Partasides C, Redfern A, Hunter M (2009) Redfern & Hunter international commercial arbitration, 5th edn. Oxford University Press, London

Collier JG, Lowe V (2002) The settlement of disputes in international law, new edn. Oxford University Press, London

Goode R (2001) The role of the lex loci arbitri in international commercial arbitration. Arbitr Int 17:19–39

Goode R, Kronke H, McKendrick E, Wool J (2007) Transnational commercial law: text, cases & materials. Oxford University Press, London

Greenberg S, Kee C, Weeramantry JR (2011) International commercial arbitration: an Asia-Pacific perspective. Cambridge University Press, Cambridge

McKendrick E, Goode R (eds) (2010) Goode on commercial law, 4th edn. Penguin, London

Mustill LJ (1987) The new lex mercatoria: the first twenty-five years. Arbitr Int 4:86–119

Paulsson J (1983) Delocalisation of international commercial arbitration: when and why it matters. Int Comp Law Q 32:53–61

Rensmann T (1998) Anational arbitral awards – legal phenomenon or academic phantom? J Int Arbitr 15(2):37–66

[25] Regardless of whether awards will ever truly be 'anational', it is agreed with Greenberg et al that at least the delocalisation debate has had the positive effect of decreasing the level of court interference at the seat of arbitration thus ensuring the greater success and utilisation of international arbitration along with having the additional side benefit of reducing the application of otherwise irrelevant local mandatory laws (Greenberg et al. [2011], pp. 79).

The Notion of Consumer Under EU Legislation and EU Case Law: Between the Poles of Legal Certainty and Flexibility

Jakob Søren Hedegaard and Stefan Wrbka

Contents

Abstract The European Commission and the European Union (EU) legislator have steadily intensified their activities in the field of consumer protection to enhance business-to-consumer (B2C) transaction in the EU. This chapter aims to comment on some of these efforts. Unlike most other contributions in the field of EU consumer law it does not dive into an analysis of rights and obligations of businesses and consumers, but discusses one of the preconditions to declare consumer law applicable – the consumer notion.

Parties to a contract that might fall under consumer laws surely benefit from understanding whether such legislation applies in the concrete case. This is best exemplified by different mandatory law standards in B2C and non-B2C cases. As

J.S. Hedegaard
Assistant Attorney, Lassen Ricard, Copenhagen, Denmark

S. Wrbka (✉)
Faculty of Law, Kyushu University, Fukuoka, Japan
e-mail: stefan.wrbka@law.kyushu-u.ac.jp

M. Fenwick, S. Wrbka (eds.), *Legal Certainty in a Contemporary Context*,
DOI 10.1007/978-981-10-0114-7_5

this chapter shows, the EU legislator – despite harmonisation efforts – has not (yet) introduced a standardised definition of the consumer notion. Although the Court of Justice of the European Union (ECJ) has repeatedly aimed to align the understandings of the diverse notions, the situation is not yet absolutely settled. From the viewpoint of legal certainty this might create some tension. This tension is intensified by certain special cases that might ask for more interpretative flexibility. In the following we will thus discuss the interplay between the EU consumer notion, EU consumer legislation, EU consumer case law, legal certainty and legal flexibility to evaluate the status quo and to take a brief look into the (possible) future.

Keywords Consumer • Consumer notion • Legal certainty • Legal flexibility • EU law • EU case law

1 Introduction

Over the past four decades, EU consumer law has advanced from occasional discussions of ideas for improving consumer protection to one of the key interests of EU law. The first two instruments that explicitly mentioned the term 'consumer' – the 1975 Council resolution on a preliminary programme of the European Economic Community (hereinafter, EEC) for a consumer protection and information policy[1] and the 1981 Council Resolution on a second programme of the EEC for a consumer protection and information policy[2] initiated a comprehensive, yet scattered framework of EU consumer legislation that started with the adoption of the Doorstep Selling Directive in 1985.[3] The EU legislator had used a sectoral approach in regulating consumer interest-related scenarios in the sense that it enacted relatively narrow directives that covered only certain situations. In addition to the Doorstep Selling Directive one should in particular mention the 1990 Package Travel Directive,[4] the 1993 Unfair Contract Terms Directive (hereinafter, UCTD),[5] the 1994 Timeshare Directive[6] and the 1997 Distance Selling

[1] Council Resolution on a preliminary programme of the European Economic Community for a consumer protection and information policy, OJ C 92, 5.4.1975, p. 1.

[2] Council Resolution on a second programme of the European Economic Community for a consumer protection and information policy, OJ C 133, 3.6.1981, p. 1.

[3] Council Directive 85/577/EEC to protect the consumer in respect of contracts negotiated away from business premises, OJ L 372, 20.12.1985, p. 31.

[4] Council Directive 90/314/EEC of 13 June 1990 on package travel, package holidays and package tours, OJ L 158, 23.6.1990, p. 59.

[5] Council Directive 93/13/EEC of 5 April 1993 on unfair terms in consumer contracts, OJ L 95, 21.4.1993, p. 29.

[6] Directive 94/47/EC of the European Parliament and of the Council on the protection of purchasers in respect of certain aspects of contracts relating to the purchase of a right to use immovable properties on a timeshare basis, OJ L 280, 29.10.1994, p. 83.

Directive,[7] all forming part of the 'consumer acquis' (in a narrow sense).[8] Although all legislative instruments that deal with consumer law questions are linked by the wish for improving consumer protection, the term 'consumer' itself is not defined in a uniform way.

The purpose of this contribution is to comment on some features of the consumer notion(s) from the perspectives of legal certainty on the one hand and legal flexibility on the other. As already shown on a different occasion[9] and as to be explained again shortly, the two concepts both represent justified interests of legal stakeholders, but at the same time can create a certain tension, as they put the focus on different and – depending on the concrete definitions of the two terms – opposing access paths to law. The emphasis in this contribution is put on (what we call) the external characteristics of the consumer notion, i.e., on the basic preconditions that have to be met to be able to consider a contractual party as being a consumer (and not a professional). Put differently (and as seen from the perspective of the good selling or service offering party), the main question lies in differentiating between business-to-business (hereinafter, B2B) and business-to-consumer (hereinafter, B2C) situations. This also means that the contribution will not aim at commenting on the question of which consumers are worthy of protection and which are not. This question, i.e., the consumer model (*Verbraucherleitbild*) – the protection-worthy consumer, a concept that adds *internal* parameters to the consumer notion – has already been subject of numerous contributions in the past.[10]

The contribution will start by taking a brief look at the two concepts of legal certainty and legal flexibility, its underlying ideas and some EU law examples. It will then move to a more detailed discussion of the consumer notion under EU law and case law. The contribution concludes with comments on the EU consumer concept from the perspective of legal certainty and legal flexibility.

---

[7] Directive 97/7/EC of the European Parliament and of the Council on the protection of consumers in respect of distance contracts, OJ L 144, 4.6.1997, p. 19.

[8] The consumer acquis (in a narrow sense) comprised in total eight directives, six contract law related directives – in addition to the already listed directives one has to mention the 1993 Unfair Terms Directive and the 1999 Consumer Sales Directive –, the 1998 Price Indication Directive and the 1998 Injunctions Directive. For Details see Wrbka (2015), pp. 162 et seq. with further references.

[9] See Wrbka (2016 forthcoming).

[10] This concepts aims to distinguish between protection-worthy consumers and those who are not, i.e., it looks at a group of people that are *already* considered being consumers. See, e.g., Benöhr (2013), pp. 16–17; Hartmann (2007); Denkinger (2007), pp. 109 et seq. (It should be noted though that this contribution deals with the consumer notion in a comprehensive way, i.e., it focuses both on internal and external characteristics); Howells et al. (2010), pp. 10–13; Weatherill (2012); Ramsay (2012), pp. 33–34; Möller (2008), pp. 77–78; Schoenmakers (2014).

2 Legal Certainty vs. Legal Flexibility

2.1 Legal Certainty and Legal Flexibility in General

As already explained in the present book,[11] legal certainty shows many facets. Depending on the circumstances, the term can refer to any of the following sub-layers: legal clarity (*Rechtsklarheit*), legal stability (*Rechtsstabilität*), legal accessibility (*Rechtszugänglichkeit*), legal peace (*Rechtsfriede*), legal enforcement (*Rechtsdurchsetzung*),[12] legal firmness and predictability (*Bestimmtheit* and *Vorhersehbarkeit*), legislative and judicial stability and continuity (*Stabilität* and *Kontinuität*) and practicability of the application of law (*Praktikabilität der Rechtsanwendung*).[13]

In particular in civil law countries with their statutory laws, legal certainty traditionally enjoys a key role in the legal order. It does not come as a surprise that commentators have referred to the certainty concept as, e.g., being one of the 'highest [legal] values'[14] or 'fundamental [legal] principles'.[15] Also more recently – in particular, in the course of the debate of a possible introduction of a European Civil Code (or at least a European Sales Law)[16] – legal certainty occupied a prominent position. Christian von Bar, Hugh Beale, Eric Clive and Hans Schulte-Nölke, four core members of the research group consortium that drafted the Draft Common Frame of Reference (hereinafter, *DCFR*)[17] identified in total 15 key elements of European and national private law and stressed that legal certainty must be considered as constituting one of them.[18] The DCFR itself categorised legal certainty under one of its four pillars.[19] Legal certainty should – so the DCFR – be seen as one expression of contractual security.[20]

---

[11] See the chapter by Wrbka in this book.

[12] For all these certainty definitions see Bydlinski (1988, p. 293, 2011, p. 325).

[13] For all these certainty definitions see Canaris (1969), p. 17.

[14] See, e.g., Canaris (1969), p. 17, where Canaris refers to legal certainty as a 'highest value' (oberster Wert).

[15] See, e.g., Bydlinski (1988), p. 173, where the author refers to legal certainty as a 'fundamental principle' (Fundamentalprinzip).

[16] In this context the discussion of a possible introduction of a Common European Sales Law has to be pointed out. For comments on the CESL, e.g., Wrbka (2015), pp. 190–262 with further references.

[17] The DCFR, published in 2009, is the result of extensive research on European private law rules primarily (but not only) focusing on contract law. For details on the DCFR see, e.g., Wrbka (2014, pp. 159–160, 2015, pp. 195–208); von Bar et al. (2009); von Bar and Clive (2009).

[18] von Bar et al. (2009), p. 10.

[19] The four pillars identified by the DCFR are: security, freedom, justice and efficiency.

[20] See Recital 22 of the DCFR Principles. Rule I. – I:102 DCFR (Interpretation and development) lists – in its third paragraph – legal certainty as one of the parameters that need to be taken into consideration in the 'interpretation and development' of private law rules (falling under the DCFR) – see Rule I. – I:102(2)(c) DCFR.

Legal flexibility on the other hand seems to be a less nuanced concept. It primarily refers to the possibility of applying legal instruments to a variety of cases (not explicitly mentioned by the wording of statutory law) or – put differently – to accommodate to special situations by broadening the application of legal rules. Putting these two concepts into a context one will realise that they principally aim at achieving different objectives. One of the main purposes of legal certainty is to create a transparent legal framework with foreseeable outcomes of (legally relevant) actions. In contrast to this, it can be said that legal flexibility adds some kind of 'fairness' or justness in a sense that the application of legal instruments is extended to linguistically not clearly covered situations, if such extension can be considered suitable and reasonable.

2.2 *Legal Certainty and Legal Flexibility in Consumer Law*

Consumer law traditionally rests on the idea that some kind of imbalance exists between a business/professional (hereinafter, business) and a consumer and that such imbalance would create unfair or unreasonable advantages for the business side.[21] Based on the argument that the consumer is the weaker or at least the (legally) less informed/experienced party,[22] national and EU consumer laws have sought to strengthen the consumer's position – either by introducing (mandatory) minimum legal standards or information obligations for the business side. More recent EU consumer laws (and legislative drafts), in particular, stress the importance of legal certainty in B2C situations to stimulate the market. Four examples should be pointed out.

In 2011 the EU legislator adopted the Consumer Rights Directive (hereinafter, CRD).[23] The CRD was one of the results (arguably the key result) of attempts to defragment the scattered consumer acquis by repealing two directives – the Doorstep Selling Directive and the Distance Selling Directive – adding one supplementary provision to each the Consumer Sales Directive (hereinafter, CSD) and the Unfair Contract Terms Directive (hereinafter, UCTD) and introducing some overarching harmonised concepts, such as a standardised passing of risk regime for sale by dispatch contracts. The CRD stressed the importance of improving legal

[21] Martijn Hesselink, for example, argues (with respect to SMEs) as follows: 'In consumer contracts SMEs are usually the stronger party' [Hesselink (2007), p. 365]. Detailed comments on the alleged consumer information deficit can be found in Becher (2008). The information deficit debate in consumer contracts has already gone beyond purely legal borders. Machteld de Hoon, for example, adds insights from sociology and psychology – for details see De Hoon (2007).

[22] On this issue in general see, e.g., Wrbka (2015), pp. 282 et seq. with further references.

[23] Directive 2011/83/EU of the European Parliament and of the Council on consumer rights, amending Council Directive 93/13/EEC and Directive 1999/44/EC of the European Parliament and of the Council and repealing Council Directive 85/577/EEC and Directive 97/7/EC of the European Parliament and of the Council, OJ L 304, 25.10.2011, p. 260.

certainty for the contractual parties. Recital 7 CRD, for example, explained as follows: 'Full harmonisation of some key regulatory aspects should considerably increase legal certainty for both consumers and traders'.[24] The EU legislator was obviously convinced that the diverse rules adopted by some national legislators that exceeded the minimum harmonised regime of the repealed rules were counterproductive from the perspective of legal certainty and that maximum harmonisation was the perfect answer to remedy the certainty deficit. By putting the emphasis on the (alleged) benefits of maximum harmonisation to improve legal certainty the legislator switched (to a very large extent) from minimum to maximum harmonisation with respect to certain issues, most notably with respect to the withdrawal period in doorstep and distance selling contracts.[25]

The CRD was not the first directive that explicitly mentioned the importance of legal certainty for B2C contracts. An older example is the 2000 E-Commerce Directive.[26] In a first attempt to standardise certain aspects of e-commerce, the directive justified its approach by arguing that its main goal should be to improve legal certainty (and as a result of this consumer confidence) in the e-commerce market. In the words of the directive this sounded as follows: 'In order to ensure legal certainty and consumer confidence, this Directive must lay down a clear and general framework to cover certain legal aspects of electronic commerce in the internal market'.[27]

One of the latest proofs of the relevance of legal certainty in EU consumer law can be seen in the new, maximum harmonised Timeshare Directive, i.e., the 2009 Timeshare Directive[28] that replaced the older, minimum harmonised version of 1994. Recital 3 2009 Timeshare Directive explained the switch from minimum to maximum harmonisation as follows:

> In order to enhance legal certainty and fully achieve the benefits of the internal market for consumers and businesses, the relevant laws of the Member States need to be approximated further. Therefore, certain aspects of the marketing, sale and resale of timeshares . . . should be fully harmonised.

Two years later, in 2011, the Proposal for a Regulation on a Common European Sales Law[29] (hereinafter *CESL Proposal*) aimed at a more comprehensive (alleged)

---

[24] Related, in some instances more precise statements can be found in Recitals 40, 41, 43, 44 CRD.

[25] For details see Article 9(1) CRD that introduces a (maximum harmonised) 14-day-withdrawal period.

[26] Directive 2000/31/EC of the European Parliament and of the Council on certain legal aspects of information society services, in particular electronic commerce, in the Internal Market ('Directive on electronic commerce'), OJ L 178, 17.7.2000, p. 1.

[27] Recital 7 E-Commerce Directive. For additional legal certainty statements within this directive see its Recitals 5 and 22.

[28] Directive 2008/122/EC of the European Parliament and of the Council on the protection of consumers in respect of certain aspects of timeshare, long-term holiday product, resale and exchange contracts, OJ L 33, 14.1.2009, p. 10.

[29] Proposal for a Regulation of the European Parliament and of the Council on a Common European Sales Law, 11.10.2011, COM (2011) 635 final.

improvement of legal certainty. The draft – if and once adopted – would introduce a standardised set of sales law rules – the Common European Sales Law (hereinafter CESL) – applicable (primarily) in certain cross-border B2C transactions.[30] In the accompanying Explanatory Memorandum the European Commission (hereinafter, Commission) argued that the CESL would improve the legal certainty situation for both the business and the consumer side. With respect to the first one, the Commission stated that 'for traders ... [the CESL] would eliminate the need for research of different national laws'.[31] In particular in terms of legal certainty consumers, too, should – in the opinion of the Commission – benefit from the CESL. The Commission is convinced that consumers 'would also enjoy more certainty about their rights when shopping cross-border on the basis of a single set of mandatory rules'.[32] On a different occasion, one of the authors of this present contribution extensively commented on these Commission assumptions and tried to prove them (to a large extent) wrong. For the purpose of this contribution it suffices to note that the EU legislator – once again – labels its (maximum) harmonisation plan with the argument of (allegedly) increased legal certainty.[33]

In all these cases, the legal certainty debate primarily revolves around the attempt to standardise B2C transaction governing provisions at a pan-EU level. Put differently, in most cases the central question lies in legislative efforts to align rules applicable in domestic transactions with those applicable at a cross-border level – or at least (e.g., in the case of the CESL) to standardise the legal cross-border setting regardless of the habitual residence/place of business of the parties to a B2C contract with the help of maximum harmonisation.

Legal certainty can, however, also be of importance in a different context. To determine whether B2C provisions are applicable at all, one needs to clarify whether a concrete transaction involves (at least) one business and (one the other side at least) one consumer. Only in such a case one could speak of a B2C transaction. This shows how important it is to correctly determine whether a transaction includes a consumer. This importance can manifest at different stages. The parties themselves might have an interest in knowing the 'status' of the other party to assess their rights and obligations correctly when entering a transaction to avoid bad surprises at a later stage. If a dispute arises, parties, their legal representatives and – if necessary – dispute solving institutions, most likely courts or ADR bodies, would have to clarify whether the scenario at hand is a B2C case or not, as this might lead to different legal consequences.[34]

---

[30] The relevance of the instrument for B2B contracts (involving at least one SME) and possible relevance for domestic scenarios – see Article 13 (a) CESL Proposal – must not be neglected. Both can, however, for the purpose of the present analysis be left uncommented.

[31] CESL Explanatory Memorandum, p. 11.

[32] CESL Explanatory Memorandum, p. 4.

[33] For details see Wrbka (2015), pp. 215–245, 274–276.

[34] For similar 'uncertainty' considerations as a result from diverse consumer definitions under EU law see, e.g., Nebbia and Askham (2004), pp. 36–38.

As will be shown in the following chapters, in most, but not all cases the EU legislator has been aware of this and has repeatedly tried to define the term 'consumer'. One complicating factor, however, is the fact that not all relevant laws have chosen the same approach, i.e., the same definition. Depending on the time of enactment of the law and the circumstances, different instruments (have) introduced different definitions. Since language is limited and the 'consumer' definitions of EU laws tend to be kept relatively short, situations might occur that pose difficulties for the correct classification of a contract as either a B2B or B2C contract. Against this background it does not come as a big surprise that case law, most notably case law found at the EU level, has provided additional parameters to determine the real 'status' of a contract. Over the years the Court of Justice of the European Union (hereinafter *ECJ*) has dealt with different issues in this respect, reaching from more fundamental differentiations between businesses and consumers to questions of mixed-purpose contracts, i.e., contracts that (on one side) involve both professional and private interests or the influence of the representation of parties. In the following we will highlight some examples of how to define consumers. Subsequent to this, we will briefly summarise and comment on the consumer notion from the viewpoint of legal certainty, on the one hand, and legal flexibility, on the other.

3 The Consumer Notion Under EU Legislation and EU Case Law

3.1 General Remarks on the Consumer Notion

The 'consumer' concept can basically be divided into two pillars. First, the question might arise whether a (natural or juristic) person can be called a consumer in a legal sense at all. For the sake of clarity we could refer to this as the 'external side' of the consumer notion. Second, and once a person is classified as a consumer in a legal sense, the question might arise whether the consumer can enjoy concrete rights under a basically suitable/applicable piece of consumer legislation. Put differently, not every consumer is necessarily treated or protected in the same way or to the same extent. Depending on the situation and the concrete legal question, consumer laws might differentiate between consumers worthy of protection and consumers who should not be given special treatment. As briefly pointed out at the beginning of this contribution, this second question refers to what is generally known as the consumer model (*Verbraucherleitbild*). This discussion tries to mitigate the (likely) negative impact or (at least) burdensome effect of consumer legislation on business interests. Consumers who are not found to be put in a bad enough (legal or balance-wise) position, should not necessarily enjoy all the same benefits as the 'truly weak' consumer. Hence, one can say that this second consumer pillar differentiates between different groups or 'classes' of consumer. For the sake of simplification one could refer to this as the 'internal side' of the consumer notion. The internal side has – as explained earlier[35] – already been subject of many contributions. Although the *Verbraucherleitbild* discussion surely is of great practical relevance, this present contribution will – due to space considerations – focus on the external side of the consumer notion.

As indicated in the previous chapter, the consumer notion is of high importance to determine whether consumer law governs a given case. Unfortunately, EU consumer legislation has adopted different consumer definitions that – as shown on a different occasion – sometimes deviate from national definitions.[36] In the following we will take a brief look at exemplary consumer definitions found at the EU level – both in the context of EU laws and EU case law.

3.2 *The (External Side of the) Consumer Notion Under EU Legislation and EU Case Law*

To date no common definition of the term 'consumer' exists at the EU level. As explained already, EU consumer law has taken a fragmented approach in the sense that the EU legislator has adopted sectoral legislation that deals with scope-wise relatively narrow issues. That does not mean, however, that every piece of consumer legislation has introduced a totally independent or unique consumer concept. Although there are certain differences, some instruments share underlying thoughts and ideas.

Arguably the most widely found consumer definition in EU legislation (adopted – with minor differences) by, e.g., the CRD, the Distance Selling of Financial Services Directive[37] and the UCTD is worded as follows (hereinafter, standard definition)[38]:

---

[35] See already supra note 10 for references.

[36] For some examples from selected Member States see, e.g., Hedegaard and Wrbka (2016). For comments from the perspective of Germany see, e.g., Ultsch (2006).

[37] Directive 2002/65/EC of the European Parliament and of the Council concerning the distance marketing of consumer financial services and amending Council Directive 90/619/EEC and Directives 97/7/EC and 98/27/EC, OJ L 271, 9.10.2002, p. 16.

[38] Article 2(1) CRD reads as follows: "'[C]onsumer' means any natural person who, in contracts covered by this Directive, is acting for purposes which are outside his trade, business, craft or profession" Article 2(d) Distance Selling of Financial Services Directive reads as follows: "'[C]onsumer' means any natural person who, in distance contracts covered by this Directive, is acting for purposes which are outside his trade, business or profession." Another example is found in Article 2(b) UCTD that includes the following definition: "[C]onsumer' means any natural person who, in contracts covered by this Directive, is acting for purposes which are outside his trade, business or profession". The definition is further adopted, e.g. by Directive 2008/48/EC of the European Parliament and of the Council on Credit Agreements, OJ L 133, 22.5.2008, p. 66 (see its Article 3(a)) and Directive 2005/29/EC of the European Parliament and of the Council concerning Unfair Business-to-consumer Commercial Practices, OJ L 149, 11.6.2005, p. 22 (see its Article 2

> Consumer means [or shall mean] any natural person who, [in situations] covered by this Directive, is acting for purposes which are outside his trade, business, craft or profession.

The CSD, on the other hand, is an example of a directive that provides for a slightly different wording:

> Consumer: shall mean any natural person who, in the contracts covered by this Directive, is acting for purposes which are *not related to* his trade, business or profession [Emphasis added].[39]

Comparing these two approaches, one might notice an interesting linguistic difference. One could argue that the CSD definition is stricter in the sense that situations might arise, where a party is not considered as being a consumer under the standard definition and not under the CSD definition. This would be the case if one understands the first one, i.e., 'purposes which are outside his trade, business, craft or profession', as an expression of purposes that relate to the *core* of the professional activities that a person engages in. If there is not relation to the *core* of the professional activities, but 'only' *some* kind of minor/'non-core' relationship, a party could qualify as a consumer under, e.g., the UCTD, but not under the CSD. If – from a material scope perspective – a disputed issue falls under both instruments (but the person would qualify as a consumer only under one of them), difficult questions as to a balanced application of the mechanisms might arise.

In contrast to the legislator (that has taken different defining approaches), the ECJ has aimed to align the consumer notions and has provided for an interpretation of the standard definition, i.e., of 'purposes which are outside his trade, business, craft or profession', that gets pretty close to the CSD definition. A prominent case in which the ECJ aimed to clarify the meaning of the standard definition was the *Pinto* decision.[40] One of the key questions was how to understand the consumer definition of the (in the meantime repealed) Doorstep Selling Directive. The wording of the consumer notion under this directive followed the standard definition. Article 2 (2) Doorstep Selling Directive read as follows: 'For the purposes of this Directive: 'consumer' means a natural person who, in transactions covered by this Directive, is acting for purposes which can be regarded as outside his trade or profession'.

In the concrete case a French national was being prosecuted for violating domestic rules on canvassing and doorstep selling that implemented the directive. Mr. Di Pinto ran a company that published a magazine in which businesses were advertised for sale. Upon initial telephone contacts Mr. Di Pinto and/or his

---

(a)). The proposed CESL Regulation takes a similar approach – see Article 2(f) CESL Regulation Proposal. In a similar way is the consumer definition under the Brussels I Regulation, that – in its Section 4/Articles 15–17 – introduces some betterments for consumers. Article 15(1) Brussels I Regulation reads as follows: 'In matters relating to a contract concluded by a person, the consumer, for a purpose which can be regarded as being outside his trade or profession . . .'. For a more recent analysis of ECJ case law in the context of the Brussels I Regulation and its consumer concept see Bisping (2014).

[39] Article 1(2)(a) CRD.

[40] C-361/89 Patrice Di Pinto.

representatives would visit potential clients to conclude an advertisement contract. Mr. Di Pinto's company usually asked for in advance payments, i.e., for payments to be made by interested businesses before the expiration of a seven day period – which, under the condition that the pertinent canvassing and doorstep selling provisions were applicable, would have been a breach of said consumer legislation. In the *Pinto* case one of the questions that arose thus was whether the canvassed traders could have been considered as consumers or not (if one followed the argument that offering businesses for sale would constitute an 'exceptional' activity that lay outside the canvassed person's trade or profession).

The ECJ answered the issue as follows:

> [T]he criterion for the application of protection lies in the connection between the transactions which are the subject of the canvassing and the professional activity of the [canvassed] trader: the latter may claim that the directive is applicable only if the transaction in respect of which he is canvassed lies outside his trade or profession. Article 2, which is drafted in general terms, does not make it possible, with regards to acts performed in the context of such a trade or professional, to draw a distinction between normal acts and those which are exceptional in nature.[41]

By this, the ECJ clarified that the decisive criterion for categorising a (natural) person as either a consumer or a professional lies in the question whether the transaction at hand has *any* connection with the person's professional activity[42] – regardless of whether it relates to the core activities or not. Hence, one could say that the ECJ opted for an objective determination (that takes account of an objective involvement of a person's business in a transaction) and not a subjective approach (that would solve the question by looking at a person's core professional activities, knowledge or skills and their link to the transaction at hand). Put differently, any transaction entered into with the purpose of benefitting or otherwise being utilized for a person's professional activity is to be considered as constituting a non-consumer transaction – regardless of whether or not the transaction lies within the professional expertise of a person in a given trade or profession. With this argumentation, the *Pinto* judgment closed the gap between the standard consumer definition and those definitions that followed the CSD approach by establishing the general criteria of a connection between the transaction and the trader's professional activity. The introduction of this overarching concept of *professional activity* merged the inconsistent implementations of 'trade', 'business', 'craft' and/or 'profession' of the standard definition under one common pillar.

The restrictive interpretation of the standard definition can be understood as an expression of the ECJ's quasi-legislative activities. From a certainty viewpoint one could both praise and criticise this approach. Aligning different consumer notions undoubtedly increases the overall clarity – since parties would be subject to standardised definitions. However, from the viewpoint of transparency one might

---

[41] C-361/89, para. 15.

[42] On the professional vs. private activity perspective see further, e.g., Howells and Weatherill (2005), pp. 285–287.

regret that the ECJ interprets the standard definition in a way that does not necessarily seem to be the most obvious one when looking at the wording. We will return to this issue later.

The *Idealservice* case[43] emphasised a *pre*-condition that needs to be fulfilled to classify a party as a consumer (under EU law). The case concerned the purchase of a drinking water dispenser by a company, i.e., a legal person, for its employees. From a legislative perspective the question revolved around the interpretation of the consumer term under the UCTD that followed the above-mentioned standard definition. The ECJ was asked to answer the questions whether a legal person could be considered as a consumer and – if so – whether in a situation where a company acquires a good for the benefit of its employees, the UCTD would be applicable. One might have expected that the ECJ would repeat its argumentation as introduced by *Pinto* to clarify the meaning of 'acting for purposes which are outside his trade, business or profession'.[44] However, the court did not even reach this stage, but determined the underlying contract as a B2B based on a different argumentation. It pointed out that the consumer definition of Article 2(b) UCTD only extends to 'natural persons' and that by this explicit wording legal persons have to considered as not being able to under the consumer concept.[45] EU consumer legislation has generally taken a similar approach as found in Article 2(b) UCTD and has been excluding legal persons from enjoying advantageous consumer protection.[46]

Going through EU consumer laws one will find additional, arguably even more indefinable consumer notions. One example can be seen in the definition used by the Price Indication Directive[47]:

> Consumer shall mean any natural person who buys a product for purposes that do not fall within *the sphere of his commercial or professional activity* [emphasis added].[48]

---

[43] C-541/99 Cape Snc v. Idealservice Srl.

[44] Article 2(b) UCTD.

[45] The judgment, albeit silent thereon, arrives at a result that could also be reached by applying the *Pinto* criteria, as the purchase was made by the company that was principally involved in *professional activities*. Pursuant to *Pinto*, the 'subjective' arguments that purchasing a drinking water dispenser lay outside the professional range of the company and that the purchase itself was not directly linked to profit making purposes on the side of the buyer could not have led to any different result, since subjective characteristics have to remain without relevance. For more comments on *Idealservice* see, e.g., Stuyck (2010), p. 29; Hondius (2006), p. 95.

[46] This does, however, not mean that Member States necessarily always take the same restrictive approach. Even some EU legislation explicitly allows Member States to broaden the consumer notion to include some 'grey areas'. An example would be the Distance Selling of Financial Services Directive, which – in its Recital 29 – explains as follows: 'This Directive is without prejudice to extension by Member States, in accordance with Community law, of the protection provided by this Directive to non-profit organisations and persons making use of financial services in order to become entrepreneurs.' See further Hedegaard and Wrbka (2016) for some national examples.

[47] Directive 98/6/EC of the European Parliament and of the Council on consumer protection in the indication of the prices of products offered to consumers, OJ L 80, 18.3.1998, p. 27.

[48] Article 2(e) Price Indication Directive.

The choice of the term *sphere* to distinguish consumers from other buyers seems unfortunate, because it appears very vague. What exactly is the 'sphere' of a commercial or professional activity? Is it the core of a commercial or professional activity? Or is it anything that (somehow) relates to a commercial or professional activity? Following the ECJ's standardising approach, one would have to opt for the latter one. Falling within the sphere of a professional activity does no necessitate that a transaction relates to core activities. Any different understanding would render the ECJ's stance as expressed in *Pinto* somewhat meaningless. One this might conclude that the different nuances used by EU consumer legislation do not create such a big problem when it comes to the basic (external) characteristics of consumers, if one affirms that ECJ case law aims quasi-harmonising the external consumer notion to the biggest possible extent. However, certain grey areas might exist, where the classification of a party as either a consumer or a business gets more complicated and controversial. In the following we would like to briefly comment on some of them.

3.3 Setting Up a Business

Reasoning similar to *Pinto*, yet in a slightly different context, was given in the *Benincasa* case.[49] Here the court had to answer the question whether activities in the course of setting up a business would already have to be considered as leading to the exclusion of consumer protection. More precisely, *Benincasa* revolved around the question of whether a person setting up a business would fall under the applicability of the advantageous, procedural consumer provisions of the Brussels I regime. The ECJ basically followed the argumentation already used in the *Pinto* case and explained as follows:

> In order to determine whether a person has the capacity of a consumer, a concept which must be strictly construed, reference must be made to the position of the person concerned in a particular contract, having regard to the nature and aim of that contract, and not to the subjective situation of the person concerned.[50]

The Court looked at the *position of the person concerned*, which can – when found to be related to a business purpose – be compared to the 'professional activity' argument introduced by the ECJ in *Pinto*. The court explained that a link must exist between the professional activity of the trader ('the position of the person') and the transaction *in the particular contract* to qualify a person as a non-consumer. Again, the court did not look at the particular skills of the party, but solely at the question whether the activities can be considered as having any connection with a business purpose (which it had in the case at hand, because the

[49] C-269/95 Francesco Benincasa v. Dentalkit Srl.

[50] C-269/95, para. 16

pre-stage activities were regarded as being close enough to the consequent, 'true' business activities).[51]

3.4 The Consumer Notion and Mixed Purpose Contracts

Another situation of practical significance is that of 'mixed purpose contracts', i.e., contracts that (clearly) show a *professional activity* dimension *as well as* a *private* purpose. The practical importance to classify such contracts as either B2B or B2C contracts lies in the fact that it is generally impossible to apply both B2B and B2C rules to one and the same legal issue. For example, if a possible withdrawal issue arises in the course of distance selling, one has to decide whether the affected party is a business or a consumer (to conclude whether the pertinent withdrawal rules are applicable – in the case of a B2C contract – or not – in the case of a B2B contract). It is not possible to withdraw to, e.g., 60% (if the consumer dimension amounts to 60% in that contract). Applying the *Pinto* reasoning is not of much help. The key issue in a mixed purpose contract is not to be seen in the question of whether we face *any* professional activity at all. In a mixed purpose contract, it clearly exists. The central problem rather lies in classifying the mixed purpose contract as either a B2B or B2C contract – despite showing characteristics of both. Put differently, in a mixed purpose contract it is not sufficient to stop after the identification of a possible professional activity. In addition, one has to clarify the impact of both the professional and private activity dimensions on the overall classification of the contract.

One of the landmark cases in this context is the *Gruber* judgment.[52] In *Gruber,* a farmer had purchased tiles for replacing the roof of his farm. The farm was used partly for professional purposes (i.e., farming) and partly as his family residence, i.e., for private purposes. When the tiles showed defects, the farmer sued the seller invoking the *inter alia* advantageous consumer jurisdiction clauses of the Brussels I Convention.[53] The question arose whether or not these rules were applicable.

[51] It should be noted though that this restrictive approach is not absolute in the sense that Member States are always asked to exclude situations of setting up businesses from their consumer notions. If granted discretion – see, e.g., the example in supra note 46 – Member States can maintain or introduce broader concepts. *Benincasa* is also a good example of a procedural law case in which the ECJ takes a similar approach to its substantive law consumer case law. Hence, the ECJ does not stop at aligning the consumer notions of only substantive laws, but transcends its borders to encompass consumer concepts found in procedural laws.

[52] C-464/01 Johann Gruber v. Bay Wa AG. Jules Stuyck points out that the *Gruber* case – despite being closely linked to the question of applicability of the Brussels I regime, must be considered as showing more general effect, i.e., also with respect to substantive law questions, as the ECJ has arrived at a more or less consistent general consumer definition in both procedural and substantive law – for details see Stuyck (2010), p. 53.

[53] In the subsequent judgment of *Ceska,* the court confirmed that the understanding set forth in the Gruber case would also be applicable with respect to the Brussels I Regulation – see C-419/11 – Ceská sporitelna, a.s. v. Gerald Feichter, para. 31. For a comment on *Ceska* see, e.g., Luzak (2013).

Since the question went beyond issues known from *Pinto* and *Benincasa*, i.e., beyond the question of whether there is any professional activity at all, the court had to go one step further. In answering the question of the impact of both professional and private purposes on the classification of a contract as either a B2B or B2C contract, the ECJ argued as follows:

> [I]t is therefore for the court seized to decide whether the contract was intended, to a non-negligible extent, to meet the needs of the trade or profession of the person concerned or whether [...], the business use was merely negligible. For that purpose, the national court should take into consideration not only the content, nature and purpose of the contract, but also the objective circumstances in which it was concluded.[54]

In addition to the objective criteria applied by the ECJ in the above-discussed cases (*Pinto* and *Benincasa*), the court looked at – what one could call – subjective circumstances. Put differently, the ECJ noted the importance of determining the shares of the professional activity dimension on the one hand and the private dimension on the other. One might argue that this contradicts the before-discussed exclusion of the subjective situation of the concerned party. But taking into consideration that the questions look conceptually different – impact of professional/private dimension (*Gruber*) vs. constituting a professional activity at all (*Pinto* and *Benincasa*) – the broadened approach taken in *Gruber* arguably is necessary.[55]

In the Gruber case, the ECJ arrived at the result that mixed purpose contracts should only be considered consumer contracts if the business character of the contract is negligible. The issue of mixed (or dual)[56] purpose contracts has not yet prompted the EU legislator to take harmonising, clarifying steps, although *some* instruments show a tendency to deviate from *Gruber*. In its Recital 17, the CRD, for example explains as follows:

> [I]n the case of dual purpose contracts, where the contract is concluded for purposes partly within and partly outside the person's trade and the trade purpose is so limited as not to be *predominant* in the overall context of the contract, that person should also be considered as a consumer (emphasis added).

The 2006 Green Paper on the Review of the Consumer Acquis (hereinafter, Consumer Acquis Green Paper)[57] takes a similar approach and addresses mixed purpose contracts under the pillar 'horizontal issues', asking whether it would be advisable to introduce any more concrete concept. Noteworthy in this context is the fact that both the CRD and the Consumer Acquis Green Paper deviate from the *Gruber* definition and suggest to differentiate between B2B and B2C contracts based on the criteria of which purpose is predominant (and not whether the business

[54] C-464/01, para. 47.

[55] For somewhat similar comments on the differentiation see, e.g., Kingisepp and Värv (2011), pp. 52 et seq.; Hondius (2006), pp. 94 (and about the objective understanding of the consumer) 95.

[56] See, e.g., Stuyck (2010), p. 54; Recital 17 CRD.

[57] European Commission, Green Paper on the Review of the Consumer Acquis, 8 February 2007, COM (2006) 744 final, p. 15. See Kingisepp and Värv (2011), p. 47.

character is negligible).[58] The same (consumer-friendlier) approach is, for example, also found in the DCFR, which defines consumer as 'any natural person who is acting *primarily* for purposes which are not related to his or her trade, business or profession' (emphasis added).[59]

3.5 The Consumer Notion and Representation

An interesting question further arises in the context of representation. In several business areas, consumers (at the buyer's side) sometimes deal with professional middlemen who – as agents – represent the seller. The second hand car business is a good example. If the seller, i.e., the person with whom the buyer concludes the contract is a non-professional, the status of the underlying sales contract might be disputable. Is it a C2C contract (because both parties to the contract are consumers) or does it constitute a B2C contract (because the buyer primarily – or even solely – deals with a professional middleman)?

The case at hand poses an interesting conceptual question: Technically speaking, such a sales contract undoubtedly constitutes a C2C contract if concluded by two private parties. One could, however, argue that the inclusion of a professional on the seller's side creates a situation that is comparable to a B2C contract if the (private) seller's only task is to sign the contract negotiated by the professional middleman on his behalf. Here a (possible) power imbalance between the professionally represented seller and the buyer comparable to an ordinary B2C contract exists. The ECJ has – to the best of our knowledge – not directly dealt with this issue yet. The situation looks, however, different when one looks at the national level. The German Supreme Court solved one of the landmark cases in 2005 in a situation similar to the above-given example.[60]

In the German Supreme Court case, the plaintiff (the buyer) argued that the sales contract had to be considered as a circumvention contract that aimed to exclude the applicability of consumer laws. The court, however, emphasised that such a construct could only be assumed under very exceptional circumstances, where there is a *clear* indication that the seller and the agent cooperate to avoid disadvantageous consumer laws. One would have to answer this in the affirmative if, e.g., the agent (and not the private seller) bore the financial risk of the sales contract.

As a conclusion of pertinent case law, one thus should note that the inclusion of middlemen does not change the character of contracts negotiated (but not signed) by middlemen (unless one could clearly consider them as circumvention transactions).

[58] For details see Consumer Acquis Green Paper, Chapter 4.1.

[59] Article I.-I:105(1) DCFR. For details on the DCFR approach see von Bar and Clive (2009), pp. 94–103. For additional, general comments see Stuyck (2010), pp. 53–54; Hondius (2006), p. 96; Reich et al. (2014), p. 397; Manko (2013), p. 2

[60] BGH, 25.1.2005, (2005) NJW, 1039. For details on this case see, e.g., Stuyck (2010), pp. 34–38.

The objective, technical construct – i.e., the question of who signs the contract – weighs stronger than possible power (im)balance issues. A similar conclusion should be drawn in the opposite case, i.e., where the professional middlemen represents a private buyer. If a sales contract is signed by a professional seller and a private buyer (but negotiated by a professional agent on his behalf), one would consequently have to arrive at the conclusion that such a contract constitutes a B2C transaction.

3.6 *Auxiliary Contracts*

We would like to conclude our excursion with comments on the significance of auxiliary contracts. In the *Dietzinger* case a son gave a guarantee to a bank in favour of his father's business to obtain credit from the bank.[61] This was done outside the bank's premises. The basic question that arose was whether the son could withdraw from the contract under the then-still applicable Doorstep Selling Directive regime. Put differently, the court needed to clarify whether the guarantee contract had to be considered as a B2C contract for which the Doorstep Selling Directive was applicable. It was beyond dispute that the contract was signed outside the bank's premises. Hence, the basic requirement for the application of the directive was fulfilled. Also without dispute was the fact that the son himself did not act in the course of his own trade or profession (which were the two options adopted by the standard definition of the Doorstep Selling Directive).[62] The ECJ, however, rejected the argument that the son could invoke the directive, by interpreting the scope of the instrument as explained by its Article 1, namely that the directive was limited to '*contracts under which a trader supplies goods or services to a consumer*',[63] in a way that one needed to take account of the nature of any combined, main contract. In the present case the ECJ arrived at the conclusion that the guarantee signed by the son was an auxiliary contract to the father's credit agreement. Since the father clearly acted in the context of his business, the guarantee had to be considered as sharing the same fate, i.e., as not qualifying as a B2C contract.[64] In the words of the ECJ this was explained as follows:

> [A] contract of guarantee concluded by a natural person who is not acting in the course of his trade or profession does not come within the scope of the directive where it guarantees repayment of a debt contracted by another person who, for his part, in acting within the course of his trade or profession.[65]

---

[61] C-45/96 Bayerische Hypotheken- und Wechselbank AG v. Edgar Dietzinger.

[62] Article 2 Doorstep Selling Directive: 'For the purposes of this Directive: 'consumer' means a natural person who, in transactions covered by this Directive, is acting for purposes which can be regarded as outside his trade or profession.'

[63] Article 1 Doorstep Selling Directive cited in C-45/96, para. 17.

[64] C-45/96, para. 18.

[65] C-45/96, para. 23.

The *Dietzinger* case is of interest primarily, because it seems to somehow depart from the earlier discussed professional activity concept. If the court had stopped at an independent analysis of the guarantee, it would have had to conclude that – due to the fact that the son himself did not act for the purpose of his own professional interests – the guarantee should have been classified as a B2C contract. However, the court broadened its evaluation and looked more deeply at the substance of the contract, i.e., the rationale behind it. Here it was not the person (having clearly been a non-professional), but solely the ultimate purpose of the guarantee that led to the determination of the guarantee as a transaction that was not governed by the Doorstep Selling Directive.[66]

4 Conclusion: The Consumer Notion from the Perspectives of Legal Certainty and Legal Flexibility

What can be concluded in terms of legal certainty and flexibility? Our excursion showed that the EU approach towards defining the consumer concept seems to put a greater emphasis on certainty in the sense that – with respect to the situation at the EU level – the EU legislator and EU case law do not allow for reacting to situations of individual imbalance. At the statutory law level there seems to be a trend towards following (what we called) the standard (consumer) definition. Though being linguistically relatively vague, EU case law contributes to this standardisation and points out that the EU consumer concept has to be understood in a comparatively restrictive way. *Pinto*, for example, explained that a standardised, objective definition (that does not take account of a party's concrete legal knowledge or skills) has to be followed to satisfy calls for legal clarity and transparency. *Stuyck*, in this context, notes that this appraoch shows that (at the EU level) the power/information imbalance between two parties to a contract is not the most important criterion. In his words this sounds as follows: 'The ECJ seems to see the consumer not as the weaker party on the basis of information asymmetry … but on the risk he is taking.'[67] The question thus lies in the decision whether the (financial) risk a party takes is a professional or 'only' private risk.

From the perspective of legal flexibility, the EU approach undeniably raises certain questions of individual appropriateness. Why should a lawyer who purchases a good for a private purpose be allowed to enjoy consumer protection whereas a legally inexperienced professional cannot enjoy the same – even if

[66] The judgment was – without explicit reference – later confirmed in *Ceska*. The ECJ – when interpreting the Brussels I Regulation – came to the conclusion that only contracts concluded "for the purpose of satisfying an individual's *own* need in terms of private consumption, are covered" [emphasis added] – see C-419/11, para. 34.

[67] Stuyck (2010), p. 53.

being in an 'imbalance situation'?[68] One answer to this might be seen in the argument of enhanced predetermination of the applicable legal framework. As illustrated with the examples of mixed purpose contracts and contracts concluded at the stage of setting up a business, knowing whether there is (enough) professional activity involved at the side of the opposite party might already cause a considerable amount of confusion. If one would add subjective criteria (e.g., concrete legal knowledge), this would further complicate the whole issue – and from the perspective of foreseeability and transparency would have be to rejected.

Depending on the concept on favours – legal certainty or legal flexibility – the outcome might be either satisfying or not. As the special cases discussed in this contribution and the pertinent literature show, the debate is not over yet. It must be expected that proponents from both sides will advocate for their respective interests. In this respect it will also be interesting to see how Member States that take a consumer-friendlier approach and apply a wider definition of the consumer concept at the national level will react to the Commission's efforts to intensify its maximum harmonisation approach .

References

Becher SI (2008) Asymmetric information in consumer contracts: the challenge that is yet to be met. Am Bus Law J 45:723–774

Benöhr I (2013) EU consumer law and human rights. Oxford University Press, Oxford

Bisping C (2014) Mandatorily protected: the consumer in the European conflict of laws. Eur Rev Private Law 22:513–544

Bydlinski F (1988) Fundamentale Rechtsgrundsätze. Springer, Vienna

Bydlinski F (2011) Juristische Methodenlehre und Rechtsbegriff, 2nd edn. Springer, Vienna

Canaris C-W (1969) Systemdenken und Systembegriff in der Jurisprudenz. Duncker & Humblot, Berlin

De Hoon MW (2007) Power imbalances in contracts: an interdisciplinary study on effects of intervention. TISCO working paper series on civil and conflict resolution systems, no. 01/2007. Available at papers.ssrn.com/sol3/papers.cfm?abstract_id=985875

Denkinger F (2007) Der Verbraucherbegriff. De Gruyter, Berlin

Hartmann B (2007) Der Begriff des Verbrauchers im nationalen und europäischen Recht. Grin, Norderstedt

Hedegaard JS, Wrbka S (2016) External characteristics of the European consumer – coherence and gaps in a multi-faceted regime, working paper, (forthcoming)

Hesselink MW (2007) SMEs in European contract law. In: Boele-Woelki K, Grosheide W (eds) The future of European contract law. Kluwer Law International, Alphen aan den Rijn, pp 349–371

Hondius E (2006) The notion of the consumer: European Union versus Member States. Sydn Law Rev 28:89–98

Howells G, Weatherill S (2005) Consumer protection law, 2nd edn. Ashgate, Aldershot

[68] See, e.g., Stuyck (2010), p. 29. Also critical on the method for defining consumers: Schueller (2012), p. 123; Reich et al. (2014), p. 53.

Howells G, Ramsay I, Wilhelmsson T (2010) Consumer law in its international dimension. In: Howells G, Ramsay I, Wilhelmsson T (eds) Handbook of research on international consumer law. Edward Elgar, Cheltenham

Kingisepp M, Värv A (2011) The notion of consumer in EU consumer Aquis and the consumer rights directive – a significant change of paradigm? Juridical International XVIII, p 47

Luzak JA (2013) Consumer's definition refined. blog entry. Available at http://recent-ecl.blogspot.co.at/2013/03/consumers-definition-refined.html

Manko R (2013) The notion of 'consumer' in EU law. Library Briefing/Library of the European Parliament. Available at http://www.europarl.europa.eu/RegData/bibliotheque/briefing/2013/130477/LDM_BRI%282013%29130477_REV1_EN.pdf

Möller S (2008) Verbraucherbegriff und Verbraucherwohlfahrt im europäischen und amerikanischen Kartellrecht. Nomos, Baden-Baden

Nebbia P, Askham T (2004) EU consumer law. Oxford University Press, Oxford

Ramsay I (2012) Consumer law and policy: Text and materials on regulating consumer markets, 3rd edn. Hart, Oxford

Reich N, Mitcklitz H-W, Rott P, Tonner K (2014) European consumer law, 2nd edn. Intersentia, Cambridge

Schoenmakers W (2014) The notion "consumer" in European private law. Master thesis. Available at http://lib.ugent.be/fulltxt/RUG01/002/163/256/RUG01-002163256_2014_0001_AC.pdf

Schueller B (2012) The definition of consumers in EU consumer law. In: Devenney J, Kenny M (eds) European consumer protection: theory and practice. Cambridge University Press, Cambridge, pp 123–142

Stuyck J (2010) Setting the scene. In: Micklitz H-W, Stuck J, Terryn E (eds) Cases, materials and text on consumer law. Hart, Oxford, pp 1–69

Ultsch ML (2006) Der einheitliche Verbraucherbegriff – §§ 13, 14 BGB: Nationale Vereinheitlichung im Lichte europäischer Vorgaben. Nomos, Baden-Baden

von Bar C, Clive E (eds) (2009) Principles, definitions and model rules of European private law. Draft Common Frame of Reference (DCFR), full edn. Sellier, Munich

von Bar C, Clive E, Schulte-Nölke H (eds) (2009) Principles, definitions and model rules of European private law – Draft Common Frame of Reference (DCFR), outline edn. Sellier, Munich

Weatherill S (2012) Consumer protection. In: Smits JM (ed) Elgar encyclopedia of comparative law, 2nd edn. Edward Elgar, Cheltenham, pp 237–245

Wrbka S (2014) The dilemma of European consumer representation in deliberative networks – the democratic deficit in the context of the drafting of the common European sales law. In: Fenwick M, Van Uytsel S, Wrbka S (eds) Networked governance, transnational business & the law. Springer, Heidelberg

Wrbka S (2015) European consumer access to justice revisited. Cambridge University Press, Cambridge

Legal Certainty and Trusts in China

Zhen Meng

Contents

Abstract The location of ownership of trust property has been a hotly debated issue among Chinese scholars since the Chinese Trust Law was enacted in 2001. This chapter describes various conventional interpretations of Chinese Trust Law submitted by legal scholars. Moreover, it develops a new, but more practical way, to explain why Chinese trust business has expanded in spite of the uncertainty of Chinese Trust Law regarding the location of ownership of trust property, using a social capital perspective. This chapter also further tries to predict what conditions would enable and make it desirable for China to clarify the location of the ownership of trust property.

Keywords Ownership of trust property • Chinese trust business • Social capital • Mutual trust • Institutionalized trust

Z. Meng (✉)
Nanjing University of Science and Technology, School of Public Affairs, Department of Law, Nanjing 210094, China
e-mail: mengzhen850925@hotmail.com

M. Fenwick, S. Wrbka (eds.), *Legal Certainty in a Contemporary Context*,
DOI 10.1007/978-981-10-0114-7_6

1 Introduction

Trust is a legal device for wealth management, which is considered to have originated in common law jurisdictions, notably England. For centuries, the trust in England had been employed as the vehicle for estate planning by families with lands, and then by urban middle class citizens. Before the mid-twentieth century, for common law lawyers, the trust had been related to testamentary and *inter vivos* personal or family trusts.[1] However, today, the trust is used not only for family settlements during life and for the flexible disposition of decedents' estates, but it also is used in many kinds of commercial transactions and business relationships, such as trust of receivables, business trust *etc*., and collective fund trust.[2] Commercial trusts are now widely utilized in many jurisdictions in the world that have a developed financial infrastructure.[3] In a modern economy, the trust, among banking, security, and insurance, is considered as one of the four mainstays of financial system.

This development of the trust leads to a recent trend in the reception of the trust in civil law jurisdictions. In a global context, by 2000, up to 53 jurisdictions worldwide possessed a statute or a code expressly or impliedly providing for trust, excluding the world's main common law jurisdictions (i.e., England, US, Canada, Australia, Hong Kong, Singapore, India *etc*.).[4]

However, from a global perspective, legislators in civilian jurisdictions have often loombergd to find solutions for theoretical and technical problems[5] when implementing trusts in their legal system. As some scholars pointed out, "perhaps the greatest difficulty the civilians have in accepting the trust is caused by the distinction between the legal and the equitable ownership."[6] It is widely considered that the "dual ownership" concept is a key feature of common law trusts. The central element of common law trust is that the trustee obtains legal ownership/title through the establishment of trust, while beneficial ownership/title of trust property is transferred to the beneficiary. A trust permits a division in the ownership of the trust property between a trustee and a beneficiary so that the trustee is compelled to act entirely in the best interests of the beneficiary in relation to the management of whatever property is held on a trust. In other words, the trustee obtains appropriate control over the trust assets in order to manage them effectively, while the beneficiary obtains the beneficial enjoyment of the assets so as to check on the trustee's powers to avoid abuses. However, it is generally acknowledged that this mechanism

---

[1] Waters (2006).

[2] Restatement of the Law Third, Trusts (US 2003), Part 1 Chapter 1 IN NT. See also McKinsey (2014); D'Angelo (2014).

[3] See D'Angelo (2014); Waters (2007).

[4] The text for each of these 53 'trusts' is supplied in Lupoi (2000). As of the present date the number is in excess of 53. See also Waters (2006).

[5] See Ho and Lee (2013).

[6] See e.g. Gretton (2000).

runs counter of important tenets of generally accepted civil law principles, particularly, the theory of "absolute ownership" and *numerous clausus* principle.[7]

The Chinese Trust Law has given rise to heated debate on the issue where the ownership to trust property is located since its enactment in 2001. It employs very vague terminology in order to conceptualize a trust, and contains paradoxical provisions with respect to the ownership of trust property. Article 2 of Chinese Trust Law provides that: "(T)rust refers to that the settler, based on his faith in trustee, *entrusts* his property rights to the trustee and allows the trustee to, according to the will of the settler and in the name of the trustee, administer or dispose of such property in the interest of a beneficiary or for any intended purposes." (emphasis added) [8] Such vagueness is causing confusion not only theoretically but also practically. The ambiguous wording of "entrust" and other relevant provisions in this Law make it uncertain who is the owner of trust property in the context of Chinese Trust Law.

This chapter will firstly describe the legal uncertainty caused by Article 2 of Chinese Trust law, and then will move on to outline the Chinese debates regarding such legal uncertainty. Subsequently, from a social capital perspective, this chapter will provide an understanding of the interaction between the uncertainty of Chinese Trust Law and the development of Chinese trust business, and will further make a prediction of the necessity to clarify the Chinese Trust Law and its conditions.

2 Legal Uncertainty Caused by Article 2 of Chinese Trust Law

It is generally understood that China, as a country employing civil law system, needs to restructure the dual ownership of trust property when accepting trust law in order to keep consistency with its overall legal system. Namely, assuming that China does not employ dual ownership, it was expected that Chinese Trust Law define whether the ownership of trust property remains at the settler of the trust, or in contrast assigned to the trustee. However, the Chinese Trust Law leaves open the fundamental questions as to whether, with the establishment of trust, the ownership of trust property is transferred from the settlor to the trustee or not, which has given rise to heated debate about who owns the trust property.[9]

Article 2 of the Chinese Trust Law states that the settlor "entrusts", rather than "transfer" which is required in common law trust as well as in several civil law jurisdictions whose trust law defines that the ownership of trust property solely

---

[7] See Bolgár (1953).

[8] The English translation of Chinese Trust Law can be found in the Database of Laws and Regulations by the National People's Congress of China. http://www.npc.gov.cn/englishnpc/Law/Frameset-page2.html. Accessed 29 August 2015.

[9] Ho (2012), pp 184-185.

belongs to the trustee (e.g. Japan), his property rights to the trustee. The requirement of transferring the trust property ownership was replaced in the last circulated draft of the Chinese Trust Law by the equivocal terminology of "entrust".[10] If the word "transfer" is used in this article, the ownership of trust property has to be assigned from the settlor to the trustee in order to establish a trust. At the time when the Trust Law was drafted, the Chinese authorities worried that the requirement of transfer of ownership of trust property might have a negative implication on the practice. According to their contention, under this requirement, people are likely to hesitate to enter into a trust contract with trust institutions, because of the risk of losing their ownership of property. Instead, the Chinese Trust Law requires the settlor to "entrust" the property rights to the trustee in order to establish a trust, which means that the Trust Law does not mandate the settlor to transfer his property rights to the trustee, though it does not prohibit any such transfer.

The terminology of "entrust" in this article caused a significant ambiguity regarding the location of the ownership of trust assets. The use of the word "entrust" raises the question as to whether it suggests an absence of vesting of property rights in the trustee (or whether the settlor remains his ownership on trust property when establishing a trust). In Chinese law, "entrustment" is not a legal term unique to the establishment of a trust; rather, it is a term typically used in the context of the creation of an agency relationship or a mandate, which do not require any transfer of property or property rights to the agent.[11] Some scholar argues that the use of "entrust" causes the ambiguity or is even a failure of legislation. It is now unclear whether, in light of the inconsistencies between the provisions themselves,[12] it is necessary for the law to define that the settlor shall transfer ownership of the relevant property in order for the trustee to set up a trust.[13]

Then, there may be two kinds of trust scheme in Chinese Trust Law: one that involves the transfer of the settlor's ownership in the underlying trust property to the trustee, and another that does not. If the trust property is not registrable, such as money or tangible movable property (but for automobiles, ships, aircrafts, etc. subject to registration similar to real estate), and the settlor does transfer the property to the trustee, the trustee will appear to the public as if he is the full owner.[14] This is because under Chinese Property Law, the rights of ownership comprise the rights of possession, use, beneficial enjoyment and disposal of the property.[15] Once a settlor transfers such types of property to the trustee by means of

---

[10] Ho (2012), p 201. For more details, *see* Bian (2002), pp 255–278.

[11] Ho (2012), p 199. Under the Contract Law of China, an entrustment contract is "a contract whereby the principal and the agent agree that the agent shall handle the affairs of the principal".

[12] For example, Article 15, 20, 28, 29, 30 are inconsistent with Article 14, 16 of Chinese Trust Law.

[13] Ho (2004).

[14] See Ho (2012).

[15] Property Law of the People's Republic of China. Its English translation available at http://www.npc.gov.cn/englishnpc/Law/2009-02/20/content_1471118.htm. Accessed 14 June 2015.

giving the possession and use of the trust property to the trustee, the trustee will have all the external representations of ownership provided in the Property Law. Moreover, the Chinese Trust Law also clearly grants the trustee the right to manage and dispose of the trust property. It is true that the trustee's rights of possession, use and disposal of the property are qualified by the beneficiaries' right to beneficial enjoyment of the property, however, such beneficial rights are not visible to the public. Accordingly, the trustee is indistinguishable from a full owner, at least from the perspective of a third party who would become possible assignee of the same trust property.

On the other hand, where the trust property is registrable, such as rights in relation to land or house or automobiles, ships, aircrafts, etc., there needs to be trust registration to make trust public to a third party. However, as of today, there are no further rules about the details of trust registration in China. One can only speculate that any such registration system will at least involve revealing and disclosing or publicizing that the trust property is subject to a trust.[16] Under such conditions, the trustee's apparent ownership will be significantly qualified by trust, because any third parties dealing with the trustee will know that his/her rights over the trust property are subject to the trust. For example, it would be made clear to the public that the trust property will not fall within the bankruptcy properties of the trustee when it is bankrupted; or the personal creditors of the trustee cannot assert claims on the trust property when the trustee is insolvent. Comparatively, according to Japanese trust law, the ownership of trust property is clearly vested to the trustee, and the registration of trust is a matter of whether the parties to trust can claim to a third party, rather than a matter of the establishment of trust.[17]

Alternatively, a settlor may retain his/her ownership of the trust property, entrusting his rights of the property to the trustee. However, the distinction between this form of trust and an agency relationship is fuzzy. Theoretically, such trusts are distinguishable from agency relationship, on the grounds of that: (1) the trustee has a general management power on the trust property, while the agent only has limited power granted by the principal; and (2) the trust property is supposed to be segregated from the settlor's own property, while the principal continues to own property entrusted to the agent, without distinction from his/her general properties.[18] However, the first distinction is only in respect of the scope of the trustee's and agent's power on the property. It is difficult for the court and also a third party to distinguish them from each other, when a principal grants a general power to the

---

[16] See Ho (2012).

[17] See Article 14 of Japanese Trust law: (its English translation available at http://www.japaneselawtranslation.go.jp/law/detail/?id=1936&vm=04&re=02)

> With regard to any property for which the acquisition, loss, and modification of any right may not be duly asserted against a third party unless it is registered, the fact that such property belongs to the trust property may not be duly asserted against a third party unless the fact that the property is under the trust is registered.

[18] Ho (2012), p 199.

agent. For the second difference, although the Trust Law provides for segregation of the trust property from the settlor and the trustee's own assets, there are no further detailed instructions as to how this is to be achieved and made visible to the public.

3 Chinese Debates Regarding the Location of Ownership of Trust Property

The ownership of trust property is deemed by Chinese legal scholars as a challenge for the traditional understanding or concept of ownership in China. As one scholar points out, "the Chinese Trust Law's lack of guidance concerning the location of ownership of trust property to a judiciary that may not yet be familiar with the trust concept is regrettable."[19] In this regard, within Chinese legal circles, the approaches of interpretation in both the academic and practical fields differ from each other. Some suggest that the ownership of trust property remains at the settlor even after the establishment of trust, whereas the trustee manages the trust property on behalf of the settlor, and the beneficiary enjoys the beneficial interest which is a right of creditor against the trustee. Others argue that the ownership of trust property is transferred from the settlor to the trustee upon the establishment of trust, and the beneficiary's right is either a new style of real right which enables the beneficiary to claim its rights on the trust property against the trustee or a third party, or a right of creditor which enables the beneficiary to obligate the trustee to manage the trust property for the benefit of the beneficiary. Still, others believe the beneficiary is the owner of the trust property. These different opinions and their expected legal consequences will be specifically explained in the following sections.

3.1 An Opinion Contending Settlor as the Owner of Trust Property

Some scholars contend that Article 2 of Chinese Trust Law is the most significant innovation of Chinese Trust Law.[20] They argue that, according to Chinese Trust Law, the ownership of trust property remains with the settlor even after the establishment of a trust.[21] In their opinion, under the Chinese law, "entrustment" is a concept typically used in an agency contract. For example, suppose that A entrusts B to sell the apartment of A. Now, A is deemed as the principal, and B is deemed as the agent. Therefore, in the deal of the sale of the apartment sale, B acts

[19] Ho (2004).
[20] See Zhang (2007).
[21] Zhang (2007).

in the name of A, and all the legal effects of the sale contract will bind A, rather than B. If B sells the apartment to a *bona fides* third party C in the name of A, in violation of the given authority or the will of A, the sale contract of the apartment shall be invalid. Also, A can claim to revoke the sale contract between B and C. The definition of the "entrustment contract" indicates that there is no transfer of property from the principal to the agent in an agency arrangement.[22] The word of "entrust" is also used in Article 30 of the Trust Law,[23] where a trustee is permitted to "entrust" others to handle the trust affairs on his behalf. This appears to be a simple authorization of the rights to manage the trust property to a third party, without transferring the ownership to the trust property to such third party. Some Chinese scholars' such understanding of Article 30 thus suggests that the transfer of trust property to the trustee is not required under Article 2 of Chinese Trust Law.[24] Besides, those scholars presented the proof that Article 20 of Chinese Trust Law states that the settlor has the right to information related to "*his* trust property" (emphasis added).[25] Articles 28[26] and 29[27] also require the trustee to segregate his own property from "the trust property of different settlors" (emphasis added). The former draft of this article, Clause 25 of the April 2000 draft of the Trust Law, only refers to "the property of other trusts", rather than that of the settlors.[28] Literally, the

[22] Article 396 of Chinese Contract Law provides that:

> An entrustment contract is a contract whereby the principal and the agent agree that the agent shall handle the affairs of the principal.

See also Lee (2009).

[23] Chinese Trust Law 2001, Article 30 provides that:

> (T)he trustee shall handle the trust affairs in person, but if there are otherwise provisions in the trust documents or there is no alternative, the trustee may entrust others to handle the affairs on his behalf. The trustee shall bear liability for the handling of the trust affairs by others to whom he entrust the trust affairs. (Emphasis added.)

[24] Lee (2009).

[25] Chinese Trust Law, Article 20 provides that:

> (T)he settlor has the right to know how *his* trust property is managed, utilized or disposed of and the income and expenses incurred therefrom, and has the right to ask the trustee to make explanations. The settlor has the right to consult, write down or duplicate the trust accounts relating to *his* trust property and other documents relating to the handling of trust affairs. (Emphasis added.)

[26] Chinese Trust Law, Article 28 provides that:

> (T)he trustee may not conduct inter transaction between his own property and trust assets or between the trust assets *of different settlors*. (Emphasis added.)

[27] Chinese Trust Law, Article 29 provides that:

> (T)he trustee shall administer the trust property separately from his own property and keep separate accounting books, and he shall do the same with regard to the trust property *of different settlors*. (Emphasis added.)

[28] Ho (2012), p 198.

wording of these articles can serve as evidence that the settlor owns the trust property after the establishment of trust. However, there are other provisions in the Trust Law that can provide evidence for the opposite opinion, as set forth above.

According to the argumentations of these scholars, in Article 15 of Chinese Trust Law, if the ownership of the trust property is deemed to be transferred to the trustee, the act of separation of trust property from the settlor's own property would have been superfluous.[29] There are provisions of the Trust Law which allow the settlor to retain extensive powers after the arrangement of establishing a trust, including power to manage the trust property, right to inspect trust documents, and even right to request the trustee to adjust the methods to manage the trust property.[30] If trust property were vested in the trustee, the settlor should retain no (beneficial) interest that would allow him to interfere with the trustee's management of the trust property. Rather, only the beneficiary has the rights to interfere the trustee's management rights to the trust property. Furthermore, these legal scholars concluded that the provisions reserving extensive powers for the settlor make it evident that even after the entrustment, the settlor remains to be the owner of the property entrusted.

According to this understanding, the settlor may possess, use, manage and dispose the trust property even after the establishment of trust; the trustee actually functions as an agent of the settlor, although the trustee may manages or disposes the trust property in his/her own name. In case of wrongful disposition of trust assets by the trustee, the settlor may rescind the wrongful disposition. The trust property will not fall within the trustee's bankruptcy estate, and cannot be seized by the personal creditor of the trustee. However, in some other scholars' view, the power of the settlor on the trust property may be too strong. They explain that Article 15 of Chinese Trust Law requires the settlor to segregate trust property from his/her private property once a trust is established. The trust property shall not fall within the settlor's bankruptcy estate, and cannot be seized by the personal creditor of the settlor as well, as long as it is segregated from other properties of the settlor. However, what if the settlor fails to meet this requirement in Article 15 of Chinese Trust Law? Because China has not yet established a registration system to make the trust public, it would be very common that, in the practice, the settlor has no means to notify his segregation to public. The difficulty for the trustee and beneficiary will

[29] Chinese Trust Law, Article 15 provides that:

> Trust property differs from other properties with which the trustor hasn't established a trust. After the trust is established, if the trustor dies or disbands according to law, or is canceled or declared bankrupt according to law, and if the trustor is the only beneficiary, the trust shall terminate and the trust property shall be deemed as his heritage or liquidation property; if the trustor is not the only beneficiary, the trust shall continue to exist and the trust property shall not be deemed as his heritage or liquidation property; but if the trustor, as a joint beneficiary, dies or disbands according to law, or is canceled or declared bankrupt according to law, the beneficial right of the trust shall be deemed as his heritage or liquidation property.

[30] See Chinese Trust Law, Article 20, 21, 22.

be that they may not know whether the settlor has segregated the trust property because the segregation of the trust property is not visible to the public in China, until it is too late. From the perspective of a third party, the trust property without registration of segregation would be deemed as part of ordinary assets of the settlor. The settlor's creditors may have recourse to the trust property in the event of the settlor's insolvency.

In light of this, some scholars criticize that if the settlor is considered to retain the ownership of the trust property, the conceptual and practical problems accompany with this understanding cannot be underestimated. They argue that, conceptually, the distinction between trust and an agency relationship is fuzzy.[31] Also, these scholars contend that from the practical perspective, such an understanding of the trust is extremely inefficient in operation. First of all, if the trustee does not hold the ownership of trust property, the trustee's power in managing the trust property will be significantly restricted. According to the Trust Law, the trustee shall manage the trust property in his own name. However, such lack of ownership of trust property will make it inconvenient for both the trustee and a third party when they want to enter into a legal relationship. For example, the owner of a piece of equipment settled an equipment leasing trust, in which the trustee, in its own name, gives the lessee of such equipment the right to use the equipment for a specified period of time for an agreed upon payment. Accordingly, the lessee arranged the schedule to manufacture the productions utilizing the leased equipment from the trustee, and made a series of sales contracts with another party to sell these products in the future. However, the lessee would be subject to the risk that the equipment lease would be overturned by the settlor, if the settlor exercises his power as an owner of the leased equipment.

Second, if the trust property is not segregated from other assets of the settlor, or is hard to be identified as a trust property, the scheme of a trust will become ineffective in order to achieve the purpose of the trustee's professional management ability, because a third party needs to pay transaction cost to identify whether the property in transaction is trust property or not. If the trustee does not have ownership of trust property, one may wonder how the trustee is to discharge his duty under Article 25 to manage the trust property with "honesty, good faith, prudence and efficiency". For example, if a settlor settles shares of a company into trust but retains ownership of them, the trustee would have no right to vote those shares in shareholders' meetings unless specifically authorized by the settlor to vote on behalf of the settlor.[32]

[31] Ho (2012), p 199.

[32] Graham and Steeny (2012).

3.2 *An Opinion Contending Trustee as the Owner of Trust Property*

Another opinion contends that the ownership of trust property is transferred to the trustee upon the establishment of a trust under the Chinese Trust Law.[33] Scholars with this view explain that the use of the word "entrust" in Article 2 of Chinese Trust Law does not necessarily suggest an absence of a transfer of property from the settlor to the trustee. In their opinion, in the relationship between the principal and the agent to an entrustment contract, the entrusted person is obliged to and expected to act *in the name of his/her principal*. Such acts of the agent are inconsistent with the requirement that the trustee manages or disposes of such property *in his/her own name*. They argue that the wording "entrust" as used in the Chinese Trust Law may have a meaning different from that of an entrustment contract in its strictest sense. Therefore, they contend that the failure to provide for a transfer of the ownership of trust property from the settlor to the trustee in the definition of trust in Article 2 should not be understood as meaning that the establishment of a trust under the Chinese Trust Law does not entail a transfer of the ownership of trust property from the settlor to the trustee. They emphasize that we should be careful about the fact Article 14 of Chinese Trust Law provides that the trustee obtains the trust property as a result of accepting the trust. This implies that Article 14 suggests that the establishment of a trust involves the acquisition of property on the part of the trustee. The trustee can only obtain property when the ownership to the trust property is transferred to him.[34] They contend that, moreover, Article 16[35] prohibits the trustee from mixing his own property with the trust property, if the ownership of trust property is not vested in the trustee, such requirements would be otiose.[36]

Also, Article 10 requires that the trust property should be registered for the purpose of publicizing the property as trust property where the relevant law or regulations so require. It is argued by the scholars contending that Article 10 means that where this provision is applicable, the trust is not effective unless the property is registered under the trustee's name.

Some other scholars admit that it is not clear who owns the trust property according to the provisions of the Trust Law, however, it is necessary to identify the owner of trust property when the trust property is involved into transactions with

---

[33] There are arguments that against this opinion, stating that the ownership of trust property held by the trustee is incompatible with the concept of the ownership in civil system. See Zhang (2007).

[34] Qu (2003). See also Lee (2009).

[35] Chinese Trust Law, Article16 provides that:

> The trust property differs from the property owned by the trustee (hereinafter referred to as inherent property for short) and shall not be deemed as the inherent property of the trustee or become part of the inherent property. If the trustee dies or disbands or terminates as a result of being canceled or being declared bankrupt according to law, the trust property shall not be deemed as his heritage or liquidation property.

[36] Qu (2003).

third parties. According to their opinion, for instance, suppose that a settlor entrusted cash to the trustee for the purpose of investment into a stock company by means of purchasing the stocks issued by the company. Who should be the shareholder of the company after purchasing such stocks? It depends on who owns the trust property from which the said investment was made. These scholars also contend that the transaction costs of transaction for the third party who attempts to make a deal related to the trust property and to protect him/herself against the risk which may arise from the transaction may increase, because the Trust Law does not clarify, and, thereby, both of the settlor and the trustee may cause such risk.[37]

In this regard, they think that it is better to interpret that the trustee is the owner of trust property in order to reduce to transaction costs, because the ownership is consisting of a bundle of rights and incidents in respect of the property, any tiny branch of such bundle remained at the settlor may cause substantial risk from the viewpoint of the third party who may attempt to deal concerning the trust property. The incidents of ownership generally comprise "the right to possess, the right to use, the right to manage, the right to the income, the right to the capital, the right to security, the incident of transmissibility, the incident of absence of term, the prohibition of harmful use, the liability to execution and the incident of residuarity."[38] Accordingly, the scholars conclude that it is obvious that the Chinese Trust Law entitles the trustee to most of these incidents, thus it would be logical and reasonable to entitle the ownership of trust property to the trustee.[39]

This point of view was supported practically as well. In a case concerning trust in 2001,[40] the court defined in the decision that trust means the act in which the settlor, on the basis of confidence on the trustee, transfers certain property rights it owns to the trustee and the trustee manages or disposes of the property rights in its own name in accordance with the intentions of the settlor and for the benefit of the beneficiary or for specific purposes; and stated that trustee is the subject of ownership to the trust property and is responsible for its own acts. The court also stated that the difference between trust and entrust lies in whether the property is transferred (from the settlor or the principal – added by the author) to the trustee or not.

From the perspective of this opinion, the beneficiary's interest can be classified as a new type of real right beside the ownership, usufructuary right, and the security interest. It seems that, according to the court, the beneficiary's interests constitute the complete real rights of the trust property together with the ownership held by the trustee. That is, by the establishment of trust relationship, there happens the alteration of real right on trust property: the owner of the property changes from

[37] Wang (2008).

[38] Lee (2009). See also Honor (1987).

[39] Yu (2010).

[40] Shandong Shipin Youxian Gongsi v. Jinan Yingda Guoji Xintuo Touzi Gongsi (Shandong Food Co. Ltd. v. Jinan Yingda International Trust and Investment Co, Ltd.), the Court of Shizhong District, Jinan, Shangdong, First Instance Civil Case No.1707 (2001).

the settler to the trustee; and a new type of real right – the beneficiary's interest – is created.[41]

In light of this understanding, some scholars contend that the trustee has the rights to possess, use, manage and dispose of the trust property in its own name and according to its own decision. Because the Chinese Trust Law requires the trustee to segregate the trust property from the other assets of the trustee, theoretically, the trust property shall not fall within the trustee's bankruptcy estate, and cannot be seized by the personal creditor of the trustee. In case of wrongful disposition of trust assets by the trustee, the settlor or beneficiary may rescind the wrongful disposition. However, implementation of the segregation of the trust property from the trustee's other assets may be difficult in practice, because the operational guidelines on separate accounting and trust registration are very rudimentary for the moment in China. To date, no further guidelines have been issued by any governmental agency (including the Ministry of Land and Resource) as to how trust registration can be made (even for real estates, the registration rules are still in the procedure of draft as of today). Therefore, the trust property is very likely to be considered to be a part of the proprietary assets of the trustee by outsiders of a trust. In the case of the bankruptcy or insolvency of the trustee, the trust property may face the risk of falling within the trustee's bankruptcy estate, or the private creditor of the trustee may assert claims on trust property, because the evidence for the independence of trust property would be very hard to provide by the trustee in the court. This perhaps is the reason why the potential consumers of trust products are hesitate to settle their property under a trust.

3.3 An Opinion Contending Beneficiary as the Owner of Trust Property

There are also scholars who hold the opinion that the ownership of trust property belongs to the beneficiary. For those scholars, the beneficiary's "beneficial right" under a trust can be regarded as an ownership interest.[42] They contend that as long as the trust comprises a right of beneficiaries against the trustee to regulate their relationship and to exclude third parties from the enjoyment of trust property, it is sufficient to constitute ownership under a Chinese Trust Law, because the beneficiary's right carries with it at least some proprietary effects.[43]

[41] Wang (2008).

[42] Wen and Feng (2005). (There are two reasons: a. Trustee's possession of the trust property might be terminated by the beneficiary (or the settlor), whereas the owner's possession of the property has no time limitation and depends on his own will. B. trustee's rights of dispose of trust property are limited within the trust contract documents and the beneficial interest.)

[43] Lee (2009).

In China, the effects of the beneficiary's interest contain: "(i) the beneficiary has the right of defense against the trustee's personal creditors when it comes to the trust property[44]; (ii) the beneficiary has the right to revoke the act of the trustee conducted in the breach of trustee's responsibility[45]; (iii) the beneficiary has the right to claim for the benefits."[46] As can be seen from this, the beneficiary's interest is an exclusive right on the trust property, and the beneficiary can defense against the third party. Besides, the system of trust registration requires the publication of trust property. They contend that beneficiary's right is real right, because of its exclusive nature, the requirement of publication, and its power of defense against a third party.[47] In their conclusion, "equitable ownership" is the real ownership under a civil law system, and a beneficial interest is the most significant incident of civil law ownership.[48]

According to this understanding, from the perspective of a third party, the trust property apparently belongs to the beneficiary, although the trustee has the rights to manage and dispose the trust property in its own name. In light of this view, the beneficiary's interests have strong protection from the Chinese Trust Law against the wrongful dispositions of trust assets by the trustee, because as the owner of trust property, the beneficiary can easily withdraw the wrongful disposition. However, since Chinese Trust Law does not require that the trust property is segregated from the assets of the beneficiary, the trust property is more likely to fall within the beneficiary's bankruptcy estate, or to be seized by the personal creditor of the beneficiary in the case of insolvency. This consequence runs counter to the purpose of the trust, which aims to provide a mechanism of ring-fenced property free from the bankruptcy of the parties to the trust, or the claim of a third party. Moreover, scholars with this view contend that since typically there are multiple beneficiaries in a trust relationship, especially, in the case of collective trust, there may be hundreds of beneficiaries, vesting the ownership of trust property in multiple beneficiaries might make the situation much more complicated.

---

[44] See e.g. Article 17 of Chinese Trust Law.

[45] This point is mainly regulated in Article 22 of Chinese Trust Law: "If the trustee disposes of the trust property against the purposes of the trust or causes losses to the trust property due to violation of the management duties or improper handling of the trust affairs, the beneficiary has the right to apply to the people's court for withdrawing the disposition; he also has the right to ask the trustee to revert the trust property or make compensation."

[46] For example, under certain circumstances, the beneficiary can demand the distribution of the profit of a trust fund, even though the trust contract between the settlor and the trustee does not have such terms.

[47] Wang (2008).

[48] Wen and Feng (2005).

3.4 Other Minor Opinions

3.4.1 An Opinion Contending That Either the Settlor or Trustee Is the Owner of Trust Property

Some of the lawyers in China also argue that, due to the ambiguity of the Trust Law, there can be two kinds of trust in China: one that involves the transfer of the settlor's rights in the underlying trust assets to the trustee, and another that does not.[49]

For example, for the securitization of credit assets, it is required by the government authorities to transfer the underlying assets of the sponsor banks (settler) to build a healthy balance sheet, which means that the settler has to transfer the ownership of trust property in order to establish a trust.[50] However, a settlor may simply retain his ownership of the trust assets, and enter into a trust contract with the trustee to "entrust" his rights to the latter.[51] For instance, for Real Estate Investment Trusts (REITs), there are huge obstacles for the transfer of the trust property in the context of Chinese legal system,[52] so those scholars argue that it may offer certain feasibility for the parties in REITs if the retention of ownership of trust property is allowed by the Trust Law.[53] In their opinion, it is not necessary to transfer the ownership of trust property in order to achieve the separate of trust property. The doctrinal basis of the trust without the requirement of the transfer of trust ownership lies in the separate of trust property, which is the sole and core feature of modern trust system.

3.4.2 An Opinion Contending That Ownership Is with Either the Settlor or the Beneficiary

In the case decided in 2006,[54] the court commented that even if ownership of the trust property has been transferred to the trustee, either the settlor or the beneficiary was the (real or substantive) owner of the trust property. In the view of the court, this is because, first, Article 2 of the Trust Law does not mandate the transfer of ownership; secondly, trustees who manage funds of multiple clients owe the duty to separate the funds "of different settlors", thus suggesting that the funds are still

[49] Ho (2012), p 196.

[50] Lou (2012).

[51] Ho (2012), p 198.

[52] REIT is a collective investment scheme where funds from investors are pooled and invested towards a specified goal as set out in the investment objective of the fund. In addition, a REIT is a fund that is invested in a portfolio of real estate assets or real estate-related assets.

[53] Lou (2012).

[54] Beijing Haidian Keji Fazhan Youxian Gongsi v. Shenzhen Xinhua Jinyuan Touzi Fazhan Youxian Gongsi (Beijing Haidian Science and Technology Development Co., Ltd. v. Shenzhen Xinhua Jinyuan Investment and Development Co., Ltd.) Chongqing High People's Court, First Instance Civil Case No.14 (2006).

owned by the settlor; and thirdly, beneficiaries have the right to obtain ownership of the trust fund upon termination of the trust, and this is explicable on the ground that the trust funds are actually owned by the beneficiaries. However, even though transferring the ownership of the trust property is not mandatory under the Chinese Trust Law, in the present case, the ownership of the trust property was indeed transferred to the trustee. Finally, the grant of ownership to beneficiaries upon termination of the trust does not necessarily entail that they own the funds during the existence of the trust.[55]

3.4.3 An Opinion That Contends the Settler, Trustee and Beneficiary Hold Partial Powers on Trust Property Respectively

According to the scholars of this opinion the power on trust property is separate from the right of ownership. They explain that the settlor, the trustee and the beneficiary separately enjoy the different incidents of ownership of trust property, which is clearly stated by Chinese Trust Law.[56] They contend that according to the Chinese Trust Law, all the three parties could have a range of powers on the trust property after the establishment of the trust,[57] which together comprise the overall ownership powers. The author agrees that the settler, trustee and beneficiary hold partial powers on trust property respectively according to Chinese Trust Law. However, this opinion does not offer any implication that can help the resolution of the problem concerning the location of ownership of trust property.

4 Legal Uncertainty and Chinese Trust Business: A Social Capital Perspective

Chinese Lawyers and legal scholars invested much effort on the issue regarding the location of trust property ownership, aiming to giving explanations that fit with the underlying civil law principles. However, one important point that is rarely taken into consideration by trust law scholars in China is the practice of the trust business itself and the ever-changing social and economic context surrounding it. The debates rarely go beyond the conflict between the abstract concept of property rights and the trust. From a social capital perspective, studying the attitudes and loomberg of the stakeholders in the trust business might be one way to understand the issue regarding the location of trust property ownership beyond the ambits of abstract principles.

---

[55] Ho (2010).

[56] Hu and Chen (2006).

[57] See Article 17, 20, 21, 22, 23, 28, 35, 40, 41/2, 50, 51/2, 53 of Chinese Trust Law.

4.1 Dense Network Facilitating the Growth of Business

China commercial trust industry has been thriving over the past decades. Back in 2004, total trust assets managed by Chinese trust companies were CNY 150 billion (approximately USD 24.51 billion). According to the China Banking Regulatory Commission (CBRC), the trust sector[58] accounted for a small portion of the finance industry, with total assets under management approximately CNY 600 billion (USD 97.93 billion) in 2007.[59] However, as data published by China Trustee Association shows, by the end of 2014, the total assets managed by the 68 trust companies in China reached a record-high CNY 13.9 trillion (USD 2.24 trillion) from around CNY 2 trillion (USD 0.33 trillion) in 2010.[60] Trust companies are becoming a more significant funding channel as well as a force in Chinese booming wealth management industry.[61]

Trusts perform an important financial function in China today, even in the absence of legal certainty concerning the location of ownership of trust property. Among other factors that have been facilitating the growth of Chinese trust industry, the concept of social capital can provide a perspective to identify other factors that are crucial to the growth of Chinese trust industry. Social capital is a concept or a context employed quite often to explain the good relationship between a pair of actors can be the resource for either or both actors to get profit from such relationship. Social capital consists of personal connections and interpersonal interaction, together with the shared sets of values that are associated with these contacts.[62] The study on social capital has given us an important suggestion that social networks have value, and actors within social networks can gain access to the value through social networks.[63] In particular, the research on social capital also suggests that (mutual) trust has substantial value in establishing commercial relationship between businesses and consumers. Research on social capital from a social

[58] One thing needs to be clarified here is that in a general sense, wealth management services provided by commercial banks, security companies, insurance companies and other financial institutions based on trust principle and trust system can be included into trust industry. But according to Chinese Trust Law, trust industry only refers to the trust business run by trust companies. In this Section, for the convenience of introduction of statistics on trust industry, the latter meaning of trust industry is taken.

[59] KPMG (2010) China's Trust Sector: The Next Chapter. https://www.kpmg.com/CN/en/IssuesAndInsights/ArticlesPublications/Documents/China-trust-sector-next-chapter-201002.pdf. Accessed 6 May 2015.

[60] China Trustee Association, http://www.xtxh.net/Trust_Statistics/19124.html (last accessed November 25, 2014).

[61] KPMG (2010) China's Trust Sector: The Next Chapter. https://www.kpmg.com/CN/en/IssuesAndInsights/ArticlesPublications/Documents/China-trust-sector-next-chapter-201002.pdf. Accessed 6 May 2015; See also Meng (2015).

[62] Field (2009), pp 15–16.

[63] Prell (2012), p 62.

network perspective tends to focus on how specific structural features of the social network affect the loomberg of actors within it.

In the case of this research, in the absence of clarity in laws and regulations on the ownership of trust property, it is submitted that social capital, among other factors, matters in promoting the personal and institutional investors in China to hand off their assets to financial service providers. China trust business is deemed to be activities among relatively small group of people or institutions. The networks of such trust business are submitted to be a dense network with tightly-knit groups. In the social network theory, the density of a given social network is found by dividing the number of all existing links between the actors by the number of potential links within the same set of actors. The higher the resulting number, the denser a network is. Dense networks are most likely to be found in small, stable communities with few external contacts and a high degree of social cohesion. Analyzing the density of networks can answer a number of potential research questions relating to how social networks might affect individuals' loomberg, attitudes, performance or beliefs.[64] The following factors provide evidences for this assumption.

4.1.1 Single Trusts Constitute a Large Percentage of Trust Business

Single trusts manage assets of a single investor. As data shows, nearly 63 % of total trust assets in Chinese trust industry is managed in form of single trusts,[65] that is to say, most of trust funds are from single institution or individual. The transaction structure of single trusts is relatively simple. Trust companies channel money from individual or institutional investors such as companies, wealthy individuals, and even banks. The cooperation between banks and trust companies constitutes a major resource for single trusts. In practice, it always goes like this: Commercial banks cannot lend to SMEs or projects in frothy industries, such as real estate, mining, or steel, where regulators see signs of overinvestment and so have instructed banks to curb lending. Then the banks take loans off their balance sheets by using trust companies as intermediaries to package and securitize loans for resale.[66] Lack of active management ability and investment ability makes trust companies in China become business channel or platform for commercial banks. The density of the network in this business model is relatively high. It is considered to be a small community with certain actors who has direct or indirect connection with one another.

---

[64] Prell (2012), p 122.

[65] China Trustee Association, http://www.xtxh.net/xtxh/statistics/22930.htm. Accessed 15 April 2015.

[66] See Zubi (2012) Murky Waters: The rapidly-evolving landscape of Chinese SME finance. http://www.geopoliticalmonitor.com/murky-waters-the-rapidly-evolving-landscape-of-chinese-sme-finance-4715/. Accessed 15 April 2015.

Banks are the most important funding source for trust assets. In particular, bank WMPs account for 28.8 % of single-unit trusts. The remaining 41.2 % is accounted for by banks' own funds and non-bank financial institutions' own funds. Although there is no detailed data on the breakdown of contribution from own funds of banks and non-bank financial institutions, industry analysts believe that banks' own funds dominate this source of single-unit trust assets, with estimates ranging from 50 to 75 %. Taken together, bank-related funds (WMPs and own funds) directly account for 50–60 % of single-unit trust assets or equivalently 35–40 % of total trust assets. Taking into account bank resources involved in combined trust and properties trust, industry analysts estimate that close to half of trust assets are directly funded by banks.[67]

4.1.2 Trust Companies Rely on Commercial Banks for Client Referrals

Collective trusts manage the assets of a number of investors. At the end of 2014, Collective trusts constitute about 30 % of total trust assets in China. In a collective trust plan, a trust company handles a pooled group of trust accounts. Although trust companies in China are making efforts in building their customer base, they currently rely heavily on commercial banks to find investors because of lack of their own client resources.

According to the *Measures for the Administration of Trust Companies' Trust Plans of Assembled Funds* promulgated by the China Banking Regulatory Commission (CBRC) in 2007 (revised in 2009), only "qualified investors" may invest in collective trust schemes.[68] As a rule, only investors with a minimum of RMB1 million (USD 160,000) to invest per trust scheme are considered. Compared with other financial institutions in China, commercial banks are the most trusted finan-

---

[67] Asian Development Bank Consultant's Report (2014) The People's Republic of China: knowledge work on shadow banking – trust funds and wealth management products. http://www.adb.org/sites/default/files/project-document/80950/shadow-banking-trust-funds-and-wmps-prc.pdf. Accessed 6 May 2015.

[68] Measures for the Administration of Trust Companies' Trust Plans of Assembled Funds, Article 6 provides that:

> The term "qualified investor" as mentioned in the preceding paragraph refers to a person that satisfies any of the following conditions and is able to identify, judge and undertake the corresponding risks of a trust plan:

1. a natural person, legal person or any other organization established according to law whose minimum investment in a trust plan is 1 million yuan or more;
2. a natural person whose aggregate individual or family financial assets exceed 1 million yuan at the time when he/she subscribes the trust plan and who can provide the relevant property certificate;
3. a natural person whose annual income exceeds 200,000 yuan for the latest 3 years or whose total annual income of husband and wife exceeds 300,000 yuan for the latest 3 years and who can provide the relevant income certificate.

cial institutions by citizens, and have most sophisticated retail networks and sizable customer bases. Most of the HNWIs in China are clients of banks, which enable banks to make the most of their network to sell trust products for trust companies. The connections between the big commercial banks and HNW customers are strong due to the improvement of, for example, relationship managers' capabilities.[69]

4.1.3 *Guanxi* Plays a Role in Relationship Marketing of Trust Products

From the documentations and interviews, we can observe the importance of the "*Guanxi*" network of managers in companies for doing financing and asset handling businesses in China. Managers in relevant companies have various connections with each other. Additionally, managers in financial institutions are required to make use of their connections to high net worth individuals for the sale of the private wealth management services or trust products. For example, in recruitment for relationship managers of Industrial and Commercial Bank of China (ICBC), it describes one of the roles of this position as: "Source new business from HNW individuals through referrals, marketing activities and personal contacts."[70]

On the other hand, there are two types of investors of commercial trusts in China: HNWIs and institutional investors (primarily commercial banks). The HNWIs are somehow, directly or indirectly, connected with one another. Individual investors are more likely to engage in activities of the same social groups (e.g. golf clubs, business association), which makes them share certain similar background. Their experience of trust products can be spread among their circle.

For current types of Chinese trust business, the degree of mutual trust seems to be relatively high as a function of a dense network. Mutual trust as social capital plays a substantial role in establishing a business contract between the service providers and consumers. Because of the relatively high degree of mutual trust between the actors within China trusts dense network, people are willing to transfer the trust property to the trustees, placing themselves at risk of losing ownership of trust property. This allows the business to flourish, even in the absence of legal certainty.

---

[69] Some of the largest trusts are closely associated with banks in terms of ownership. For example, CITIC Trust and CITIC Bank are subsidiaries of the CITIC Group. CCB Trust's controlling shareholder is the China Construction Bank. Industrial Trust's majority owner is Industrial Bank of China.

[70] Industrial and Commercial Bank of China (ICBC) Relationship Manager. http://www.gulftalent.com/uae/jobs/relationship-manager-167871. Accessed 30 August 2015.

4.2 Nascent Transformation of Chinese Trust Business

Although commercial trusts in China have developed at a rapid speed, most professionals have realized the potential long-term unsustainability of the business. They predict that Chinese trust business is facing a dilemma. For one thing, the demand for trusts in China is predictably increasing. Chinese HNWIs population generates great demand for investment products and assets management services. For the other thing, the trust industry is observed to be in its decline stage of the business life cycle. Growth in funds managed at the Chinese trusts may slow to 20–30 % a year from a 50 to 60 % pace since 2008, according to the estimation of some professionals.[71] The data published by China Trustee Association also show that trust companies' assets under management climbed 6.4 % to 12.5 trillion yuan ($2 trillion) as of June 30 of 2014 from 3 months earlier.[72] That's the slowest growth since the first quarter of 2012.[73] At this point, Chinese trust industry is predicted by many professionals to be stepping into the decline stage.

In order to avoid this decline and maintain a positive business life cycle, trust companies have started to change in various innovative ways their business model. With the transition of Chinese trust industry in terms of the business model, the number of potential consumers (HNWIs) for assets management services increases dramatically. As the size of the network becomes larger, the actors within the network will be sparsely connected with each other, with most actors having only few links. Sociologists have shown that network density tends to attenuate as the network grows larger.[74] Predictably, the Chinese social network surrounding the trust industry will expand, and the density of this network would accordingly become lower. In addition, there are also possibilities that the urbanization, the way of people's work, the nuclear family, *etc.* can be accelerate the society becoming sparse. It is proposed in this research that the network of Chinese trust business in the near future will be qualitatively a sparse network.

A sparse network is connected by a fewer number of links only. In a sparse network, links are more difficult to create. Actors within a sparse network are less likely to have social capital that they can rely on to achieve cooperation. In a sparse network, lack or low degree of mutual trust between actors within the network is more likely to happen. In a sparse network, institutionalized trust is essential for the efficient operation of a business. Institutional factors including legal regulations,

---

[71] China Trust Industry Growth to Slow by Half, Huabao Says (Aug. 2, 2013), available at http://www.bloomberg.com/news/articles/2013-08-01/china-trust-industry-growth-to-slow-by-half-huabao-says (last accessed June 23, 2015).

[72] China Trustee Association (2014) Main Business Data of Trust Companies (1st Quarter 2014). http://www.xtxh.net/xtxh/statisticsEN/20044.htm. Accessed 15 April 2015.

[73] Bloomberg (2014) China trust asset growth slows in shadow banking campaign. http://www.bloomberg.com/news/articles/2014-08-12/china-s-trust-asset-growth-slows-amid-shadow-banking-crackdown. Accessed 11 May 2015.

[74] Mayhew and Levinger (1976).

professional codes of conduct, corporate reputation, industrial standards, and other formal and informal norms of behaviour, can build an individual's confidence in the institutional mechanisms that make the other party honest and consistent.[75] In an economy characterized by a high level of institutionalized trust, actors are able to enter into transactions with only limited information about their partner's specific attributes, with the scope of trust extending beyond the number of people that are know personally.[76]

An important way to build institutionalized trust might be the clarification of the law. The high degree of trust in law can serve as a form of social capital which can be utilized by the actors within the network of an industry. In the potential sparse network of Chinese trust industry, a clear provision about the location of ownership of trust property may reduce the concerns of potential consumers.

However, it must be not overestimated what the law can do in this regard. The clarification of the trust law should be backed by a certain degree of trust from the citizens in the trust institutions. Additionally, the process of the replacement of personal trust relationship by institutionalized trust is "partial" and "incremental". It is noted that with the ever-increasing complexity of society, relationships like *guanxi* in China may play a less important role in social actions, but it will be relatively slow to be replaced by institutionalized forms of trust. It seems unlikely that institutionalized trust can be easily established by the clarification of the law alone. Chinese trust companies would be obliged to build social trust from potential consumers over time. Only if consumers' trust in trust companies reaches a certain degree, is the time ripe for the clarification of Chinese Trust Law as to the location of ownership of trust property.

5 Conclusion

This chapter described the legal uncertainty caused by Article 2 of Chinese Trust Law, and outlined the following interpretations by Chinese scholars: (1) ownership of trust property is transferred to the trustee by the settlor when establishing a trust; (2) ownership of trust property remains with the settlor even after the establishment of a trust; (3) ownership of trust property is with the beneficiaries upon the establishment of a trust; (4) ownership of trust property is with either the settlor or the trustee depending on whether the settlor had transferred ownership of trust property to the trustee; (5) ownership of trust property is with either the settlor or the beneficiary; (6) the settler, trustee and beneficiary hold partial powers on trust property respectively.

In spite of such legal uncertainty, Chinese commercial trust industry has been thriving over the past decades. It was suggested in this chapter that the concept of

[75] Bachmann and Inkpen (2013), p. 460.

[76] Smallbone and Welte (2006).

social capital can provide a perspective to identify factors, among others, that are crucial to the growth of Chinese trust industry in spite of the lack of certainty in the law. In this chapter, Chinese trust business is deemed to be activities among relatively small group of people or institutions. The network of such trust business is submitted to be a dense network. Because of the relatively high degree of mutual trust between the actors within China trusts dense network, people are willing to transfer the trust property to the trustees, placing themselves at risk of losing ownership of trust assets. This allows the business to flourish, even in the absence of legal certainty.

This chapter also predicted that the network of China trust business in the near future is likely to transform towards a sparser network. In a sparse network, actors are more likely to reserve their ownership rights rather than put themselves into risk, unless institutionalized trust is built between service providers and potential consumers. An important way to build institutionalized trust might be the clarification of the law. However, the clarification of the trust law should be backed by a certain degree of trust from the citizens in the trust institutions. Only if consumers' trust in trust companies reaches a certain degree, is the time ripe for the clarification of Chinese Trust Law as to the location of ownership of trust property.

Acknowledgments This paper is supported by "the Fundamental Research Funds for the Central Universities", No.AE15001_16.

References

Asian Development Bank Consultant's Report (2014) The People's Republic of China: knowledge work on shadow banking – trust funds and wealth management products. http://www.adb.org/sites/default/files/project-document/80950/shadow-banking-trust-funds-and-wmps-prc.pdf. Accessed 6 May 2015

Bachmann R, Inkpen AC (2013) Understanding institutional-based trust building processes in inter-organizational relationships. In: Costa AC, Anderson N (eds) Ttrust and social capital in organizations, vol II, Trust in institutions: organizational and inter-organizational level trust. Sage, London, pp 455–481

Bian Y (ed) (2002) Zhonghua renmin gongheguo xintuofa shiyi (Annotation of the trust law of the People's Republic of China). Law Press China, Beijing

Bloomberg (2014) China trust asset growth slows in shadow banking campaign. http://www.bloomberg.com/news/articles/2014-08-12/china-s-trust-asset-growth-slows-amid-shadow-banking-crackdown. Accessed 11 May 2015

Bolgár V (1953) Why no trusts in the civil law? Am J Comp Law 2:204–219

D'Angelo N (2014) Commercial trusts. LexisNexis, Butterworth

Database of Laws and Regulations by the National People's Congress of China. http://www.npc.gov.cn/englishnpc/Law/Frameset-page2.html. Accessed 29 Aug 2015

Field J (2009) Social capital, 2nd edn. Routledge, New York

Graham T, Steeny P (2012) The Chinese trust. Trusts & Trustees 18(1):36–42

Gretton GL (2000) Trusts without equity. Int Comp Law Q 49:599–620

China Trust Industry Growth to Slow by Half, Huabao Says (2013) http://www.bloomberg.com/news/articles/2013-08-01/china-trust-industry-growth-to-slow-by-half-huabao-says. Accessed 23 June 2015

Ho L (2004) The reception of trust in Asia: emerging Asian principles of trust? Singap J Leg Stud 2004:287–304

Ho L (2010) China trust law and practice since 2001. Trusts & Trustees 16(3):124–127

Ho L (2012) Trust laws in China. In: Smith L (ed) Re-imaging the trust: trusts in civil law. Cambridge University Press, Cambridge/New York, pp 183–221

Ho L, Lee R (2013) Reception of the trust in Asia: a historical perspective. In: Ho L, Lee R (eds) Trust law in Asian civil law jurisdictions: a comparative analysis. Cambridge University Press, Cambridge/New York, pp 10–26

Honor T (1987) Making law bind: essays legal and philosophical. Clarendon, Oxford

Hu G, Chen Q (2006) Quanneng fenge: lun woguo xintuofa zhi xintuo caichan suoyouquan (Separating the right and the power: trust property proprietary rights in Chinese trust law). J Zhengzhou Univ 39(6):84–88

Industrial and Commercial Bank of China (ICBC) Relationship Manager. http://www.gulftalent.com/uae/jobs/relationship-manager-167871. Accessed 30 Aug 2015

KPMG (2010) China's trust sector: the next chapter. https://www.kpmg.com/CN/en/IssuesAndInsights/ArticlesPublications/Documents/China-trust-sector-next-chapter-201002.pdf. Accessed 6 May 2015

Lee R (2009) Conceptualizing the Chinese trust. Int Comp Law Q 58(3):655

Lou J (2012) Xintuo caichan de dulixing yu xintuocaichan guishu de guanxi (Relationship between the trust property segregation and the ownership of trust property). J Guangdong Soc Sci 2:242–250

Lupoi M (ed) (2000) Trust laws of the world: a collection of original texts. ETI Editore, Rome

Mayhew B, Levinger R (1976) On the emergence of oligarchy in human interaction. Am J Sociol 81:1017–1049

McKinsey (2014) Global wealth management survey 2014: an attractive sector in transition. http://www.mckinsey.com/~/media/mckinsey%20offices/france/pdfs/global_wealth_management_survey_2014.ashx. Accessed 29 Aug 2015

Meng Z (2015) Should China clarify the ownership of trust assets? A social network perspective. Trusts & Trustees 21(5):492–500

Prell C (2012) Social network analysis: history, theory and methodology. Sage, London

Qu C (2003) The doctrinal basis of the trust principles in China's trust law. Real Prop Prob Trust J 38:345–376

Smallbone D, Welte F (2006) Conceptualising entrepreneurship in a transition context. Int J Entrep Small Bus 3(2):190–206

Wang Y (2008) Lun xintuofa yu wuquanfa de guanxi: xintuofa zai minfa faxi zhong de wenti (Relationship between trust law and property law: toward the questions of trust law in civil law system). J Peking Univ Philos Soc Sci 6:93–101

Waters D (2006) The future of the trust (Part I). J Int Tax Trust Corp Plann 13(4):179–223

Waters D (2007) The future of the trust (Part II). J Int Tax Trust Corp Plann 14(1):1–22

Wen S, Feng X (2005) Lun xintuo caichan suoyouquan (Ownership of trust property). Wuhan Univ J Philos Soc Sci 58(2):203–209

Yu H (2010) Lun yingmei xintuo caichan shuangchong suoyouquan zai zhongguo de bentuhua (Localization of dual ownership of trust property in China). Modern Law Sci 32(3):159–168

Zhang C (2007) Woguo xintuo caichan suoyouquan guishu de taidu jiqi fali shenshi (An examination of the Chinese attitude towards the ownership of trust property). J Gansu Inst Polit Sci Law 91:7–14

Zubi H (2012) Murky waters: the rapidly-evolving landscape of Chinese SME finance. http://www.geopoliticalmonitor.com/murky-waters-the-rapidly-evolving-landscape-of-chinese-sme-finance-4715/. Accessed 15 Apr 2015

Part II
Perspectives from Criminal Law

Multilingual Norms in European Criminal Law

Georg C. Langheld

Contents

Abstract European norms are equally authentic in 24 different languages. To truly know the law, we need to analyse all of them. In practice, the versions which constitute a norm do not state identically the same but differ from one another. The European ECJ of Justice (ECJ) has to choose which version really reflects the content of the norm and prevails over others. At the same time, the ECJ does not grant the individual a right to invoke the wording of a version he or she can understand. This conflicts with the principle of legality, particularly in criminal cases.

The article tracks the genesis of supranational elements of crime, takes a look at their interpretation and proposes a framework of how we should analyse discrepancies between several versions describing a single multilingual norm. The article aims to show that the ECJ could solve the individual's misery of not knowing what the law really says by following through on existing case-law. While interpretative standards do not need to change, the individual must have the right to invoke a particular version under European law, especially in defence against criminal prosecution.

G.C. Langheld (✉)
Noerr LLP, Munich, Germany
e-mail: Georg.Langheld@noerr.com

M. Fenwick, S. Wrbka (eds.), *Legal Certainty in a Contemporary Context*,
DOI 10.1007/978-981-10-0114-7_7

Keywords Multilingualism • European Union • Interpretation • Theory of Norms • Elements of crime • Supranational law • Skoma-Lux

1 Introduction

Japan's culture of cultivating cherry trees is renowned and admired all over the world. As a token of her friendship, Japan has bestowed many of these cherry trees to foreign governments and institutions. Let us assume, for the sake of this paper, that one of these trees stands rooted in Brussels, Belgium, which many consider the capital city of Europe for its close links to law-making at the European level. Imagine this tree starts to bloom sometime during the spring and will eventually bear fruit. If you were to wonder about the taste of these cherries, there is but one way to find out: You would have to try one. Let us further assume that we have a representative from each of the 28 Member States of the European Union pick a cherry from this tree and taste it. While the first 27 of these representatives would announce that this tree bears sour cherries, the last one of them would swear that the cherries taste sweet. Who is right? Or in other words: Is anybody wrong?

2 The Case of Lubella

This simple story serves as an allegory for the language situation in the European Union. More specifically, it refers to the case of Lubella decided by the European Court of Justice in 1996.[1] At that time, European law had set a minimum price for sour cherries and charged importing companies a countervailing amount to avoid competition below the minimum price. So they did in the case of the German company Lubella. Lubella challenged this decision before court and claimed that the regulation only referred to sweet cherries and not to sour cherries. Lubella based its case on the German version of the regulation, which did in fact use the word for sweet cherries ("Süßkirschen"). All other versions explicitly referred to sour cherries. What might provoke especially criminal lawyers for such a clear and obvious violation of the wording did not stir the ECJ at all. The ECJ simply referred to its well-settled case-law according to which

> the need for a uniform interpretation of [Union] regulations makes it impossible for a given piece of legislation to be considered in isolation and requires that, in case of doubt, it should be interpreted and applied in the light of the versions existing in the other official languages.[2]

---

[1] C-64/95, Lubella.

[2] C-64/95, para. 17.

Since all but the German version referred to sour cherries, the ECJ ruled in their favour. For the purposes of that regulation, Süßkirschen ("sweet cherries") must therefore be understood to mean Sauerkirschen ("sour cherries").

So much for the case of Lubella, which did not involve criminal or administrative sanctions. The facts also suggest that Lubella had not acted in good faith when relying on the German version. I have omitted these facts to keep it simple. When it comes to criminal law, this approach described above becomes dangerous.

3 Supranational Elements of Crime

Let us take a step back and look at how criminal law provisions in European law came into existence. As a general rule, criminal justice in Europe lies still within the hands of national legislators. We have provisions on homicide, murder, theft and fraud in all of the 28 national jurisdictions that form the European Union. A European criminal code with comparable criminal laws does not exist. Scholars and practitioners agree that the European Union does – generally speaking – not have the competence to enact its own supranational criminal law provisions.[3]

The European Union must not act unless there is an express competence embodied in one of the European Treaties, which confers the power to legislate upon the Union.[4] Within the scope of its competences, the Union may enact regulations that are directly applicable in all Member States.[5] This is what we will call supranational law because it is applicable in all of the Member States *eo ipso*. There is no need for national legislators to implement these European provisions in their domestic legal systems. Instead, these provisions are directly binding on national courts and administrative authorities. The European legislators, notably the Council of the European Union and the European Parliament, have enacted regulations to govern many legal areas, many of which are of a technical nature. They concern for example fishing quota or the making, marketing and distribution of wine and other alcoholic beverages. Due to this technical nature, many European citizens go about their daily routines without much concern for European provisions.

Although the European Union has over the years reached out to legislate in many different fields, it has left the field of criminal law relatively untouched. Member States have always regarded the criminal justice system a peculiar aspect of their national sovereignties and have consequently defended this domain.[6] This lack of

[3] Cf. Satzger (2012), § 6 paras. 18 et seq. for a detailed analysis of the EU competences in this regard.

[4] Art. 5(1) and (2) TEU.

[5] Art. 288(2) TFEU.

[6] Satzger (2001), pp. 166 et seqq.

criminal law competence leaves the European Union dissatisfied. While it may on the one hand regulate large legal areas with the greatest precision and respect for details, its hands are tied with regard to enforcing these provisions and to punishing perpetrators. Therefore, the law of the European Union requires the Member States to

> ensure in particular that infringements of [Union] law are penalised under conditions, both procedural and substantive, which are analogous to those applicable to infringements of national law of a similar nature and importance and which, in any event, make the penalty effective, proportionate and dissuasive.[7]

The national criminal justice system must therefore serve to protect the interests of the Union by imposing penalties, not necessarily criminal sanctions, for violations of Union law. The easiest way to fulfil this obligation would be to transpose the European regulation into national law and to provide for a sanction in case of violations thereof. The ECJ, however, has expressly prohibited Member States from transposing supranational into national law provisions. The ECJ fears that such implementing measures might conceal their European origin[8] (and threaten the ECJ's mandate to interpret supranational law). The only way forward is therefore to enact so called blanket criminal law provisions.

Consider Section 19 para. 1 of the German Substances Control Act,[9] which provides:

> A prison sentence of up to five years shall be imposed on anyone who
> 2. (. . .) contrary to Art. 3 para. 2 of regulation (EC) no. 273/2004 possesses or places on the market scheduled substances of category 1 of Annex I.

This German (blanket) criminal law is in itself incomplete. To learn what conduct is punishable, we need to read Art. 3 para. 2 of regulation (EC) no. 273/2004[10] (which the blanket criminal law incorporates):

> *(. . .) shall be required to obtain a licence from the competent authorities before they may possess or place on the market scheduled substances of category 1 of Annex I. (. . .)*

Reading these provisions together, we now know that i.a. possessing a substance listed in Annex I without a licence is prohibited and punishable. Similar national legislation has been enacted in all other Member States as well.[11] Supranational elements of crime therefore exist as references in national blanket criminal laws.

---

[7] C-68/88, Greek Maize, para. 24; C-367/09, SGS Belgium, paras. 40 et seq.

[8] C-34/73, Variola, paras. 9 et seq.

[9] BGBl I 2008, 306. Translation from the German original by the author.

[10] OJ 18 Feb 2004, L 47/1.

[11] Council Framework Decision 2004/757/JHA, OJ 11 Nov 2004, L 335/8.

4 Interpretation of Supranational Elements of Crime

Before we turn to the consequences for the principle of legal certainty, let us briefly look at how these supranational elements of crime must be interpreted. Since the purpose of the national blanket criminal laws is to establish sanctions for violations of supranational norms, the interpretation of the blanket criminal laws must follow the interpretation standards provided for the norms themselves.

As the ECJ repeatedly states:

> It must be borne in mind that [Union] legislation is drafted in several languages and that the different language versions are all equally authentic. An interpretation of a provision of [Union] law thus involves a comparison of the different language versions. It must also be borne in mind, even where the different language versions are entirely in accord with one another, that [Union] law uses terminology which is peculiar to it. Furthermore, it must be emphasised that legal concepts do not necessarily have the same meaning in [Union] law and in the law of the various Member States.[12]

Thus, European norms have their own nomenclature. Their words have to be interpreted autonomously and by taking into account all of the official versions. It is needless to say that there is probably not a single person in Europe, presumably not even a single linguistic expert working at the ECJ, who is capable of comparing technically phrased regulations in 24 languages. It seems absurd to assume this to be possible. The ECJ, however, has clung to its established standard of interpretation. It has done so, in my view, because it fears to take any step towards giving particular versions more weight. Over decades, the ECJ has fought vigorously against national courts, even constitutional courts, and their attacks on the supremacy of Union law. By maintaining that no particular version may be superior to others, the ECJ has managed to get a firm grip on Union law and to secure its mandate as the sole interpreter.

5 Deficits under the Principle of Legal Certainty

We should distinguish two different types of deficits with regard to the principle of legal certainty: concrete and abstract deficits.

5.1 Concrete Deficits

Let us take a look at Art. 5 of regulation (EC) no. 423/2007,[13] which prohibited the rendering of certain “brokering services” to Iran. Any violation of this prohibition

[12] C-283/81, CILFIT, paras. 18 et seq.

[13] OJ 20 Apr 2007, L 103/1.

was punishable under a German blanket criminal law. The regulation defined the term “brokering services” as follows:

> (. . .) activities of persons, entities and partnerships acting as intermediaries by buying, selling or arranging the transfer of goods and technology (. . .)

The German version read:

> (...) Tätigkeiten von Personen, Einrichtungen und Partnerschaften, die als Vermittler beim Kauf, beim Verkauf oder bei der Organisation des Transfers von Gütern und Technologien tätig sind (...)

Readers who understand both languages and read carefully will note a striking difference: according to the English version an intermediary is a contracting party in a chain of subsequent exchanges or transfers of a prohibited good as is indicated by the term “by buying, selling”. The German version merely requires an intermediary to facilitate the buying and selling by others. An assisting role suffices. The German version does not require an intermediary to personally become a contractor.

This example illustrates a concrete deficit with regard to the principle of legal certainty. The German and English versions do not match as to this particular aspect. If the ECJ were asked to determine the meaning of this definition, it would have to opt for either the German or the English version. In case the ECJ prefers the German version by merely requiring a supporting role of the intermediary (instead of him or her becoming part of a chain of transactions), English speakers might claim a violation of the principle of legality since the English wording is phrased more narrowly.

5.2 Abstract Deficits

Beyond concrete examples, in which versions do not seem to match, there is a general, systemic deficit to the principle of legal certainty. In a multilingual legal environment, we simply do not know what the law says. We assume that the jurist-linguists working in their Brussels offices do a perfect job of translating all working documents literally and correctly before they become the law. Everyday experience of working with different languages, however, challenges this assumption. This systemic deficit cannot be explained by intrinsic limits to the principle of legality which we accept today. This principle, as envisioned by its inventors, Charles de Montesquieu and Cesare Beccaria, stipulates that any law must be phrased as precisely as necessary to trigger the same thoughts and ideas in any person’s mind and convey exactly the notion of what is legal and what is prohibited.[14] We have learned to limit this bold demand. But the language of a legal text remains a trustworthy source for interpreting the law.

[14] Montesquieu (1750), Book 11, Chapter 6; Beccaria (1764), Chapter 4.

However, the problems posed by Union law are of a different quality. If the ECJ continues to interpret Union law autonomously from national interpretations and with due regard to literally all of the official languages, one particular language may no longer provide a satisfactory means of orientation. One simply does not know to what Union law refers. Instead, we need to estimate the law based on our (limited) understanding. Who can tell if the version one can understand correctly reflects the law (as interpreted by the ECJ)? In one of the first proceedings before the ECJ, at a time when there were only four authentic languages, Advocate General Maurice Lagrange put these considerations in a nutshell by stating:

> As you know, all four languages are authentic, which means that no single one of them is authentic.[15]

As we will see in the following, the ECJ is well aware of these consequences.

6 The View Taken by the ECJ

The ECJ has acknowledged the principle of legal certainty long ago. The ECJ did this first in the context of administrative sanctions for illegal cartels[16] but has willingly extended this principle to the field of criminal law subsequently. The ECJ acknowledges

> that legislation must define clearly offences and the penalties which they attract. That requirement is satisfied where the individual concerned is able, on the basis of the wording of the relevant provision and, if need be, with the help of the interpretative guidance given by the courts, to know which acts or omissions will make him criminally liable.[17]

Although the ECJ seems to base the assessment whether the content of an incriminated norm is phrased in a sufficiently clear way on the ability of the "individual concerned", such individual must "if need be" take recourse to the "interpretative guidance given by the courts". It is fair for the ECJ to acknowledge limits to the principle of legality which are inherent to the use of language. It will never be possible to trigger the same thoughts in everybody's minds by using abstract legal terms. But the ECJ's jurisprudence suggests that the principle of legality is nothing but a formal guarantee which the individual can hardly ever invoke if we continue to go by the ECJ's interpretation, as we will see in the following.

In recent years, the ECJ has had and continues to have the opportunity to refine the role of particular versions of European regulations due to the recent accession of central and eastern European countries to the European Union. A large number of

[15] C-13/61, Opinion by Advocate General Lagrange.

[16] C-85/76, Hoffmann-La Roche, paras. 128 et seq.

[17] C-405/10, Garenfeld, para. 48; C-546/09, Aurubis Balgaria, paras. 41 et seq., each with further references.

countries, such as Poland, the Czech Republic, Slovakia or Hungary, acceded to the European Union in 2004. Romania and Bulgaria followed in 2007, Croatia in 2013. When these countries joined, the entire Union legislation had to be translated into the new official languages. This amounted to a Herculean task and was not accomplished by the legal interpreters in due time. Not surprisingly, these countries became official Member States before Union legislation in its entirety became available in their official languages. It so happened that individuals from these countries were fined for violating regulations which at the time of the violation had not yet been published in the official journal. They claimed that this was a violation of the principle of legality and the ECJ concurred with their views. In the case of Skoma-Lux, which was decided in 2007, the ECJ held

> that the principle of legal certainty requires that Union legislation must allow those concerned to acquaint themselves with the precise extent of the obligations it imposes upon them, which may be guaranteed only by the proper publication of that legislation in the official language of those to whom it applies.[18]

The ECJ seemed to acknowledge language as a means that would allow an individual to inform him - or herself about the content of the norm before the alleged offence. When Kurcums Metal, a Latvian company, tried to invoke this reasoning in a case in which the Latvian version existed but differed from the other languages to have a fine annulled, the ECJ stopped short of assigning any substantive meaning to the principle of legality. In its own words:

> The problem (...) is not that of a failure to publish [the regulation] in the Official Journal of the European Union, which was indeed published inter alia in Latvian, but that of a divergence between the Latvian language version of Article 1 of that regulation and the other language versions of that provision.[19]

While this may already be read as rejecting any material consequences from the Skoma-Lux judgment, the ECJ made this clear explicitly:

> It is settled case-law that the wording used in one language version of a provision of European Union law cannot serve as the sole basis for the interpretation of that provision, or be made to override the other language versions in that regard. Such an approach would be incompatible with the requirement for uniform application of European Union law. (...)[20]

The ECJ handed down the judgment in the case of Kurcums Metal on November 15th, 2012. This is where we stand today: The ECJ seemingly considers the publication of all versions to be important for letting the individual know what is expected of him or her. The ECJ implies that a particular version has the potential of sufficiently informing individuals about their duties under Union law. However, once a particular version has been published officially, it is only of subordinate relevance – if it is of relevance at all. In case of differences between versions, the individual may not invoke what he or she could have relied on if it was missing.

---

[18] C-161/06, Skoma-Lux, para. 38.

[19] C-558/11, Kurcums Metal, para. 47.

[20] C-558/11, para. 48.

7 The Way Forward

Assuming that the ECJ will not put the uniform application of Union law at stake by allowing national courts to give preference to the wording of a particular version, what approach should the ECJ pursue instead? To solve the problem, we should distinguish norms and sanctioning provisions.[21] While norms contain imperatives directed at individuals, sanctioning provisions contain the rules for dealing with possible infringements. With regard to the example mentioned above (relating to the law on export control), the regulation concerning certain measures against Iran contains explicit prohibitions, while the German blanket criminal law merely provides legal consequences for those who do not abide by the referenced norms.

It is not necessary to alter the rules governing the interpretation of Union norms, i.e. the prohibition under European law in the example. Civil law and (to some extent) administrative law could still tie legal consequences to the norm (as derived from a comparison of all versions). We may, however, change the way we look at national sanctioning provisions from the perspective of the principle of legality in criminal law. We would then limit the scope of application for the norm in particular cases in which the individual cannot understand the true meaning of a norm. In these cases, the ECJ should allow invoking the wording of a particular version, and only with regard to the legality of the sanctioning provision, rather than the underlying norm as such. National courts would then be tasked to assess whether a particular version of a Union norm reflects the actual content of this norm (as interpreted by the ECJ). This solution would reconcile the need for a uniform interpretation of Union law (which takes every particular version into account) with the need for reasonable foreseeability. Most cases – presumably – would not take a different outcome. Many official translations are defective but not in all aspects. The ECJ would be required to take a leap of faith towards national courts and trust their prudent application of the principle of legality (or rather legal certainty).

Let us briefly identify follow-up questions. The solution described above does not address the limits to the individual right to invoke the text of a particular version. First, may anyone invoke a text that he or she does not understand? In the spirit of European integration the answer might be yes. After all, it is the institution's fault, not the individual's. But then the individual right would go beyond what is necessary to preserve individual liberty. Second, may anyone invoke a text although he or she personally could have known from another version what the true content of the norm would be? The answer seems to be no. Since European integration aims to promote the understanding of language, why should anyone benefit from not acquiring the skills to communicate in other languages?

[21] As was first done by German legal scholar Karl Binding in his Theory of Norms ("Normentheorie").

Although we leave these questions unanswered for now, I believe that establishing the right to rely on a particular version is a necessary step towards ensuring the liberty of the individual in European criminal law. It seems to be the only way to uphold the equality of all authentic languages on the one hand and to give the principle of legality on the other hand some substantive meaning. The formal approach so far endorsed by the ECJ is a dead end. When deliberating whether and how we must adapt our thinking to address legal issues with which we have not been confronted in the past, we should seek to maintain the substantive cores of our fundamental rights.

To sum up the state of legal certainty in European criminal law, let us honour Japan's literary traditions by concluding with a haiku poem.[22]

In Brussels, there blooms
A cherry tree and its fruits
Taste both: sweet and sour.

References

Beccaria C (1764) On crimes and punishments
Montesquieu (1750) The spirit of the laws
Satzger H (2001) Die Europäisierung des Strafrechts. Carl Heymanns, Cologne
Satzger H (2012) International and European criminal law. Nomos, Baden-Baden

[22] I kindly ask to excuse my feeble attempt.

Empirical Judgement in Criminal Proceedings

Sebastian Stehle

Contents

Abstract Empirical judgement is a multi-layered term and considered to be difficult to approach. It can be cloudy and hard to handle in respect of objectivity. Moreover, the good of legal certainty is of superior importance within the legal system of a constitutional state. Whenever objectivity is threatened in legal processes, legal certainty is threatened at the same time. Circumstances can become especially severe in matters of criminal proceedings – a legal field that inevitably takes a direct and substantial impact on individual constitutional rights for granted.

This contribution aims to analyze the issue from a fundamental viewpoint. I will outline the essentials of the concept of empirical judgement beginning beyond jurisprudence. An empirical understanding of experience as sense perception will be the philosophic basis for the following exploration of the relevance of empirical judgement within criminal proceedings. The German Code of Criminal Procedure shall serve as an object of study to demonstrate that empirical judgement is an indispensable tool to gain cognition within criminal proceedings. Yet inconsiderate or even arbitrary application of empirical judgement threatens the adherence of the German Constitution in which the principle of legal certainty is granted as a

S. Stehle (✉)
Faculty of Law, Munich University (LMU), Munich, Germany
e-mail: scs.stehle@gmail.com

M. Fenwick, S. Wrbka (eds.), *Legal Certainty in a Contemporary Context*,
DOI 10.1007/978-981-10-0114-7_8

fundamental principle. This dichotomy of logical indispensability on the one hand and practical hazardousness towards the protection of constitutional rights on the other hand constitutes the legal area of conflict this contribution attempts to turn the spotlight onto. Finally approaches to enhance objectivity whilst applying empirical judgement within criminal proceedings will be considered concisely.

Keywords Empirical judgement • Experience • Legal certainty • Equal treatment • Degrees of suspicion • Criminal procedure • Consideration of evidence • Criminology

1 Introduction

Considered from the viewpoint of criminal proceedings, the term "empirical judgement" is multi-layered and difficult to approach. It is often said to be cloudy and hard to handle in respect of objectivity.[1] However, handling empirical judgement in criminal proceedings in an objective way is essential to ensure legal certainty. Therefore, it is the neither minor nor easy task of legal science, criminology, jurisdiction and decision-makers in criminal investigation proceedings to concretize and objectify the usage of empirical judgement in criminal proceedings.

Empirical judgement is an important tool in criminal proceedings. This contribution aims to analyze as well the functionality of empirical judgement in general as to present examples from the German code of criminal procedure (StPO), where empirical judgement becomes crucial. Amongst others empirical judgement is used to determine which measures provided by the code of criminal procedure in general can be used in a certain case. Eventually empirical judgement allows measures of impact to constitutional rights. Accordingly it is of major importance to ensure that the right of legal certainty and the right of equal treatment (codified in article 20 section III and article 3 of the German Constitution) are not violated.[2]

I am going to outline the significance of the tool in criminal proceedings using the German Code of Criminal Procedure as the object of study and I am going to demonstrate which dangers loom in the arbitrary application of empirical judgement. Conclusively, conceptions of possibilities to improve objectivity in handling empirical judgement shall be presented.

[1] Soiné (2010a), p. 345 and (2010b), p. 275.

[2] Soiné (2010b), p. 279.

2 A Definition of Empirical Judgement

Despite the fact that empirical judgement is a cloudy and multi-layered term, it is nevertheless possible to shape it more clearly. In a first approach the term "experience" needs to be examined more closely. Afterwards, the functionality of empirical judgement can be examined in greater detail.

2.1 Experience as the Basis of Empirical Judgement

Experience can be seen as the basis of empirical judgement. A definition of experience could be the process of seeing and perceiving any event in life and thus knowing more than before. It can also refer to the enhancement of routine and familiarity in handling certain work stages by repetition.[3] It is thus possible to gain knowledge from experience in a process of cognition. Rules of empirical judgement are based on experience and formed in a process of cognition. They can then be used to gain knowledge about the most likely course of events in a period of time in the past that is unknown or about the most likely development of events in the future.

To put it in other words, there is experience that consists of sense perception, on the one hand.[4] However, sole experience is of hardly any use. It needs a process of cognition on the other hand, logical hypotheses, verification and falsification, to form a rule of empirical judgement that can finally be used to gain knowledge.

2.1.1 Sole Experience

Basically there can be two meanings of experience, as seen before. Experience as repetition of work stages and experience as sense perception of life-events.[5] Repetition of work stages often refers to the handling of certain devices, such as a machine, a tool, sports equipment or a musical instrument.[6] However, this understanding of experience has no meaning besides the mere enhancement of unconscious factual know-how in operating the device. It does only lead to a plus of dexterity. Taken this understanding of experience as a basis, experience cannot lead directly to a plus of theoretical knowledge without further processes of cognition.[7]

---

[3] Dudenredaktion (2011), p. 532.

[4] Soiné (2010b), p. 275.

[5] Soiné (2010b), p. 275.

[6] The science of neuropsychology names this process procedural or implicit learning: Edelmann and Wittmann (2012), p. 111.

[7] However, of course knowledge can be gained from the observation of this process. This again would be experience in an understanding of sense perception.

Thus, from now on I will refer to experience as sense perception of life-events leading to a plus of theoretical knowledge, the recognition of certain facts that can be processed by cognition and expressed verbally.[8] This understanding leads to an approach towards the forming of rules of empirical judgement. The line that separates experience from a rule of empirical judgement can be drawn where a single sensual perception steps back and a generalizable finding, a rule of empirical judgement, emerges.

This understanding of experience as sense perception provides a basis to analize how rules of empirical judgement can be formed from experience. It is an empirical understanding of experience, seeing experience as the indispensable basis of cognition. In the beginning there is a sense perception, an experience. Subsequently it takes a process of cognition to form a rule of empirical judgement from it.[9]

2.1.2 The Process of Forming and Using Rules of Empirical Judgement

Having said that in the beginning there is a first experience and in the end there is a gain of knowledge, the crucial question is what happens in between. This is where empirical judgement becomes vital.

2.1.2.1 Abduction

From a single perception a reliable rule of empirical judgement cannot be formed. We can only presume that certain conclusions could be drawn. Therefore the first and sole experience is no suitable basis to gain knowledge. Still this first experience is the beginning of the process of gaining knowledge, as it leads to a first logical hypothesis within a process of cognition. This first process of cognition can be called abduction in philosophical terms.

Example We see (sense perception) event B happening. We presume (cognition) that event A could have happened before or event C might happen next. But yet we do not really know.

2.1.2.2 Induction

Repeating the experience made and studying similar events can broaden the basis of experience and lead to a suitable fundament to form a first rule of empirical

[8] The science of neuropsychology names this process declarative or explicit learning: Edelmann and Wittmann (2012), p. 111.

[9] This conception of experience, perception and cognition dates back to classical empirism, shaped and represented by scholars such as Hobbes, Locke, Berkeley and Hume: Brockhausredaktion (2009), pp. 102, 107, 109, 448.

judgement. This again happens in a process of cognition: We mentally process the existing information (consisting of experience) to find a more generally applicable rule – a rule of empirical judgement. Now we have a broadened fundament of experience and can therefore form a more reliable rule of empirical judgement. This second process of cognition is called induction.

Example We see (sense perception) event B happening again and again. We also see similar events B-1, B-2, B-3 (...) happening. We conclude (cognition) that event A must have happened before or event C will happen next. Still we do not know this by absolute certainty, but we have achieved a relatively high level of reliability – provided we have performed all processing correctly.

2.1.2.3 Enhancement of Reliability

Still the rule of empirical judgement found is not entirely reliable. If a rule of empirical judgement is meant to be only statistical, the degree of reliability achieved might nevertheless be sufficient. In this case the rule only serves to provide a presumption of probability.[10] However, passing through a process of falsification and verification repeatedly can lead to a larger quantity of sole experiences and therefore continuously broaden the basis of the rule of empirical judgement found. This can improve the reliability of the rule up to a point, where we can consider it as a generally valid, deterministic rule of empirical judgement.[11]

However, it seems impossible to achieve absolute certainty. It is thus necessary – but difficult – to determine which degree of reliability makes for a hypothesis, a statistical rule of empirical judgement or a generally valid, deterministic rule of empirical judgement.[12]

In any case, the reliability of rules of empirical judgement is enhanced by repetition of the second process of cognition, the induction. Verification and falsification broadens the basis of experience by sense perception and thus allows the formation of more reliable rules of empirical judgement by induction.[13]

---

[10] Such statistical rules of empirical judgement (also called relative rules of empirical judgement or rules of empirical judgement leading to a presumption of propability) cannot lead to compelling conclusions but only to a certain "objective propability", Kraatz (2011), p. 86. Still they have to be minded e.g. by judges regarding consideration of evidence. Refer to: Kraatz (2011), p. 142. To enable conclusions as a reliable instrument in judicial proceedings, however, additional facts have to join in. Refer to: Kraatz (2011), pp. 89 et seq., 92.

[11] Soiné (2010b), pp. 275 et seq.

[12] Refer to further examination related to judicial consideration of evidence (§ 261 StPO) further down (3.1.6).

[13] Modern brain research questions increasingly if human being is free in cognitive decision making. It might be determined, which conclusions are drawn by a certain brain, if certain information input is processed. Possibly, we do not have a free will. Refer to: Singer (2004), pp. 30 et seq.

2.1.2.4 Deduction

Finally a rule of empirical judgement can be applied in order to tell more about the most likely course of events in the past during a period that is unknown or the future. This third process of cognition is called deduction.

Example Any event of a fictional "B-class" happened. This is a fact. We can now apply rules of empirical judgement to tell e.g. that a certain "A-class-event" must have happened before or a certain "C-class-event" is very likely to happen next.

2.1.2.5 Interim Summary

This entire process of forming and using rules of empirical judgement begins with a first experience and a logical hypothesis formed by cognition (abduction). The basis of experience available has then to be broadened by repeated sense perception to form a rule of empirical judgement in a second process of cognition (induction). By verification and falsification this step has to be repeated several times to improve the reliability of the rule found. In a third process of cognition the rule of empirical judgement can be used to tell more about the most likely course of events in the past or the future (deduction).[14] The reliability of the final result (conclusion) is determined by the quality of all of the processes mentioned above, especially the quality and objectivity of the processes of cognition.

Example We see (sense perception) a pen dropping to the ground, if released in Germany by person X. This first experience leads to a logical hypothesis that could read "A pen is dropping to the ground, if released in Germany by person X". Still this first logical hypothesis is not very reliable and has a small area of application. Repeatedly studying similar experiences broadens the basis of experience. We see other pens dropping to the ground in other places released by other persons or maybe even robots. By induction we can now form a rule of empirical judgement that could read "All pens are dropping to the ground if released". Still we need to pass through the process of verification and falsification to further enhance the reliability of the rule of empirical judgement. For example, we would find out that the rule stated above is not verified if tried in space. Knowing the law of gravity (by a degree that matches current physical science, as far as I can tell) we could then repeat the process of induction and form an improved rule that might read "Pens are moving in relation to a reference frame according to the force of gravity if no other force interferes with or equals the force of gravity". By deduction we can finally gain knowledge. If someone is holding a pen on planet earth and releases it, we can tell by using the rule of empirical judgement found that it is going to drop to the ground (telling the future). Alternatively, if we know that someone has been holding a pen (fact 1) and the pen is lying in front of that person on the ground

[14] Soiné (2010b), p. 277.

one second later (fact 2) we can link these facts by application of empirical judgement and tell that the person in question very likely released the pen within the second between, even if we have not seen or recorded this latter event (telling the past).[15]

This example (the functioning of the law of gravity) can be seen as a generally valid, deterministic rule of empirical judgement. It is remarkable that it is possible to use and gain knowledge from it, even though one has not studied physics and disposes only of ordinary everyday knowledge about physical science.

2.1.2.6 Using Someone Else's Rules of Empirical Judgement

We learn from this fact that – of course – not every human being has to form all rules of empirical judgement all over again as it is possible to refer to acknowledged and ascertained rules of empirical judgement found by others. However, we have to distinguish between generally established rules and such that require certain knowledge, skills or education.[16] Nevertheless, we can even use some scientific rules that we would not have been able to develop by ourselves due to a lack of knowledge and education in a performance-minded way, if they count to common knowledge (such as the functioning of gravity as shown above). The exact understanding of the scientific coherences is not necessary to know the rule and to gain knowledge from it up to a certain degree.

It is noticeable that it is not only possible, but the most common case to gain knowledge from rules of empirical judgement found by others and not by ourselves. A significant number of humans or even human kind as such can thus develop a treasure of experiences and rules of empirical judgement we collectively can benefit from. I would like to call this "collective experience".

2.2 *The Relevance of Empirical Judgement Within Criminal Proceedings*

On the basis of an understanding of empirical judgement as an experience-based instrument used to gain knowledge by cognition, the meaning of this instrument for criminal proceedings can now be examined. We hereby need to separate mere criminalistic life-experience from rules of empirical judgement found by criminologic and forensic science.[17]

[15] Both varieties of applying empirical judgement – telling the past and telling the future – become vital in the course of criminal proceedings, what will show up further down.

[16] Soiné (2010b), p. 276.

[17] Soiné (2010a), p. 345.

2.2.1 Criminalistic Life-Experience

I will refer to the term "criminalistic life-experience" as the sum of general experiences and rules of empirical judgement gathered by a decision-maker during his professional life.[18] It becomes obvious that criminalistic life-experience is a gateway for general life-experience to (inadvertently) break into criminalistic decision-making. Compared to mere life-experience the treasure of criminalistic life-experience does not provide specific or exclusive rules of empirical judgement – if anything it is linked to mere life-experience in many ways and might even overlap with the latter.[19] Though criminalistic life-experience mainly consists of experiences made during professional training and life, a purposeful and conscious development of criminalistic life-experience is hard to achieve. Rules assigned to mere life-experience are likewise formed by processes of cognition. The processes of induction and deduction often are executed unconsciously; absolute separation between rules assigned to *criminalistic* life-experience and such assigned to *mere* life-experience is impossible because facts coming up in professional life inevitably relate to experiences made in private life.[20] Not least the majority of people and society probably wishes to maintain the speed of everyday working life and fast work frequently (not necessarily) contradicts quality work.

However, awareness can be raised. In matters of criminalistic professional education the fact that one can gain knowledge from rules of empirical judgement found and experiences made by others is used.[21] A well structured professional education may shape the structure of criminalistic life-experience of a single decision-maker and therefore enhance the objectivity of his decision and thus improve the adherence of legal certainty.

2.2.2 Further Distinction

Besides criminalistic life-experience it is possible to distinguish between individual, collective and institutional experience (and rules of empirical judgement).

In order to distinguish the term from criminal-technical rules of empirical judgement,[22] the foregoing explanations relate to "criminalistic life-experience" as the entirety of *non-technical* rules of empirical judgement available to a certain

---

[18] Worthwhile and instructive about the influence of life-experience in judicial proceedings: Kraatz (2011), pp. 89 et seq.

[19] Refer to: Walder and Hansjakob (2012), p. 173.

[20] Soiné (2010b), p. 276.

[21] At least this is the ambition of professional education. However, reality may deviate. E. g. Soiné states insufficient education of law students that have in mind to become criminal judge or public prosecutor: Soiné (2010b), p. 276.

[22] For further explanations refer to: 2.2.3.

criminalistic decision-maker. This understanding relates to criminalistic life-experience as a kind of individual experience.

However, the entirety of all experiences and rules of empirical judgement gathered by a *group of individuals* sums up to a collective treasure of empirical judgement – a treasure of collective experience. Still this collective experience would not be more than the sum of all single experiences and rules of empirical judgement it consists of.

Related to criminalistic institutions (e.g. the police) a superior treasure trove of experiences and rules of empirical judgement opens up and is filled by overlapping experiences and rules out of each individual's treasure trove of experiences and rules. From this superior viewpoint a selection of experiences and rules of empirical judgement that have been proved especially reliable emerges. Together they form a higher level of criminalistic experience that can be named institutional criminalistic experience.[23] Institutional criminalistic experience has to be distinguished from criminal-technical rules of empirical judgement that can be assigned to institutions as well.[24]

Things come full circle when experiences and rules of empirical judgement pass over from institutional to individual criminalistic experience by interaction between colleagues and integration of institutional experience into professional education programs. By this process a constant renewal of institutional as well as individual and thus collective experience is granted.[25]

2.2.3 Criminal-Technical Rules of Empirical Judgement

Forensic science deals with crime and methods of analyzing and clearing up criminal offence in a scientific-technical way, such as the securing of evidence. Forensic methods for example are DNA analysis or the analysis of fingerprints.[26] Hence criminal-technical rules of empirical judgement are of a scientific kind and not usable without specific professional education and knowledge. Because of the high degree of scientific knowledge the application of a criminal-technical rule requires, judges may not use these rules within the frame of judicial interpretation of evidence and judicial independence on their own – but of course an expert can be appointed.[27] Because of their scientific nature these rules of empirical judgement are formed by technical, systemic, empirical and experimental knowledge acquisition. They are highly objective and factual.

[23] Eisenberg and Conen name institutionalised strategies of suspicion in relation to internal instructions and standards: Eisenberg and Conen (1998), p. 2245.

[24] Soiné (2010b), p. 276.

[25] About the exchange of experiences in matters of spezialised professional proceedings in workgroups: Walder and Hansjakob (2012), p. 174.

[26] Schwind (2013), p. 11, m.n. 27.

[27] Soiné (2010a), p. 346.

3 The Necessity and Functionality of Empirical Judgement Within the German Code of Criminal Procedure (StPO)

Subject of the following is to show examples out of the German Code of Criminal Procedure – StPO – where rules of empirical judgement become vital. Empirical judgement is an instrument that is not codified explicitly. Nevertheless, the StPO presupposes the application of rules of empirical judgement. Looking at these gateways for empirical judgement in criminal proceedings from a viewpoint of legal certainty highlights the importance of an objective and equitable application of this instrument.

3.1 Gateways for the Application of Rules of Empirical Judgement in German Criminal Proceedings

3.1.1 Reasonable Suspicion, § 152 II StPO

§ 152 II StPO stipulates the principle of legality. According to that principle public prosecution is obliged to initiate criminal proceedings, if there is reasonable suspicion indicating criminal offence has been committed.[28] There has to be reasonable suspicion,[29] which is present when concrete facts indicate that any situation in life contains a crime committed.[30] If such facts don't exist, the StPO legitimates no antedated examinations to initially detect reasonable suspicion.[31] Basically, to start criminal proceedings and to open up the catalogue of competencies of the StPO facts need to indicate by reasonable suspicion that criminal offence has been committed.

The answer to the question whether such facts exist in a certain case or not can only be given by a presumption of probability, because the actual course of events lying in the past is precicely unknown. As outlined above rules of empirical judgement serve to find knowledge about unknown courses of events. Accordingly the question whether facts indicate by reasonable suspicion that criminal offence has been committed or not can only be answered by an application of rules of empirical judgement.[32] It can be stated that the crucial criterion of § 152 II StPO is filled up by empirical judgement. Due to a lack of knowledge about the course of events in the past, a different method is logically unthinkable (given evolution refrains from raising human kind onto a higher dimension of cognition).

[28] Diemer (2013b), m.n. 7; Pfeiffer (2005), m.n. 2.

[29] Beukelmann (2015), m.n. 2.

[30] Beukelmann (2015), m.n. 4; Pfeiffer (2005), m.n. 1a; Diemer (2013b), m.n. 9.

[31] Beukelmann (2015), m.n. 6.1.

[32] Diemer (2013b), m.n. 7; Pfeiffer (2005), m.n. 1a; BGH NJW 1989, 96, 97; BVerfG NJW 1994, 783, 784; BVerfG NStZ-RR 2004, 206, 207.

However, it is important that rules of empirical judgement may only serve the interpretation of facts. It is not sufficient for reasonable suspicion in the meaning of § 152 II StPO that according to general criminalistic hypotheses it seems possible or likely that criminal offence has been committed at a certain place and time.[33] Mere general suspicion and theoretical possibilities of crime are insufficient to substantiate reasonable suspicion. It is forced to be based on certain facts.[34]

It shows up that already at the very beginning of criminal proceedings the decision-makers are dependant on rules of empirical judgement. As it is impossible to always apply rules of empirical judgement in exactly the same way – which is going to be outlined further down – the decision-maker has a certain margin of appreciation which is of limited controllability by the courts.[35] In order to make use of this margin of appreciation the decision-maker uses mainly rules of empirical judgement assigned to individual criminalistic life-experience.

Ultimately the question whether facts indicate by reasonable suspicion criminal offence has been committed or not asks for a determination by certain degrees of suspicion. The term "reasonable suspicion" indicates a humble degree of suspicion is sufficient – however any unreasonable minimum of suspicion definitely is not sufficient.[36] § 152 II StPO itself makes for a distinction of degrees of suspicion as the norm states that *reasonable* suspicion must be on hand – conversely this implies that *unreasonable* suspicion must exist as well.[37] The question is, which degree of suspicion is sufficient and which not. This distinction can only be performed by normative means[38]; "it is impossible to prove mathematically precisely whether indications [leading to suspicion] are reasonable".[39] Eventually the task of answering the question whether reasonable suspicion results from certain *facts* is always governed by a weighing of all aspects of an individual case. Therefore the final conclusion will always be influenced by the treasure of criminalistic life-experience of the single decision-maker.

[33] Diemer (2013b), m.n. 7.

[34] BGH NStZ 1994, 499, 500; OLG Hamburg NJW 1984, 1635, 1636; Soiné (2010b), p. 277; Pfeiffer (2005), m.n. 1a.

[35] Beukelmann (2015), m.n. 5; Diemer (2013b), m.n. 8; BGH NJW 1989, 96, 97; BGH NStZ 1997, 398, 400. However, discretion is not to be excersized: Pfeiffer (2005), m.n. 3. Critical: Eisenberg and Conen (1998), p. 2248, 2249.

[36] Pfeiffer names the degree of reasonable suspicion a certain threshold of suspicion that can as well be undershot: Pfeiffer (2005), m.n. 1c.

[37] Comprehensively about degrees of suspicion and the definition of reasonable suspicion: Schulz (2001), pp. 527 et seq. Schulz names the phrasing "reasonable" in § 152 II StPO a bridge between what is factual and what is normative: Schulz (2001), p. 528.

[38] Reasonable suspicion in § 152 II StPO neither means ample nor urgent suspicion and it does not need to give reason for filing of action: Diemer (2013b), m.n. 7; Pfeiffer (2005), m.n. 1a. Still it is questionable whether this negative statement can concretize the term "reasonable suspicion". Schulz assumes that reasonable suspicion has to be defined positively: Schulz (2001), p. 527. Likewise: Eisenberg and Conen (1998), p. 2243.

[39] Rogall (1997), p. 400.

In reality police officers will often act autonomously when investigating (though public prosecution is competent predominantly, § 152 II StPO)[40] and it can be stated that characteristics such as appearance, behaviour, gender, age, color of skin etc. substantially affect decisions.[41] A look and a behavior deviating from standards combined with facts related to location and time of day are circumstances tendentially substantiating suspicion according to public opinion. It is to be feared that such subjective judgement – often mere prejudices – leading to social stereotypes of suspicion based on public opinion can be hardly blanked out by decision-makers.[42]

This shows that rules of empirical judgement assigned to *criminalistic* life-experience are situated quite close to *general* life-experience. Nonetheless they make up a large part of criminalistic decision-making in matters of determination of degrees of suspicion. For their tendencially subjective kind this can lead to a lack of objectivity and therefore a lack of legal certainty. The process of weighing is shaped not only by objectively approved experiences and rules of empirical judgement, but as well by subjective, personal thinkings that cannot be entirely verified. Different decision-makers can even legally come to different conclusions in one and the same case and as long as a certain decision cannot be found arbitrary it lies within the margin of appreciation conceded to the decision-maker.[43] Certain variations in decision-making are therefore tolerable and have to be acquiesced. Of course a contradiction arises here, as the principle of legality shall guarantee steady and consistent criminal proceedings. Legal certainty (Art. 20 III GG) and equal treatment (Art. 3 GG) demand for an objective and predictable treatment of the question whether criminal proceedings have to be initiated or not – and it has to based on certain facts.[44]

3.1.2 Identification Measures, § 81b StPO

§ 81b StPO is a legal basis for repressive means as well as preventive identification measures.[45] Empirical judgement becomes vital in two different ways.

On the one hand measures according to § 81b StPO are only allowed against an accused. For this, reasonable suspicion in the sense of § 152 II StPO has to be given; just any vague suspicion is not sufficient.[46] However, the initiation of investigation proceedings shall not be a compulsory requirement as long as the will of public

[40] Eisenberg and Conen (1998), p. 2245.

[41] Eisenberg and Conen (1998), p. 2246.

[42] Detailed: Eisenberg and Conen (1998), pp. 2246 et seq.

[43] BGH NJW 1989, 96, 97; BVerfG NJW 1984, 1451, 1452.

[44] Eisenberg and Conen (1998), p. 2241.

[45] Ritzert (2015), before m.n. 1; Senge (2013), m.n. 1; Pfeiffer (2005), m.n. 1; Beulke (2012), p. 163, m.n. 243.

[46] Senge (2013), m.n. 2; Pfeiffer (2005), m.n. 1.

prosecution to pursue emerges clearly.[47] As shown before empirical judgement is a necessary tool in determining whether there is reasonable suspicion indicating a crime has been committed or not. Indirectly empirical judgement becomes vital for § 81b StPO via the term of reasonable suspicion.

But empirical judgement is also needed directly in applying § 81b StPO. Identification measures are assigned to police law and executed by the criminal investigation department of the police.[48] They also relate to the procedural position of an accused. Only measures that are *required* are allowed. This is for the measures evolve impact on constitutional rights of the respective accused and the principle of proportionality has to be retained (amongst others).[49] Specifically this means that according to rules of empirical judgement there have to be facts indicating that the respective accused will be involved in prospective criminal investigation proceedings again (relating to similar as well as different kinds of criminal offence) and that the identification measures taken will then support these prospective proceedings by incriminating or exonerating the accused. In this decision all circumstances of the individual case have to be considered. These can be the kind and the weightiness of the crime the accused is suspected to have committed in the proceedings of reason and the method of committing the crime. Furthermore, these can be circumstances related to the accused himself, such as his personality and the period of time in which he has been noticeable in criminal matters.[50]

In general identification measures are possible disregarding the course and the results of the proceedings of reason; they do not become illegal and can still be "required" even if the accused will be acquitted or the proceedings ceased.[51] These preventive identification measures mainly relate to the question whether it is likely that the accused will be involved in prospective criminal proceedings again – a question that has to be answered using rules of empirical judgement. To put it in another way, the general danger of repetition of (any) criminal offence according to rules of empirical judgement is crucial.

Even if the accused is noticeable in criminal matters the first time in his life during the proceedings of reason, the prediction regarding his danger of repetition can be unfavorable. There shall be rules of empirical judgement speaking for a higher degree of danger of repetition in matters of certain types of criminal offence (such as sexual offence, battery or drug offence) due to personal penchants that are hard to overcome.[52] However, if such rules of empirical judgement are not proved scientifically (e.g. by criminologic methods, empirical studies, medical studies) but

[47] Senge (2013), m.n. 2; Pfeiffer (2005), m.n. 1. Opposing viewpoint: Ritzert (2015), m.n. 1.

[48] Ritzert (2015), before m.n. 1 and m.n. 7; Senge (2013), m.n. 5.

[49] Ritzert (2015), m.n. 5.

[50] BVerwG NJW 1983, 772, 773; VGH Mannheim NJW 2008, 3082, 3083; OVG Münster BeckRS 2010, 49130; OVG Bautzen BeckRS 2011, 45233; VG Braunschweig NVwZ-RR 2008, 30, 31; Soiné (2010b), pp. 277, 278; Ritzert (2015), m.n. 5; Pfeiffer (2005), m.n. 5.

[51] Ritzert (2015), m.n. 5a.

[52] VG Braunschweig NVwZ-RR 2008, 30 f.; Soiné (2010b), p. 278.

simply taken from (mere) *criminalistic* life-experience, there is a danger of slipping into *general* life-experience or even sheer public opinion and thereby crossing the line towards prejudices. This again shows the weakness of empirical judgement: The application of alleged but not suffiently reliable rules of empirical judgement leads to a lack of objectivity and therefore a lack of equal treatment and legal certainty.[53]

However, in matters of § 81b StPO the concretization of the legal term "required" underlies full controllability by the administrative courts, leading to a high chance of rectification in case of defective decisions. Still the decision regarding the prediction whether the accused is likely to be involved in criminal proceedings again underlies limited controllability (arbitrariness-control) due to the margin of appreciation granted to the decision-maker.[54]

3.1.3 Searching of Homes, § 102 StPO

§ 102 StPO allows the searching of the home of a suspect. One requirement for this measure is the likelihood that criminal offence has been committed. Basically reasonable suspicion in the meaning of § 152 II StPO is sufficient here,[55] but a search that is only supposed to lead to reasonable suspicion is not permitted.[56] Again it is necessary to apply empirical judgement in order to answer the question whether reasonable suspicion is given.[57]

The procedural position of an accused in investigation proceedings initiated is no requirement,[58] but the suspect must be of the age of criminal responsibility.[59]

Empirical judgement becomes furthermore vital related to the intended goal of the search (seizure of evidence or of a suspect), as an important requirement for a legal searching is that facts – interpreted by cognition using rules of empirical judgement – must indicate that the goal of the search can be achieved.[60] Insofar courts have already applied rules of empirical judgement assigned to *general* life-experience explicitly.[61]

---

[53] Critically, but finally agreeing to an unfavorable prediction due to a margin of appreciation granted to executive by legislation: VGH Mannheim NJW 2008, 3082, 3083 et seq. In this case the police came to an unfavorable conclusion in a first-offender-case related to sexual offence and child pornography applying an alleged but not scientifically proved rule of empirical judgement telling a high danger of repetition.

[54] VGH Mannheim NJW 2008, 3082, 3083; VGH Mannheim NVwZ-RR 2004, 572, 573; Soiné (2010b), p. 278.

[55] Hegmann (2015), m.n. 1; BGH NStZ 2000, 154, 155; BGH NJW 2000, 84, 85.

[56] Hegmann (2015), § 102, m.n. 3.

[57] Bruns (2013), m.n. 3; Hegmann (2015), m.n. 1; Pfeiffer (2005), m.n. 1; Soiné (2010b), p. 278.

[58] However, the suspect will achieve the formal position of an accused through the search: Bruns (2013), m.n. 1; Hegmann (2015), m.n. 2; BGH NStZ 1997, 398, 400; BGH NStZ 2007, 653.

[59] Hegmann (2015), m.n. 2; Bruns (2013), m.n. 1.

[60] Bruns (2013), m.n. 2, 3; Pfeiffer (2005), m.n. 3.

[61] BGH NStZ 2000, 154, 155.

Because of the impact on constitutional rights it is important that *facts* indicate that the goal of the search will be achieved.[62] Thus, empirical judgement may only serve to link facts and the conclusion that the search will probably lead to seizure of evidence or of a suspect.

3.1.4 Admonition and Hearing, § 136 StPO

Whether someone is heard as an accused in the meaning of § 136 StPO depends significantly on an act of incrimination by public prosecution. A specific degree of suspicion is not required.[63] Nevertheless the position of an accused can also result from a high degree of suspicion without any act of incrimination, as public prosecution is not allowed to refuse this procedural status against adversing suspicion.[64] However, public prosecution has a relatively broad margin of appreciation here.[65] All circumstances of the single case have to be considered. If there is a very high degree of suspicion, it is arbitrary and an procedural error to withhold the status of an accused.[66]

According to § 136 I S. 2 StPO the accused has to be admonished prior to the hearing. If the admonition remains undone, there is nonetheless no restraint of utilization in front of court as far as it is assured that the accused had known his right to silence anyway.[67] But there is no rule of empirical judgement that certain groups of people (such as formerly accused) or people of certain professions (such as doctors) generally know their right to silence.[68]

3.1.5 Investigative Custody, § 112 StPO

§ 112 StPO allows to take the accused into investigative custody if there is urgent suspicion. Accordingly the accused does not necessarily have to be the delinquent – a certain (higher) degree of propability is sufficient.[69] In the same way rules of empirical judgement were needed to determine whether reasonable suspicion is given or not they are needed here.[70]

---

62 BVerfG NJW 1991, 690, 691. About the impact on constitutional rights of a search and the principle of proportionality: BVerfG NJW 1994, 2079.

63 Diemer (2013a), m.n. 4; Pfeiffer (2005), m.n. 2; BGH NStZ 1997, 398, 400.

64 Beulke (2012), p. 72, m.n. 110.

65 Diemer (2013a), m.n. 4; Pfeiffer (2005), m.n. 2; BGH NJW 1990, 2633, 2634; BGH NJW 1992, 1463, 1466; BGH NStZ 1997, 398.

66 BGH NStZ 2007, 653, 654.

67 Monka (2015a), m.n. 21; Diemer (2013a), m.n. 27; Pfeiffer (2005), m.n. 4.

68 BGH NJW 1992, 1463, 1466.

69 Kraatz (2011), p. 299.

70 Krauß (2015), m.n. 3, 6; Graf (2013), m.n. 6, 8; Pfeiffer (2005), m.n. 2.

Furthermore, grounds for detention are required, § 112 I S. 1, II StPO, which can e.g. be the danger of absconding or the danger of suppression of evidence. To determine whether such grounds are given rules of empirical judgement are used.[71]

Danger of absonding, § 112 II Nr. 2 StPO, shall be given when there is a higher degree of probability that the accused will abscond than that he will not abscond from the trial.[72] Especially considerable for the decision are personal conditions and the behaviour of the accused towards the investigation authorities. Criteria like age, family ties, occupation, contacts abroad, earnings, assets (especially such abroad), fettle, sicknesses or drug addiction shall be crucial as well as kind and weightiness of the crime in question.[73] However, there is no rule of empirical judgement telling that foreign citizens generally have good contacts abroad.[74] Though the seriousness of the expectable sentence matters, there is no rule of empirical judgement telling that an expectable custodial sentence of at least 1 year irrefutably leads to danger of absconding.[75]

3.1.6 Consideration of Evidence, § 261 StPO

Within the frame of free consideration of evidence during the main trial, § 261 StPO, rules of empirical judgement play a decisive role.[76] The bench reconstructs the circumstances of the crime according to given evidence and testifies.[77] This is an empirical process, as no one can tell with absolute certainty what really happened.[78] Just like any human being judges can only approach reality by exploring the objective truth on a subjective basis of convincement.[79] The judicial interpretation of things heard and seen during trial (experiences, sense-perception) is a process of cognition applying rules of empirical judgement and leading to a conclusion (deduction).[80] Hereby all kinds of rules can be used and even rules assigned to general life-experience of the judges can influence the decision. The

[71] Hereby the committing magistrate shall even be allowed to use rules of empirical judgement in relation to typical modes of behaviour regarding terrorists or spys: Graf (2013), m.n. 9.

[72] Graf (2013), m.n. 16.

[73] Examples for offences that speak for a higher danger of absconding are treason, terrorism and organized criminality: Krauß (2015), m.n. 15; Graf (2013), m.n. 23; OLG Stuttgart, BeckRS 2008, 22224.

[74] Pfeiffer (2005), m.n. 6.

[75] OLG Celle NJW 1950, 240; Graf (2013), m.n. 20.

[76] Kraatz (2011), p. 136.

[77] Eisenberg (2015), m.n. 914 et seq.

[78] BGH NJW 1995, 1930 et seq.

[79] Albrecht (1983), p. 486 and p. 489; Pfeiffer (2005), m.n. 2. Refer also to: Brockhausredaktion (2009), pp. 460, 446. Kraatz discusses the required degree of convincement and the relevance of doubt elaborately: Kraatz (2011), pp. 133 et seq.

[80] Eisenberg (2015), m.n. 7.

danger of a lack of objectivity and a lack of attention paid to the individual case due to schematic thinking in categories of typical types of offences impends.[81]

Though it is generally accepted that rules of empirical judgement are needed for judicial consideration of evidence, judges are not entirely free in applying them.[82] General rules out of acknowledged criminalistic life-experience and criminal-technical rules that are scientifically proven are suitable to gain cognition by a very high degree of certainty. Due to their high validity the bench is obliged to use these rules – if they are applicable in the concrete situation.[83] The same pertains for acknowledged rules of empirical judgement that are considered not absolutely, but highly reliable.[84] Statistical or relative rules of empirical judgement leading to a mere presumption of propability have to be minded by judges, however, they do not force compelling conclusions[85] and thus leave a relatively large margin of appreciation to the applying judge. In contrast, judges are not allowed to use not suffiently approved rules of empirical judgement or make up new rules.[86] If a decision is made in violation of these principles it is defective regarding § 261 StPO.[87] Still sparsely approved criminal-technical rules are applicable after hearing an expert.[88] Only immature and obviously not suitable or unreliable methods have to be rejected.[89]

If technical rules of empirical judgement require specialized knowledge it is obligatory to hear an expert, but the expert may not replace the decision-maker. His only task is to supply the decision-maker with information needed to understand the functionality of the technical coherences. The legal consideration concluding from the technical rule of empirical judgement behooves to the bench.[90]

Furthermore all decisions made during *investigation proceedings* based on rules of empirical judgement can and have to be revised and rectified during main trial in order to grant they do not violate logical laws of thinking, are not arbitrary and do not contain contradictions. Hereby the margin of appreciation granted to the decision-maker and the principle of limited controllability have to be minded.[91]

---

[81] Eisenberg (2015), m.n. 915. This phenomenon is already recognizeable during law studies. In exams students often tend to conceptionally cut off individual details of a case if it is similar to a famous or known case: Beulke (2013), p. 2, m.n. 4 and p. 1, m.n. 2.

[82] Albrecht (1983), p. 488.

[83] Albrecht (1983), p. 489; Eschelbach (2015), m.n. 37; Kraatz (2011), p. 137.

[84] Eschelbach (2015), m.n. 38.

[85] Kraatz (2011), pp. 142 et seq.

[86] Examples out of jurisdiction from years back are alleged rules telling that all Turkish citizens lie in front of court or that all adulterers are thiefs: Albrecht (1983), p. 489. Of course, decisions based on such obviously not existent rules of empirical judgement have been rectified by the courts of higher instance.

[87] BGH NStZ 1982, 478, 479.

[88] Eschelbach (2015), m.n. 36; Soiné (2010b), p. 278.

[89] E.g. the use of polygraphs according to permanent jurisdiction: Monka (2015b), m.n. 27; BGH NStZ 2011, 474, 475. Refer also to: Soiné (2010b), pp. 278 et seq.

[90] BGH NJW 1955, 840, 841.

[91] Soiné (2010b), p. 279.

The jurisdiction of the Federal Supreme Court seems to be fairly generous in accepting logical conclusions made by judges in matters of consideration of evidence. It shall be sufficient that conclusions are rationally based on facts and seem possible and comprehensible. They do not have to be compelling.[92] Of course, this jurisdiction can lead to a lack of predictability and controllability of court decisions, which in turn leads to a lack of legal certainty.[93] Furthermore, when decisions are essentially based on statistical or relative rules of empirical judgement, individual life-experience can easily enter the decision – turning it not only unpredictable but also incomprehensible, unless the (alleged) rules of empirical judgement applied are outlined clearly and precisely within the reasoning of the verdict.[94]

3.2 *Difficulties and Possibilities of Enhancement*

3.2.1 Initial Overview: Lacks of Objectivity

Even the Federal Constitutional Court admits that depending on personal experiences and differing usage of Empirical Judgement it is legally possible that different decision-makers will come to different conclusions (and therefore decisions) in one and the same case.[95] According to the Federal Constitutional Court this is self-evident and does not necessarily lead to a violation of constitutional law. This shows how difficult it is to objectify empirical judgement.

Mere life-experience often breaks its way into criminalistic empirical judgement leading to decisions based on alleged rules of typical behavior and courses of events, providing fallacious certainty. And yet these alleged rules can be shaped by subjective thinkings or even prejudices rather than approved objective coherences.[96] Visceral conclusions can lack of a rational basis and therefore are often unreliable or even false.[97]

---

[92] BGH NStZ-RR 2008, 370.

[93] Therefore Kraatz demands for a clarification of the jurisdiction within the Federal Supreme Court regarding the required degree of probability when considering evidence: Kraatz (2011), p. 135.

[94] Kraatz (2011), pp. 189 et seq.

[95] BVerfG NJW 1984, 1451, 1452.

[96] Eisenberg (2015), m.n. 916.

[97] Widmaier et al. (2014), para 84, m.n. 24.

3.2.2 Supreme Rights in Danger: Legal Certainty (Art. 20 III GG) and Equal Treatment (Art. 3 GG)

Altogether objectivity in handling empirical judgement is of major importance – as a lack of objectivity rapidly leads to a lack of legal certainty. And a lack of legal certainty is irreconcilable with the German constitution, Art. 20 III GG. Legal certainty shall grant reliability of jurisdiction to the addressees of law. This task is considered one of the most upscale duties of the state.[98] The principle of legal certainty itself addresses the power of the state and requires that all sovereign acts are comprehensible, predictable and calculable. State power must never be used arbitrarily.[99]

In detail it is required that law is of such clarity and certainty that the addressee can adapt his behavior to it.[100] This does not necessarily exclude the use of vague legal terms, discretion and comprehensive clauses as long as interpretation and concretization in jurisdiction and a comprehensible and predictable application of law is possible.[101] These requirements are raised higher in matters related to individual constitutional rights where incriminating measures causing restrictions of freedom can be taken by state power. This is especially the case if these measures can (partly) be taken secretly.[102] Criminal (investigation) proceedings are such a legal area.

Applying rules of empirical judgement is a way of interpreting and concretizing law to make it fit every individual case. In order to not to violate the principle of legal certainty and therefore the constitution it has to be ensured that the factual application of a rule of empirical judgement is reliable, predictable and calculable for the addressee. Besides legal certainty the principle of equal treatment, Art. 3 GG, is also threatened if empirical judgement is used in a misguided way.[103]

To protect these constitutional principles of supreme value it shall be demanded that all decisions in matters of suspicion that bother constitutional rights have to be of full controllability by the courts.[104] However, such an approach on a secondary level is not entirely satisfying. In criminal proceedings we have to seek for approaches already taking effect on the level of the first decision in order to objectify the use of empirical judgement.

---

[98] Huster and Rux (2015), m.n. 181.

[99] Grzeszick (2014), m.n. 50.

[100] Grzeszick (2014), m.n. 58.

[101] Huster and Rux (2015), m.n. 182; Grzeszick (2014), m.n. 62, 63.

[102] Grzeszick (2014), m.n. 65.

[103] Refer to: Soiné (2010b), p. 279.

[104] Refer to: Eisenberg and Conen (1998), pp. 2248 et seq. (in relation to reasonable suspicion).

3.2.3 Possibilities of Objectifying and Structuring the Application of Empirical Judgement Within Criminal Proceedings

Whereas general logical conclusions and cognitive estimations are sufficient in everyday life, higher standards have to be met in criminal proceedings. Hermeneutic methods are a possible measure to achieve this goal.[105]

3.2.3.1 Development of Rules of Empirical Judgement

One approach is to develop rules of empirical judgement by scientific means. Social sciences (such as criminology) provide fundamental methods to comprehend crime.[106] An empirical study consists of a conceptual stage, an inquiry or elicitation and an evaluation. At the beginning there is a hypothesis, forming the basis of the study (abduction). It must not contain any contradictions and be deniable as well as verifiable.[107] To deny or verify the hypothesis is the goal of the study. The hypothesis contains variables that have to be defined precisely to enable reliable results.[108] It is permissible to use vague legal terms as long as they are already concretized and clearly interpreted by jurisdiction.[109]

Following the hypothesis the method of inquiry has to be determined. Possible methods are the evaluation of case files or social studies and psychological tests.[110] Finally, the data raised has to be analized and thus the hypothesis will be verified or falsified.

At the end of this process a rule of empirical judgement can be formed. In the best case it has the reliability of a scientific rule of empirical judgement. Still even scientifically formed rules of empirical judgement need to be steadily validated. In particular, social rules of empirical judgement can become outdated, as social structures are subject to change over time.

3.2.3.2 Hermeneutic Methods in Concrete Cases

Developing reliable rules of empirical judgement alone cannot ensure objective criminal proceedings. Therefore, hermeneutic methods in proceeding individual cases are of great significance.

---

105 Soiné (2010b), p. 277.

106 About the difference between criminalistics and criminology: Schwind (2013), p. 10, m.n. 24.

107 Schwind (2013), p. 171, m.n. 5, 6, 12.

108 Schwind (2013), p. 171, m.n. 9.

109 Examples: motor-vehicle, public road traffic. About operational defining of terms: Schwind (2013), p. 173, m.n. 19.

110 About factual problems concerning inquiry: Schwind (2013), p. 181, m.n. 38.

To avoid premature conclusions and typed interpretations without taking care of the individual characteristics of a case hermeneutic methods provide appropriate possibilities like a structured operative case analysis. The principle basically requires to split up a criminalistic process in detailed pieces of information gathered and interpretated systematically according to reliable rules of empirical judgement. Analizing charts, schemes and checklists provided to the decision-maker support reliable and objective criminal proceedings clear of prejudices and subjective opinions.[111]

An example would be a method called "criminalistic cycle" that includes elements of the "intelligence cycle" developed by the Central Intelligence Agency. According to this method, five steps have to be passed through: phrasing a suspicion, analyzing facts that lead to suspicion, setting up hypotheses, comparing the case with the requirements of the norm to be applied, gathering of missing data.[112]

4 Concluding Summary

Empirical judgement is an indispensable tool of interpreting circumstances and forming conclusions in criminal proceedings. For it is impossible to find absolute truth about a course of events in the past or to know what is going to happen in the future, the decision-maker is compelled to rely on a perception of the case that he thinks is as close to the objective truth as possible. Coming to that conclusion he applies rules of empirical judgement that link facts and conclusion and therefore are the basis of what can be named "subjective truth".

Whilst applying rules of empirical judgement constitutional rights – especially legal certainty – are affected. Inconsiderate or even arbitrary application of rules of empirical judgement can impair legal certainty, equal treatment and other rights of superior significance. Therefore it has to be the aim of jurisdiction, jurisprudence and every single decision-maker to objectify the application of rules of empirical judgement as far as possible. It has to be ensured that decisions are based on profound facts and that rules of empirical judgement applied are reliable. Hermeneutic methods can support this goal. Only by these means fair, equal and predictable criminal proceedings are enabled.

References

Albrecht P (1983) Überzeugungsbildung und Sachverständigenbeweis in der neueren strafrechtlichen Judikatur zur freien Beweiswürdigung (§ 261 StPO). NStZ 1983:486–493

Beukelmann S (2015) § 152 StPO. In: Graf J (ed) Strafprozessordnung – Beck'scher Online Kommentar. C.H. Beck, München

[111] Refer to: Roll (2010), p. 411.

[112] Hansjakob (2012), pp. 662 et seq.

Beulke W (2012) Strafprozessrecht. C.F. Müller, Heidelberg
Beulke W (2013) Klausurenkurs im Strafrecht I. C.F. Müller, Heidelberg
Brockhausredaktion (2009) Der Brockhaus Philosophie. Wissenmedia, Gütersloh
Bruns M (2013) § 102 StPO. In: Hannich R (ed) Karlsruher Kommentar zur Strafprozessordnung. C.H. Beck, München
Diemer H (2013a) § 136 StPO. In: Hannich R (ed) Karlsruher Kommentar zur Strafprozessordnung. C.H. Beck, München
Diemer H (2013b) § 152 StPO. In: Hannich R (ed) Karlsruher Kommentar zur Strafprozessordnung. C.H. Beck, München
Dudenredaktion (2011) Deutsches Universalwörterbuch. Bibliographisches Institut, Mannheim
Edelmann W, Wittmann S (2012) Lernpsychologie. Weinheim, Beltz
Eisenberg U (2015) Beweisrecht der StPO – Spezialkommentar. C.H. Beck, München
Eisenberg U, Conen S (1998) § 152 II StPO: Legalitätsprinzip im gerichtsfreien Raum? NJW 1998:2241–2249
Eschelbach R (2015) § 261 StPO. In: Graf J (ed) Strafprozessordnung – Beck'scher Online Kommentar. C.H. Beck, München
Graf J (2013) § 112 StPO. In: Hannich R (ed) Karlsruher Kommentar zur Strafprozessordnung. C.H. Beck, München
Grzeszick B (2014) Article 20 GG. In: Maunz T, Dürig G (eds) Grundgesetz – Kommentar. C.H. Beck, München
Hansjakob T (2012) Der kriminalistische Zyklus. Kriminalistik 2012:662–666
Hegmann S (2015) § 102 StPO. In: Graf J (ed) Strafprozessordnung – Beck'scher Online Kommentar. C.H. Beck, München
Huster S, Rux J (2015) Article 20 GG. In: Epping V, Hillgruber C (eds) Grundgesetz – Beck'scher Online Kommentar. C.H. Beck, München
Kraatz E (2011) Der Einfluss der Erfahrung auf die tatrichterliche Sachverhaltsfeststellung. Walter de Gruyter, Berlin
Krauß M (2015) § 112 StPO. In: Graf J (ed) Strafprozessordnung – Beck'scher Online Kommentar. C.H. Beck, München
Monka C (2015a) § 136 StPO. In: Graf J (ed) Strafprozessordnung – Beck'scher Online Kommentar. C.H. Beck, München
Monka C (2015b) § 136a StPO. In: Graf J (ed) Strafprozessordnung – Beck'scher Online Kommentar. C.H. Beck, München
Pfeiffer G (2005) Strafprozessordnung – Kommentar. C.H. Beck, München
Ritzert S (2015) § 81b StPO. In: Graf J (ed) Strafprozessordnung – Beck'scher Online Kommentar. C.H. Beck, München
Rogall K (1997) BGH: Vernehmung eines Beschuldigten als Zeugen. NStZ 1997:398–400
Roll H (2010) Operative Fallanalyse. In: Wirth I (ed) Kriminalistik-Lexikon. Kriminalistik, Heidelberg
Schulz L (2001) Normiertes Misstrauen – Der Verdacht im Strafverfahren. Klostermann, Frankfurt
Schwind H (2013) Kriminologie. Kriminalistik, Heidelberg
Senge L (2013) § 81b StPO. In: Hannich R (ed) Karlsruher Kommentar zur Strafprozessordnung. C.H. Beck, München
Singer W (2004) Verschaltungen legen uns fest: Wir sollten aufhören, von Freiheit zu sprechen. In: Geyer C (ed) Hirnforschung und Willensfreiheit. Suhrkamp, Berlin, pp 30–65
Soiné M (2010a) Kriminalistische Erfahrung. In: Wirth I (ed) Kriminalistik-Lexikon. Kriminalistik, Heidelberg
Soiné M (2010b) Kriminalistische Erfahrung als Rechtserkenntnisquelle. Kriminalistik 2010:275–281
Walder H, Hansjakob T (2012) Kriminalistisches Denken. Kriminalistik, Heidelberg
Widmaier G, Müller E, Schlothauer R, Schütrumpf M (2014) Münchener Anwaltshandbuch Strafverteidigung. C.H. Beck, München

The Multiple Uncertainties of the Corporate Criminal Law

Mark Fenwick

Contents

Abstract Corporate criminal law refers to the body of legal norms that imposes criminal liability on the corporation, rather than individual members of the corporation, such as directors, officers, managers or employees. This chapter begins by suggesting that the reach of corporate criminal law has greatly expanded over the last three decades. A second striking feature of recent corporate criminal law is the degree to which the substantive criminal law in this field is often plagued by a lack of legal certainty as to the scope of the offence. Examples of legal "uncertainty" are introduced from securities law and anti-corruption law. The chapter goes on to argue that the legal basis for the new corporate criminal law – the doctrine of corporate legal liability – is similarly characterized by uncertainties of various kinds. The discussion highlights how a concern with legal certainty seems to run up against other policy considerations, notably the pragmatic need to take meaningful action against corporate wrongdoing. The chapter concludes with the suggestion that in the context of contemporary corporate criminal law, the meaning of legal certainty has been transformed from a fundamental principle of criminal justice to one of a number of competing policy considerations that have to be resolved in responding to socially undesirable corporate behavior. The combined effect of this net-widening and legal "uncertainty" has been to greatly increase legal

M. Fenwick (✉)
Faculty of Law, Kyushu University, Fukuoka, Japan
e-mail: mdf0911@gmail.com

M. Fenwick, S. Wrbka (eds.), *Legal Certainty in a Contemporary Context*,
DOI 10.1007/978-981-10-0114-7_9

risk for companies and to provide a strong incentive to invest in internal governance mechanisms aimed at social enforcement, i.e. corporate compliance.

Keywords Corporate criminal law • Legal certainty • Social enforcement • Corporate corruption • Corporate compliance

1 Introduction

Corporate criminal law refers to the body of law that imposes criminal liability on the corporation rather than individual members of the corporation, such as directors, officers, managers or employees. This chapter begins by suggesting that the reach of corporate criminal law has greatly expanded over the last three decades, particularly in the fields of market regulation, anti-corruption, anti-money laundering, and securities laws. The term – the *new corporate criminal law* – will be used to describe the resulting body of substantive and procedural norms. The focus of this chapter will be examining these issues in the context of US Federal and English law, but the framework offered has more generally applicability. In addition to this process of "net-widening", a second striking feature of the new corporate criminal law is the degree to which the substantive law is plagued by concerns about a lack of legal certainty. A couple of illustrative examples of this new legal "uncertainty" will be introduced from securities law and anti-corruption law. One effect of this uncertainty is a corresponding increase in prosecutorial and regulatory discretion.

The chapter goes on to argue that the legal foundation for the new corporate criminal law – namely the doctrine of corporate legal liability – is also pervaded by multiple uncertainties, both as to the appropriate legal standard and the underlying rationale and effects of the doctrine. More generally, it is suggested that a concern with legal certainty repeatedly runs up against other competing policy considerations, notably the need to address in an effective and meaningful way the problem of corporate wrongdoing. In the context of corporate criminal law, therefore, the meaning of legal certainty has been transformed from a fundamental principle of criminal justice to one of a number of competing policy considerations that have to be resolved in responding to socially undesirable corporate behavior. The chapter ends with the suggestion that a combined effect of this uncertainty has been to greatly increase the legal risk for companies, thus obliging them to invest heavily in compliance mechanisms aimed at ameliorating legal risk.

2 The New Corporate Criminal Law, Net-Widening & Legal Certainty

The idea of a corporate criminal law is not new; in its modern form, its origins can be traced to English law in the early decades of the nineteenth century.[1] The historical position of modern legal systems was that although individual members of a corporation could be criminally liable for offences committed in the course of their occupation, the corporation *itself* could not be liable. Criminal liability lay with members of the corporation – directors, managers or employees – but not with the corporation itself. As such, the corporation fell outside the domain of criminal responsibility. From the perspective of the criminal law, a corporation was an incorporeal entity that lacked the necessary degree of fault or blameworthiness that is a necessary condition for the imposition of criminal liability.

Blackstone, for example, regarded it as self-evident that criminal liability was confined to natural persons and that any other approach would constitute an anthropomorphic error; a corporation is incapable of acting with the requisite moral fault necessary for the criminal law.[2] Moreover, he characterized the corporation as an impoverished legal subject and identified a number of practical difficulties that would arise in applying criminal law and procedure to corporations. In particular, a corporation cannot appear in court "in person" to offer a defense (resulting in a trial *in absentia*), a corporation cannot swear an oath, nor can a corporation be arrested, imprisoned or executed. For Blackstone, at least, it seemed fairly obvious that corporations could not be subjected to the discipline of the criminal law.

The origins of modern corporate criminal liability rules can be traced back to the early decades of the nineteenth century when, in the context of rapid industrialization, corporations acquired a greater social presence as the scope and impact of their activities expanded dramatically.[3] In response to this socio-economic transformation, English law gradually extended the application of the criminal law to juristic persons, such as municipalities and then corporations. This change was initially a result of judicial rather than legislative action, and involved cases of criminal omission resulting in public nuisance. The scope of this new form of criminal liability gradually expanded, however, to include acts as well as omissions and finally crimes requiring intent and not just absolute liability offences. Within half a century, Blackstone's more theoretical concerns had been swept away by the pragmatic need to address the pressing issue of corporate misconduct.

A similar story can be told about the emergence and development of corporate criminal liability in a US context.[4] The early US history of corporate criminal

---

[1] For the early modern history of corporate criminal liability in English law, see Wells (2001).

[2] Blackstone (1979), p. 464.

[3] Wells (2001), ch. 2.

[4] See, generally, Bernard (1984).

liability, for instance, culminated in 1909 with the US Supreme Court decision in *New York Central & Hudson River Railroad v. United States*. Constitutional concerns about Federal anti-trust legislation that explicitly imposed criminal liability on corporations were set aside in favor of the more pragmatic view that corporate criminal liability represented the "only means" to "control" errant corporations.[5]

By the early-decades of the twentieth century, the idea of corporate criminal liability was well established in the main jurisdiction of the common law world. Nevertheless, for much of its history, corporate criminal law was marginalized from the mainstream of criminal justice, even in those jurisdictions that embraced the doctrine. In practice, criminal prosecution of corporate suspects remained something of an exception, perhaps reflecting both the power of large corporations and a recognition on the part of the state that prosecuting such cases was always going to be difficult and that – even in the best case – a conviction might result in socially undesirable collateral damage to innocent third parties.

Moreover, most civilian jurisdictions rejected the idea of corporate criminal law, preferring instead to focus on the personal liability of managers.[6] This approach reflected the view that the liability of legal persons is properly dealt with as part of public administrative law rather than the criminal law. Many countries in Europe (such as Germany, Italy and Spain) began to confront the growing power of business enterprises by introducing systems of administrative regulation, similar to "public welfare" offences in the United States or regulatory offences in the UK. These infractions are enforced by administrative agencies and have neither the status of criminal sanction and are thought to be morally neutral and lacking the element of condemnation and moral fault associated with criminal liability.

The consequence was that corporate criminal liability occupied a marginal position both in the imagination and practice of modern criminal justice.[7] As with white-collar offenders, more generally, the early history of corporate criminal law is a familiar tale of economically powerful elites being insulated from the intrusive gaze of the criminal justice system.[8]

Over the last three decades, however, this situation has changed – or, at least, the picture has become somewhat more complicated – and corporate criminal law has acquired a new significance in the "mix" of regulatory strategies for responding to corporate wrongdoing.[9] Across multiple jurisdictions, a process of "net-widening" has occurred that has significantly expanded the scope of corporate criminal law.[10]

---

[5] New York Central & Hudson River Railroad v. US, (1909) 212 U.S. 481.

[6] For an important discussion of the principles underling the traditional continental European approach, see Leigh (1977).

[7] On this controversy and marginalization more generally, see Hamdani and Klement (2008), Khanna (1996), Laufer (1994).

[8] See Sutherland (1949) for the class statement of this position.

[9] For more on this issue, see Orland (2007).

[10] For the original formulation of net-widening, see Cohen (1985).

Although we should not be naive in underestimating the capacity of the business community to limit the degree of intrusion into their activities, an effect of this new emphasis on corporate criminal law is that business enterprises can no longer afford to ignore corporate criminal law and they are now obliged to incorporate it into their decision-making processes, policies and practices, and organizational structure.

Firstly, many civilian jurisdictions that did not previously have provision for corporate criminal liability have now introduced it.[11] The administrative law approach to corporate wrong doing has gradually been supplemented by the introduction of corporate criminal liability. In a European context, this seems to have largely been the result of pressure from regional and international organizations that identified a regulatory gap, which – it was believed corporate criminal responsibility could fill.

The second piece of evidence for net-widening in corporate criminal law has been the expansion in the scope of corporate criminal law and the creation of multiple new categories of criminal offence.[12] Even a cursory list of the main fields of contemporary corporate criminal law highlights the breadth of the law in this area; anti-corruption law, anti-money laundering law, fraud law (including investment fraud, securities fraud, government fraud, mortgage fraud, consumer fraud and false advertising), competition law, tax law (including off-shore tax evasion), accounting standards law, marketing law, export controls & sanctions law, labor law, health & safety law, and environmental law. Moreover, these are just the general fields of law; there are also many industry specific laws that impact upon corporations operating in particular sectors of the economy. These are all areas that have significantly expanded over the last three decades.

A third trend is to apply corporate criminal law extra-territorially or alternatively to apply it to the acts of foreign companies for acts committed in a third state, if such a company issue securities in the home state or conducts a significant part of its business in the home state. This issue will not be explored here, but the effect of this trend is to transform domestic criminal law into a form of transnational law, as companies find themselves obliged to meet the legal requirements of multiple jurisdictions.[13]

Paralleling this expansion in the number of criminal offences and extended territorial reach has been a corresponding tendency to weaken the *mens rea* requirements for corporate crimes. The emergence and expansion of strict liability (i.e. "no-fault" or public welfare) offences is the most obvious example of this transformation. It is no coincidence that many strict liability offences are concerned with corporate activities, such as pollution and health and safety where there is a clear public interest at stake in halting the proscribed acts. And yet, there has also been a more general trend on the part of legislators to move from relatively "high level" *mens rea* requirements, such as intent or knowledge, to relatively low-level

[11] See Duber (2013).

[12] See, Braithwaite and Drahos (2000) for a comprehensive overview.

[13] For more on this issue, see Fenwick (2015).

requirements, such as recklessness and negligence. As with strict liability, this general trend has also been particularly important in the context of corporate regulation.

The final element in the widening of the criminal justice "net" is a more aggressive attitude towards enforcement. Enforcement actions have increased substantially, particularly over the past decade. There is a great deal of discussion of a "new era" of enforcement in multiple fields of corporate criminal law, notably anti-corruption law, anti-money laundering law, securities law and competition law.[14] There has also been a corresponding increase in the size of sanctions. Sentencing guidelines for organizations have been upwardly adjusted and enforcement agencies are more aggressive in pursuing larger penalties.

A further – and in this context, more relevant – feature of contemporary white collar and corporate criminal law is the degree to which legal certainty has been compromised in this net-widening process. Two examples will be introduced to illustrate what, it would be argued, is a more general trend to blur the lines of criminal liability by making the full scope or "outer limits" of the criminal offence unclear. The examples are taken from US Federal criminal law, but given the territorial reach of these prohibitions they clearly impact business entities from multiple jurisdictions.

Firstly, in the context of securities law there has been a trend to blur the lines of liability for insider trading. Insider trading law traditionally imposed liability on (i) corporate "insiders" who traded on material non-public information in breach of a duty owed to their corporation, or (ii) corporate "outsiders" who "misappropriated" and traded on such information in breach of a duty owed to the *source* of the information.[15] Recently, however, the lines of liability have become increasingly uncertain and liability has been imposed on defendants where it is unclear whether they owe a duty to the corporation or the source of the information.[16] For example, there have been recent convictions where confidential information has been unwillingly thrust on a person, who then trades on that information; cases where the entity whose information was taken and used denied that it was owed a duty; and cases where a duty is found to have arise where the insider and an inadvertent recipient of that information happen to be friends. In all such cases, neither of the traditional theories seems to apply and the result of this more aggressive enforcement policy is to create ambiguities in the scope of the offence.

Moreover, post-2008 there has been the use of insider trading against hedge funds (the New York Times has spoken of a "crackdown"). For example, Steve A. Cohen's SAC Capital Advisors was indicted in July 2013 for securities fraud, which led investors to withdraw from the fund. Many in the financial services sector believe this to be highly controversial. The traders at *SAC* weren't corporate

---

[14] On the new era of enforcement in corporate criminal law, see Koehler (2014).

[15] See Green (2007), ch. 18.

[16] For a review of recent case law, see Crimmins (2013).

insiders nor outsiders seeking personal gain, rather they were investors looking for information about corporations whose shares they were thinking of buying, selling or shorting. Skeptics asked whether highly aggressive "diligent" traders be criminalized in this way? The activity of hedge funds helps speed the flow of information to financial markets, thus enabling more efficient and accurate pricing of the shares of corporations. Uncovering things about corporations that management would rather not disclose is something professional money managers are *supposed to do.* i.e. hedge funds perform a valuable public interest function. The key point, however, is that such an enforcement policy seems to expand the scope of the offence to encompass behavior that was previously thought to fall outside the scope of the norm.

A second example of how uncertainties have been introduced into contemporary white collar and corporate criminal law can be seen in anti-corruption law, particularly anti-corruption laws targeting corporate corruption conducted overseas, such as the US *Foreign and Corrupt Practices Act* [*FCPA*] (1977) or the more recent UK *Bribery Act* (2010).[17] Multiple uncertainties can be found in these laws. The US law, for instance, prohibits a company of its agents of paying or offering to pay money or anything of value to a foreign official to obtain or retain business. The statute defines a "foreign official" in part as "any officer or employee of a foreign government or any department, agency, or instrumentality thereof . . ."[18] However, uncertainty and surrounds the interpretation of the term, "instrumentality", which is not defined in the statute. The Department of Justice and SEC have taken advantage of this uncertainty. To take one of a number of controversial cases, in an action against American construction company KBR, the DOJ and SEC alleged that KBR made improper payments to employees of Nigeria LNG Limited.[19] The government claimed that these employees were foreign officials under the *FCPA* despite the fact that the only connection with the Nigerian government was that the Nigerian government held a minority ownership stake in LNG Limited. KBR settled the case to avoid the possibility of a damaging conviction. Given an aggressive enforcement policy, on the one hand, and the textual uncertainty of the law on the other, it is extremely difficult for companies to decide *ex ante* whether companies are sufficiently state-owned or state-controlled to qualify as an instrumentality of a foreign official, that is to say whether the *FCPA* applies to a particular transaction or business relationship.

In both the example from securities law and anti-corruption law, therefore, the "outer limits" of the core offence – the boundary between permissible and impermissible conduct – seems to have become increasingly blurred as a result of a combination of executive (i.e. regulatory), legislative or judicial action.[20] The scope for aggressive enforcement is thus hugely expanded and the legal risk for

---

[17] On US law, see Koehler (2012). For the UK law, see Engle (2011).

[18] 15 U.S.C. §§ 78dd-1(f)(1)(A).

[19] For other similar cases, see Juedes (2013), pp. 43–47.

[20] For more on this trend, see Orland (2007).

any company concomitantly increases. From the perspective of legal certainty, such a trend would seem to be highly problematic.

3 The Multiple Uncertainties of Corporate Criminal Liability

The above discussion introduced the new corporate criminal law and suggested that a key feature of this area of law is that the criminal justice "net" is both widening and that, at the same time, the outer limits of criminal liability are becoming less certain.

In addition to the uncertainties created by these developments, multiple uncertainties also surround the legal doctrine that underlies *all* corporate criminal law, namely the doctrine of corporate criminal liability. These uncertainties will be considered under two headings, namely doctrinal uncertainties and normative uncertainties. It is worth noting from the outset that these uncertainties are not new; critics of corporate criminal liability have pointed to these issues for many years, but these concerns take on a greater significance as the scope of corporate criminal law has continued to expand and greater efforts are devoted to enforcement.

3.1 Doctrinal Uncertainties

At least in the Anglo-American world, the traditional approach to corporate criminal liability has been variations on so-called imputation doctrines.[21] Such an approach requires the identification of a single human offender whose crime is then imputed – attributed – to the company. By way of introduction to the uncertainty that pervades different forms of imputation, an interesting contrast can be made between the imputation approaches of the US Federal Courts and that employed in English law. In what follows, it will be suggested that both exhibit various doctrinal uncertainties, but that resolving these uncertainties has been accorded less weight than the competing desire to establish a legal standard that can be effective in tackling corporate wrongdoing.

Since the early twentieth century, US Federal courts have tended to adopt a broad vicarious liability standard whereby the criminal act of any employee "regardless of rank" that occurs in "the scope of employment" and which intends, "at least in part, to benefit the company", can be imputed to the company itself.[22]

[21] For a comprehensive review, see Lederman (2000).

[22] See the Supreme Court ruling in New York Central & Hudson River Railway Company v. United States 212 US 481 (1909).

A company can be convicted for any crime – including crimes of intent – based on this standard.

The rationale for this broad approach is that without the threat of criminal liability there is little incentive for companies to curb illegal but profitable activities that place innocent parties at risk. However, the obvious difficulty with such a standard is that it seems unreasonable to expect a large corporation – particularly one operating transnationally – to take responsibility for the acts of *all* of its employees. This is particularly so if the consequences of a criminal conviction for the corporation may cause negative effects that extend to innocent third parties, such as other employees, investors and customers. And even if a particular company adopts all reasonable measures to prevent its staff from committing an offence, it could still be subjected to criminal sanctions under the vicarious liability standard. Stated bluntly, if the company faces the risk of conviction regardless of its actions what incentive exists to invest too heavily in preventive measures or compliance? The legal standard seems to be too open-ended placing companies in a state of permanent non-compliance.

The English approach, therefore, has been to ameliorate the extreme consequences of the vicarious liability standard by limiting the "class" of employees whose criminal acts can be imputed to the company.[23] This is the so-called identification doctrine. Specifically, only those actions and thought patterns of certain high-ranking individuals within the company – the so-called "directing mind" of the company – are regarded in law as the acts of the company itself. Criminal acts committed by those individuals are regarded as being committed by the company, i.e. their acts are "identified" with the company. In the leading English case, the supermarket company, Tesco, was acquitted of falsely advertising prices on the grounds that the "brains" of the company were unaware of the wrongdoing even though the store manager had the requisite degree of knowledge.[24] Under the US vicarious liability approach, the company would have been convicted in such a case.

Although the rationale for this more restrictive approach is clear, it has resulted in a number of difficulties. Firstly, it has proven extremely difficult for English courts to arrive at a sufficiently clear and consistent definition of who is the "directing mind". Similar difficulties have occurred in Canada, Hong Kong and Australia in their use of identification standards.[25] Formalistic definitions of the "directing mind" that focus on those individuals that occupy particular positions within a company – such as the Board of Directors or CEO – often fails to capture the real power distribution in complex modern organizations. Moreover, they would seem to be easily circumvented by the delegation of criminal activities to lower ranked employees. However, a more substantive approach to defining the

[23] Canada, Australia, Hong Kong & several US states also adopt variations on this approach.

[24] Tesco Supermarkets Ltd. v. Natrass [1972] AC 153.

[25] For a review of the Canadian situation, see Department of Justice (Canada), Corporate Criminal Liability Discussion Paper (2002); and for Hong Kong, Lau (2003). Australia is discussed below.

"directing mind" has proven too vague in a criminal law context, as it requires the court to identify various functions or substantive powers – the power to direct company policy, for example – that are not amenable to precise definition. Both a formalistic and a substantive approach to defining the directing mind of the company seem highly problematic in a criminal law context, and the result is that the core concept in the identification approach is surrounded by ambiguities.

In addition to the definitional challenge, a further against identification is that it has been almost impossible for prosecutors to secure convictions against corporations in such cases because high managerial agents – however defined – are going to be relatively well placed to insulate themselves against criminal investigation (i.e. they are "judgment proof"). A series of high profile acquittals – most notably in the case against P&O for the sinking of the ferry, the Herald of Free Enterprise – due to the failure to secure a case against senior management reinforced public perceptions of injustice and fueled a perception that identification is tantamount to immunity for corporations.[26] This perception of injustice is particularly so when low ranking employees are convicted for their role in the same incident.[27]

Judicial dissatisfaction with the identification standard can also be seen in a 1995 case, *Meridian Global Funds Management Asia Ltd. v. Securities Commission*, when Lord Hoffman in an important and influential judgment of the Privy Council suggested that although there is a presumption in favor of identification in English law, vicarious liability may be adopted if the purpose of a statute is better achieved by adopting the broader standard.[28] The *Meridian* formula has been criticized on the grounds that the policy of a statute may be hard to find and it is unlikely that the words of the relevant provisions will provide a clear answer as to "who" constitutes the company. As such, the new approach seems to introduce an enormous amount of uncertainty into the criminal law. The result seems to pile uncertainty – which standard is going to apply for this particular statute? – onto uncertainty – what is the definition of the "directing mind".

Moreover, the more flexible *Meridian* approach does not really address certain fundamental problems with both forms of imputation. Firstly, all imputation standards presume that an individual person has committed a criminal offense. In complex modern organizations where corporate decisions and actions are the result of a combination of individual acts this may be an unrealistic assumption.

Secondly, by focusing on the criminal acts of only one person, the *collective* nature of corporate criminal liability is not captured. Stated bluntly, there is simply no concept of *organizational* fault with imputation doctrines. Criminal liability is derived from the criminal acts of a certain class of employees and this seems a weak

---

[26] P&O European Ferries Ltd [1991] 93 Cr App Rep 72.

[27] Attorney Generals Reference (No. 2 of 1999) [2000] QB 796. In this case, a rail company and the driver were both charged for offenses connected to serious rail accident near London. The driver was convicted but the court dismissed the case against the rail company on the grounds that there was no evidence that any corporate officers had engaged in any criminal act.

[28] [1995] 3 All ER 918. *Meridian* involved the criminal acts of investment managers therefore the broader US standard was required in order to ensure a conviction against the company.

basis for the imposition of a criminal sanction against an organization. Finally, corporate criminal liability for crimes of intent runs contrary to one of the basic principles of criminal law – punishment of the morally blameworthy – since it relies upon vicarious guilt rather than personal fault.

A number of jurisdictions have therefore attempted to develop alternatives to imputation. The necessity of these moves highlights the limited applicability of the traditional criminal law model to corporations. The first alternative emerged in the US Federal Courts in the late 1980s, so-called aggregation doctrine. The need for aggregation arises when no one individual has committed an offence but the combined effect of several individual actions is criminal. The classic example of this is the *Bank of New England* case from 1987, when a US bank was charged with knowingly violating the federal Currency Transaction Reporting Act.[29] This statute required financial institutions to report to the US Treasury all transactions in excess of $10,000. In this case a customer of a bank withdrew cash from the same account but from three different branches of the bank. The total sum for the three transactions was greater than $10,000. The bank failed to report the transactions and was subsequently prosecuted. Under imputation doctrines the bank would have been acquitted since no one individual employee had violated the rules. However, the court allowed the three acts to be aggregated in order to establish the corporation's guilt. The rationale behind a doctrine of this kind is clear: it prevents corporations evading criminal liability by compartmentalizing their activities.

The principle difficulty with aggregation is that "the total seems to exceed the sum of the parts".[30] Two innocent states of mind are being added together to produce a guilty state of mind. Several non-culpable states (the acts of the individual bank tellers in the *Bank of New England* example) are combined to result in a culpable state. Again this seems to run against basic notions of criminal responsibility. Of course, to those who favor aggregation it is precisely the fact that the conviction of a company does not carry any implication that the workers are guilty of any offence that means this approach is preferable for grounding organization fault. However, there is something disturbing about the suggestion that the "company" committed a crime in the absence of any single criminal act.[31] Another difficult is deciding which individual acts should be aggregated (any employees or those identified with the company?) and justifying the distinction. As such, we arrive back at earlier debates about which employees are to be identified with the company and the attendant difficulties in such an approach.

Aware of many of the difficulties in this area, several jurisdictions have sought to develop new models that address the limited ability to stretch in a fair and legitimate way familiar criminal law categories (such as personal responsibility)

---

[29] United States v. Bank of New England 821 F 2d 844 (1st Cir) (1987).

[30] Gobert and Punch (2004), p. 84.

[31] It is on this basis that aggregation was rejected by English courts, see Attorney Generals Reference (No. 2 of 1999) [2000] QB 796, p. 798.

to the context of corporate wrongdoing. Again though, they seem to have various difficulties from the perspective of legal certainty.

One alternative, for example, is a so-called risk management model of corporate criminal liability. This can be found in various proposals of the English Law Commission to establish a new offense of "corporate killing" as well as a 2001 reform in Italian law.[32] In both cases, the issue of criminal responsibility is framed in terms of whether the company's behavior fell below what could be reasonably have been expected in the circumstances. That is to say, criminal liability is imposed on a company if there has been a corporate failure to manage risk in a reasonable manner. Unlike the imputation and aggregation doctrines the company would be liable not for what its agents had done or thought, but for the organization of its policies and practices pertaining to risk management.

The draft *Involuntary Homicide Bill* attached to English Law Commission on corporate criminal liability report illustrates this approach. A company would be liable for the crime of corporate killing if (i) "management failure" by the corporation is cause of a person's death, and (ii) that "failure constitutes conduct failing far below what can reasonably be expected of the corporation in the circumstances". Many criticisms have been made of this proposal, but one issue is whether policy evaluation of the kind envisaged by the draft law is an appropriate task for a criminal court (especially in those jurisdictions with juries or lay-panels).

A similar, but even more radical, example of attempting re-think the legal basis of corporate criminal liability is found in the Australian Federal Criminal Code of 1995. Under this reform, liability is imposed on the corporation if "a corporate culture existed within the body corporate that directed, encouraged, or tolerated" criminal acts.[33] The law goes on to define corporate culture expansively as "an attitude, policy, rule, course of conduct, or practice existing within the body corporate".[34] Companies are thus prevented from hiding behind codes of conduct or other policy statements if the reality of corporate practice is very different. Again, this approach is not without difficulties. At the very least one is obliged to distort language in ascribing criminal guilt to a corporate body on the grounds that it is responsible for the emergence of a morally blameworthy corporate culture.

Even the briefest discussion of the liability standard of companies in a criminal law context reveals how various uncertainties pervade the discussion, and how various competing policy interests need to be resolved in arriving at an appropriate standard. In particular, there is a tension between, on the one hand, finding a fair and workable standard appropriate in dealing with large, modern business organizations and, on the other hand, finding a standard that is sufficiently certain. Against this background, it is perhaps not surprising that concerns of legal certainty have often taken second place to a more pragmatic desire to find a standard that is going to be

[32] For an extensive discussion of both English proposals and the Italian Law reform, see Gobert and Punch (2004), ch. 3.

[33] Australian Federal Criminal Code 1995, section 12(c)(2).

[34] Ibid. Section 12(c)(3).

workable in complex cases involving highly-motivated and resourced corporate suspects and defendants.

3.2 Uncertainties as to Purpose & Effect

The uncertainties surrounding these doctrinal questions are further compounded when one considers the uncertainties that surround the policy reasons for adopting corporate criminal liability in the first place. Again, a great deal of ambiguity seems to surround the underlying purpose of corporate criminal liability and how – and whether – it might function to achieve such a purpose.

The normative justification for corporate criminal liability, in general, has conventionally been provided by arguments from deterrence and prevention, rather than retribution.[35] Although there is an academic literature defending retribution as a legitimate aim of corporate criminal law, the dominant approach amongst policy-makers, judges and academics has been to focus on how corporate criminal liability contributes to the deterrence and prevention of corporate wrong doing.[36]

This general unwillingness to advance versions of retribution as a justification for corporate criminal law can be explained by a reluctance to cause economic harm – by punishing a corporation – without some possibility of a clear countervailing social benefit (in the form of a reduction in future wrong doing). Nevertheless, although retribution has not usually functioned as an independent justification for imposing criminal liability on corporations, it has served as a partial constraint upon the law in this area, in the sense that *some* blameworthiness on the part of the corporate defendant – either in terms of fault or harm – is required for almost all offences.

The main focus of the normative discussion, however, has been on the question of whether and how the goal of reducing corporate wrongdoing might be achieved. In examining this issue, it is helpful to treat deterrence and prevention as separate justifications for corporate criminal liability. In order to avoid terminological confusion, the process whereby a person desists from criminal conduct as a result of the threat of criminal sanction will be referred to as deterrence. In contrast, the process whereby the threat of criminal sanction motivates persons to monitor *other* persons to ensure that crimes do not occur will be termed prevention.

Taking deterrence first; imposing criminal liability on the corporation might seem incompatible with the aim of deterrence because a corporation is a fictional legal entity that cannot itself be "deterred" in the way that a natural person can, i.e. a corporation cannot experience the feeling of being threatened, therefore it cannot be deterred. Corporate criminal liability therefore aims to deter the unlawful acts or omissions of a corporation's agents.

---

[35] For an excellent overview of these issues, see Khanna (1996).

[36] See, for example, Laufer (1994).

Although the criminal justice system could focus exclusively on deterring such wrongdoing via *individual* criminal liability, a system of purely personal criminal liability has various limitations from the viewpoint of deterrence. In particular, the state faces significant administrative costs in identifying individual offenders within large, complex organizations and proving, beyond a reasonable doubt, that criminal wrongdoing has, in fact, taken place. Such difficulties greatly reduce the likelihood of detection – and hence the risks of crime for any prospective offender – and the resulting sense of security might embolden an individual contemplating wrongdoing. Holding the corporation liable therefore represents a cost-effective way to overcome the shortcomings of a system based purely on personal liability. The threat of *corporate* liability deters individual agents of the company from participating in wrongdoing because of the negative outcome that an individual will suffer if the company is convicted and they are implicated in such wrongdoing.

In addition to deterring individual agents of the company from wrongdoing, advocates of corporate criminal liability also argue that is has the additional advantage of preventing wrong doing by creating a strong incentive for *all* of the stakeholders within a company to monitor one another for wrongdoing and to correct any wrongdoing that is uncovered. In this way, corporate criminal liability motivates a company to reduce its liability exposure by assuming the task of policing the agents of that company.[37] Moreover, companies are particularly well placed to perform this monitoring function. At least, it can be convincingly argued that they are better placed than the state or other third parties negatively affected by corporate wrong doing to engage in such monitoring. A company can thus introduce internal controls and *ex ante* measures for detecting agents contemplating wrongdoing. In addition, a company can react to wrongdoing by taking action against those involved in wrongdoing, reporting them to the authorities or implementing reforms to ensure that there is no recurrence of wrongdoing. In this way, corporate criminal liability can contribute to a reduction in corporate crime.

It is worth emphasizing the differences between corporate and individual criminal liability on this point. When an individual is punished or threatened with punishment, the goal of that punishment or threat of punishment is to inhibit rather than to mobilize. As Brent Fisse noted: "The message conveyed [to the natural person by the criminal law] is "refrain from committing that offence", rather than "refrain from committing that offence and take such steps to improve your physiological and psychological capacity for self-control as are necessary to guard against repetition". By contrast, when a corporate offender is punished or threatened with punishment, *the message is catalytic as well as inhibitory*. The message conveyed, for corporate offences of commission as well as for those of omission, is "refrain from committing that offence and take such steps as are necessary organizationally to guard against repetition (my emphasis)"."[38]

[37] See Simpson (2002).

[38] Fisse (1983), p. 1160.

This reliance on *both* the "inhibitory" (i.e. deterrence) and "catalytic" (i.e. prevention) functions distinguishes corporate criminal liability from the criminal law as it is applied to natural persons. One of the central aims of the new corporate criminal law has been to bolster this catalytic function of corporate criminal liability and to promote internal efforts at ensuring compliance.[39]

A key premise of both the deterrence and prevention justification for corporate criminal liability is the claim that the *threat* of corporate criminal liability provides a strong behavioral incentive for all individuals to either desist from offending or to monitor others and prevent them from offending. The belief that corporate criminal liability can have this kind of impact on individuals within business entities seems to be widespread among policy makers, judges, prosecutors, regulators and commentators. It is therefore important to look, in more detail, at the nature of the threat created by the existence of corporate criminal liability and some of the uncertainties that surround the assumption that this threat provides the necessary behavioral incentives.

Both the criminal justice system and society in general impose sanctions on any corporation found criminally liable; the criminal justice system sanctions via the formal sanction imposed (e.g. a fine) and society sanctions the company in the form of reputational damage. Moreover, informal sanctions can arise from the fact of an indictment or criminal investigation and are not necessarily contingent on a conviction. It is the *combined* threat of both types of sanction that deters wrongdoing and provides the incentive for corporations to engage in crime prevention. It is therefore worth considering the threat that these two types of sanctions pose. The key question is whether this threat is sufficiently severe and certain to have purchase over the behavioral incentives of those individuals contemplating wrongdoing or in a position to engage in crime prevention. In the following, it will be suggested that finding a clear answer to this question is not simple.

Taking formal sanctions first; judges and administrative agencies are empowered to impose a range of formal sanctions if a company is convicted, most obviously fines and loss of license, although shaming penalties are increasingly used. Traditionally, fines are used as the primary sanction in the context of corporate crime. The rationale for the fine seems fairly simple: the primary goal of all corporate activity is to make money and corporations can thus be deterred from wrongdoing and motivated to invest in prevention by the threat of monetary sanctions that can directly impact upon a companies central purpose. Additional advantages of the fine as a sanction are that they are cheap to administer and there is some (financial) benefit to the state. In general, fines do not extend to allow for compensation for victims, although this may be possible in some circumstances. Further advantages are that fines are flexible and can be calibrated to the specific facts of the case. Finally, in extreme cases a fine can be imposed that is large enough to deprive a corporation of all of its assets and drive the company out of business (what can be thought of as a corporate death sentence).

---

[39] See Fenwick (2015).

However, many commentators have criticized fines, as ineffective in either deterring or preventing corporate wrong doing.[40] It is often suggested that fines have traditionally been set too low in the case of corporate crime and that, as a consequence, fines are seen as the "price" to engage in criminal behavior. It has also been suggested that fines are ineffective because the company may easily transfer the burden to innocent third parties, such as customers, shareholders, or employees. If the effects of the fine can be reduced then the threat of the fine is significantly reduced and increasing the level of the fines would merely mean imposing a greater burden on these third parties.

The effect of this kind of consideration is to introduce uncertainty as to the scale of the threat posed by the fine and, in consequence, to drastically reduce the incentive to prevent wrongdoing. A common response to this argument is to suggest that the various "third parties" who ultimately bear the cost of the fines – e.g. shareholders or employees, perhaps even consumers – are not innocent parties because they benefited – either directly or indirectly – from the illegal activity in the form of higher share dividends, share price, wages, or product prices. Even though these parties may not be directly responsible for the illegality, it might seem fair to deprive them of these unlawfully obtained gains, and it is precisely this possibility, which is designed to motivate various "third parties" to engage in social enforcement. The key issue is whether the loss of a job or a decrease in the value of an investment is proportionate given the lack of direct responsibility and whether this possibility can actually be sufficiently powerful to incentivize these third parties to engage in social enforcement. Moreover, in the case of shareholders the possibility of such harm may have a chilling effect on investment and reduce the capacity of companies to capitalize via securities markets. Either way, doubts seem to be cast over the capacity of the law to have a clear and predictable impact on behavioral incentives.

Of course, fines are not the only formal sanctions that are available in cases of corporate crime. Other sanctions can be imposed – such as loss of license or shaming – can, and depending on the nature of a corporation's business these may be equally important and a conviction can have disastrous consequences for a company, even if there is only a small fine imposed.[41]

A consensus amongst most commentators is that informal sanctions constitute a more significant threat to a company than formal sanctions.[42] The ability of any company to succeed is contingent on having and maintaining a reputation for probity. Given the importance that the market attaches to corporate reputation, it is often suggested that large business entities will struggle to survive even an indictment, let alone a trial or conviction. This seems particularly true in some

---

[40] See Simpson (2002).

[41] See Bucy (1995), p. 693.

[42] See Bharara (2007), p.73 ("[C]orporate defendants, subject as they are to market pressures, may not be able to survive indictment, much less conviction and sentencing").

sectors, such as financial services. Even an investigation can be hugely damaging for any firm that depends on public trust as a key element of its business model.

Although it is difficult to verify empirically the claim that the threat to corporate reputation is the primary threat posed by corporate criminal liability, the behavior of corporate executives in seeking to evade criminal investigation provides strong circumstantial evidence for the claim that executives place a premium on corporate reputation. Corporations that are under criminal investigation will often take drastic measures to avoid indictment, including waiving various legal professional privileges and disclosing the findings of any internal investigation, assisting the investigation of individual employees, and entering into pre-indictment agreements of various kinds (e.g. deferred prosecution agreements) many of which impose a significant and on-going burden on the company.

Business leaders clearly regard corporate reputation as a valued asset of a company that both improves profits and facilitates other objectives. The most obvious benefit of corporate reputation is the impact it has on customers. Consumer good will is clearly directly connected to increased corporate profits.

But a positive corporate reputation has a number of other less obvious financial benefits. For example, banks will be more likely to offer credit during financial difficulties to companies with a positive reputation. The reputation of a company also affects the culture within an organization, which has the potential to boost performance and facilitate attracting the best talent. A positive reputation may also bring benefits in dealing with the state. A company with a positive reputation may have more political influence when lobbying over state action likely to impact upon a company's sphere of business operations.

Adverse publicity may also trigger a variety of other non-financial bad effects for a corporation. Most significantly, negative publicity spotlight may trigger further unwanted attention to the corporation and trigger more government or media interest, and potentially private litigation (so-called "spotlight syndrome").

Reputation thus helps a corporation to achieve a wide range of important corporate goals and the threat posed by corporate criminal liability to that reputation has the potential to alter behavioral incentives in such a way as to deter and prevent corporate crime. However, all of the above seems to depend on various empirical claims and the particular circumstances of a particular company. We can, therefore, see that in addition to the various doctrinal uncertainties discussed above there are various uncertainties about the underlying rationale for corporate criminal liability, in particular relating to the purpose of this form of liability, and the various processes that seem necessary in order to achieve the underlying purpose, however it is defined.

4 Uncertainty, Legal Risk & Incentivizing Social Enforcement

One effect of the increased legal uncertainty created by the new corporate criminal law is to greatly expand the legal risk facing companies. Managing this new legal risk obliges companies – particularly larger companies – to invest heavily in meaningful, flexible and adaptable "compliance" mechanisms within organizational governance that aim at minimizing the liability exposure that has been created by uncertainties as to the scope of the law and liability. In the following, such internal governance mechanisms will be characterized as social enforcement. The suggestion is that social enforcement is a response, at least in part, to the combined facts of net-widening and legal uncertainty, and the new legal risk that such developments have created.

Social enforcement aims at ensuring that meaningful self-regulatory capacities – a culture of compliance – become firmly embedded in the structure and culture of an organization. In this context, a culture of compliance can be characterized by a generalized awareness of relevant legal obligations, putting in place incentive structures that encourage compliance with those obligations and establishing institutionalized control mechanisms for monitoring corporate conduct and implementing corrective action in the event of non-compliance.

In this way, the new corporate criminal law transfers much of the responsibility, functions and administrative costs associated with "policing" compliance from the state to private actors. This approach can be justified on the grounds that the corporation is best placed to monitor for, and, when necessary, correct wrongdoing at least cost to society. Public enforcement – in the form of indictment, trial and possible conviction – is regarded as a measure of last resort to be employed in the event of a breakdown or failure in social enforcement.

A key organizing principle of the new corporate criminal law seems to be to provide corporations with incentives to engage in social enforcement. This is not to suggest that other principles more traditionally associated with criminal justice, such as punishment or deterrence, are irrelevant in the context of the new corporate criminal law. Modern legal systems have a complex character in the sense that they can simultaneously embed multiple, possibly competing, principles. Nevertheless, the contemporary emphasis on social enforcement gives the new corporate criminal law a distinctive character and that it offers a better interpretive and explanatory fit with a wide range of recent developments than more traditional justifications for imposing criminal liability. The point to be emphasized in this context is that uncertainty as to the legal risk profile of a company might function as a powerful incentive to bolster social enforcement. In this way, uncertainty might contribute to achieving socially desirable policy objectives.

Corporate compliance can be understood as the institutional means adopted by firms to achieve the goal of social enforcement. Stand-alone compliance departments developed in the early 1960s, initially in the US. Prior to that time, the legal department would have responsibility for compliance functions. However, the legal risks associated with the new corporate criminal law, as well as the proliferation of regulation more generally, has triggered an expanded role for the discourse and practice of compliance in contemporary business enterprises.

Significantly, many legal systems increasingly offer incentives to implement effective compliance programs. That is to say, the criminal justice system offers "rewards" for implementing compliance structures in the event that wrongdoing does occur, i.e. in the event of a breakdown in social enforcement companies will be "rewarded" for having had compliance in place at the time any offending occurred. Modern corporate criminal law is predicated on a recognition that perfect compliance is impossible and that demanding perfection may be counter-productive. Such an expectation has a "chilling effect" on a firm's willingness to invest in what will often be regarded as a non-revenue generating activity.

There are a number of examples of legal measures designed to "reward" compliance. Firstly, compliance can function as a justification, that is to say, a full defense against criminal liability. A company that can show it had adequate compliance procedures in place at the time an offence occurred is not criminally liable. The UK Bribery Act, for example, offers a full defense against liability for the payment of bribes, if – at the time the offence occurred – the corporation had "adequate" compliance mechanisms in place.

Secondly, compliance can provide mitigation at the sentencing phase.[43] The US Sentencing Guidelines for Organizations include compliance as a key factor in the reduction of sentence. Finally, compliance can provide a company with leverage in any settlement negotiations that take place prior to indictment. Pre-indictment diversion, in the deferred prosecution agreements, is increasingly common so the advantages to a corporation of having adequate procedures can be important at that stage.[44]

In each of these different ways, therefore, the legal system offers clear and additional incentives for a corporation to implement compliance processes and procedures aimed at social enforcement.

5 Conclusion

The new corporate criminal law seems to be characterized by simultaneous processes of net-widening (i.e. more offences applied to companies, often with lower *mens rea* requirements) and diminishing legal certainty (i.e. ambiguity as to the "outer limits" of these offences). In addition, multiple normative and empirical uncertainties continue to surround the legal doctrine underlying this whole field of

[43] See Koehler (2012) for a comparative analysis of the compliance defense in different jurisdictions.

[44] On the rise of the deferred prosecution agreement in the context of corporate criminal procedure, see Garrett (2014).

law, namely corporate criminal liability. A concern with legal certainty in corporate criminal law constantly seems to run up against other competing policy considerations and resolving the various interests in favor of legal certainty is becoming increasingly difficult. In particular, political pressure to be seen to be doing something about socially undesirable corporate behavior means that legal certainty is often compromised in the name of some counter-veiling policy argument. Whether such derogation is legitimate or not is a discussion for another occasion. The point here has been to suggest that, at least in the context of contemporary corporate criminal law, the development of new corporate criminal law seems to have transformed the meaning of legal certainty. Certainty no longer seems to function as a fundamental principle of criminal justice that trumps other considerations or, at least, creates a strong presumption of excluding other reasons. Instead, legal certainty seems to have taken on a more modest role as one of a number of competing considerations that have to be resolved in addressing the response of the criminal justice system to socially undesirable corporate behavior.

The chapter suggested that one important effect of this change has been to contribute to a significant expansion in the legal risk facing companies, obliging them to invest in meaningful and flexible "compliance" mechanisms within organizational governance that aim at managing this new legal risk. This trend towards social enforcement – i.e. transferring much of the responsibility, functions and administrative costs associated with "policing" compliance from the state to private actors – seems to be a distinctive feature of the new corporate criminal law. This trend towards social enforcement seems to be closely connected to the difficult and on-going task of managing the complex profile of legal risk that has emerged, partly as a result of the diminishing certainty of the law.

References

Bernard T (1984) The historical development of corporate criminal liability. Criminology 22:3–17

Bharara P (2007) Corporations cry uncle and their employees cry foul: rethinking prosecutorial pressure on corporate defendants. Am Crim Law Rev 44:53–79

Blackstone W (1979 [1765–1769]) Commentaries on the laws of England. University of Chicago Press, Chicago

Braithwaite J, Drahos P (2000) Global business regulation. Cambridge University Press, Cambridge

Bucy PH (1995) Civil prosecution of health care fraud. Wake For Law Rev 30:720–737

Cohen S (1985) Visions of social control. Polity, Cambridge

Crimmins S (2013) Insider trading: where is the line? Columbia Bus Law Rev 2:330–368

Duber M (2013) The comparative history & theory of corporate criminal liability. New Crim Law Rev 16:203–240

Engle E (2011) Understanding the UK bribery act by reference to the OECD convention and the foreign and corrupt practices act. Int Law Am Bar Assoc 44:1173–1188

Fenwick M (2015) The new corporate criminal law & transnational legal risk. In: Fenwick M, Wrbka S (eds) Flexibility of law & its limits in contemporary business regulation. Springer, New York

Fisse B (1983) Reconstructing corporate criminal law. Calif Law Rev 56:1141–1246

Garrett BL (2014) Too big to jail: how prosecutors compromise with corporations. Belknap, Cambridge
Gobert J, Punch M (2004) Rethinking corporate crime. Butterworths, London
Green S (2007) Lying, stealing & cheating: a moral theory of white collar crime. Oxford University Press, Oxford
Hamdani A, Klement A (2008) Corporate crime & deterrence. Stanford Law Rev 61:271–310
Juedes D (2013) Taming the FCPA overreach through an adequate procedures defense. William & Mary Bus Law Rev 4:37–66
Khanna VS (1996) Corporate criminal liability. Harv Law Rev 199:1477–1534
Koehler M (2012) The story of the foreign corrupt practices act. Ohio State Law J 5:930–1013
Koehler M (2014) The foreign corrupt practices act in a new era. Edward Elgar, London
Lau MJ (2003) Director's criminal liability in Hong Kong. Corp Pract 12:1–19
Laufer WS (1994) Corporate bodies & guilty minds. Emory Law J 43:647–730
Lederman E (2000) Models for imposing corporate criminal liability. Buffalo Crim Law Rev 4:641–708
Leigh L (1977) The criminal liability of corporations and other groups: a comparative view. Ottawa Law Rev 9:247–302
Orland L (2007) The transformation of corporate criminal law. Brooklyn J Corp Fin Comm Law 1:45–87
Simpson S (2002) Corporate crime, law & social control. Cambridge University Press, Cambridge
Sutherland E (1949) White collar crime. Holt, Rinehart & Winston, New York
Wells C (2001) Corporations and criminal responsibility. Oxford University Press, Oxford

Types of Offenders—A Criminological Perspective in Historical Contexts

Katrin Höffler

Contents

Abstract There is a long tradition of classifying offenders based on certain attributions in penal law as well as in criminology. Classifying offenders is, especially when oversimplifying, considered as a negative approach. It carries the risk of excluding certain delinquents in the sense of labeling. But a closer look reveals the fact that recent models and methods also make use of classifications, especially when it comes to the overlap of deviant behavior, delinquency and psychiatric disorders (e.g. psychopaths or paedophiles). The problem is, that this classification takes place without becoming conscious. As a result neither the benefit nor the potential risk of this classifying approach is sufficiently taken into

This article picks up, considerably shortened, some of the historical and criminological aspects of the authors' inaugural lecture, published in German in ZStW 2015, issue no. 4.

K. Höffler (✉)
Faculty of Law, Goettingen University, Goettingen, Germany
e-mail: katrin.hoeffler@jura.uni-goettingen.de

M. Fenwick, S. Wrbka (eds.), *Legal Certainty in a Contemporary Context*,
DOI 10.1007/978-981-10-0114-7_10

account. Some types of offenders, resulting from particular attributions, have a long tradition. They are considered as simply existing among lawyers, judges and state's attorneys (just think about the classification of offenders introduced by *von Liszt:* "offenders by opportunity", "treatable offenders" "non-treatable offenders"). A systematic analysis of the historical contexts of existing types of offenders will help to answer the question whether classifying delinquent behavior is an appropriate way to deal with offenders and the consequences of delinquent behavior in our times.

Keywords Types of offenders • Lombroso • Franz von Liszt • Life course research

1 Introduction

The German penal law and its codified sanctions are today based on committed criminal acts, not on the criminals themselves. That means that someone will be punished for having committed a theft – but not for being a thief. So the starting point for punishing is human *behavior*, but not a human *being* or a *type of offender*.[1] Of course, this cannot be taken for granted. In 1939, Freisler, a Nazi-judge and former president of the highest Nazi-court during WW II, said: "The legislator simply put him (the offender) there – so that the judge may look at him and say: this subject deserves to be hanged".[2] Freisler strongly pushed the idea of focusing on the offender instead of the criminal act.

Being a certain type of offender has never been the only reason for punishment in the past. But still there is a long tradition of classifying offenders based on certain attributions in penal law as well as in criminology.

By systematically analyzing types of offenders in the past and today, this article will work out their role in penal law and criminology as well as the risks and benefits of using classificatory approaches in the context of penal sanctions.

2 Some Historical Remarks

2.1 von Liszt

Franz von Liszt, one of the most important German jurists in the past, proclaimed in 1882 that penal sanctions should not be backward-looking ("*quia peccatum est*") but reach out for the future ("*ne peccetur*").[3] In his opinion the punishment itself had absolute origins – but the way of punishing needed to be developed by

[1] Bockelmann (1957), p. 29.

[2] Freisler (1939), p. 1451.

[3] von Liszt (1883), p. 1.

considering new insights. Starting from the crime itself as a matter of fact, punishments should provide protection for the legal system and society by infringing the criminals' rights.[4] Therefore he strongly focused on the criminal person. Based on his idea that the purpose of punishing was deterrence, treating and securing, he developed three types of offenders: offenders who can and need to be treated; offenders who cannot be treated; and offenders who do not need to be treated.[5]

But we have to keep in mind: Von Liszt was convinced that criminality was caused both by disposition and environmental influences.[6]

2.2 *Lombroso's Concept: The Born Delinquent*

Years before von Liszt, Lombroso, an Italian criminal anthropologist and psychiatrist, presented his concept "*l'uomo delinquente*", the "born delinquent".[7] In his view, environmental influences such as social and economic conditions had little or even no influence at all on the question whether someone would become criminal or not. On the contrary individual dispositions would be much more important. Lombroso tried to prove his theory by defining a *homo delinquens* as an anthropological type and opposing this type to the *homo sapiens*. He then started looking at sculls of detainees and mental patients and felt confident of identifying essential variations between these two types of persons. By discovering atavistic differences he concluded that not only mental patients and delinquents but also "normal people" and delinquents showed crucial differences and that crimes of born delinquents were not based on their free will but determined by their disposition. His entire concept was based on the offender as a person, not on the crime committed.[8]

2.2.1 Interim Conclusion

Lombroso has not only been heavily criticized but his concept soon was rebutted. However, in the following years the dispute between his followers and the followers of the so called "French school", which went back to Lacassagne and Tarde,[9] who were convinced that only social factors would cause delinquency, could not be resolved. Von Liszt pursued his combined idea, incorporating both disposition and environmental influences.[10]

4 von Liszt (1883), p. 21.

5 von Liszt (1905), p. 170.

6 von Liszt (1905), p. 234.

7 Lombroso (1876).

8 Lombroso (1876).

9 See Meier (2007), § 2.

10 von Liszt (1905), p. 234.

3 Types of Offenders in Penal Law

But what about "the offender" in German penal law at the present moment? Although the current substantive law links punishments primarily to criminal acts and not to criminals, there do exist some categories of delinquents which are more or less obvious when having a closer look at single provisions .

Categorizations also exist in the German law of sanctions, which means the chapter of law that deals with the questions of which kind of punishment or treatment an offender should undergo. Here you can find genuine types of offenders as well as modified forms. However, the existing types of offenders must not be put on a level with the types that had existed during the Nazi-regime[11] or that *Lombroso* had in mind. And – unlike the substantive law – the law of sanctions *must* focus on the delinquent person in order to implement preventive strategies.

The question is how these different types and categories can be systemized. As they can be found on all kind of levels, in this analysis a new model will be developed which is composed and sorted by criminological, psychological and sociological features.

The base level consists of the delinquent's feelings,[12] characteristics[13] and environment. The second level addresses the internal state – knowledge, will and motivation. What is important to be aware of is that this inner state is mostly shaped by the characteristics of the first level. The delinquent's behavior can be located at the third level. This third level is the interface between the delinquent and criminal act. In contrast to everything that happens at level one and two, facts at level three are visible. And here comes the crucial point: we draw conclusions from what we see at level three and believe that we know what is happening at level one and two. But the link between the levels is not as straight as imagined. And it may not be forgotten that the conclusions drawn from this might be wrong.

4 Types of Offenders in Criminology

4.1 Criminological Concepts

4.1.1 General Remarks

Upon closer investigation of the different types of offenders in criminology, it becomes clear that certain types of offenders are especially interesting for criminological research, such as spree killers, sex offenders or stalkers. But all these types have several aspects in common which are examined in the following.

[11] Dahm (1940).

[12] See Wirtz (2014), p. 636.

[13] See Wirtz (2014), p. 442.

4.1.2 Life Course Research

Criminological life course research focuses on the personal and delinquent development of offenders during a long period of time (longitudinal studies). The theoretical background is formed by theories such as the interactional theory of delinquency by Thornberry (1987) or the theory of diverse socialization and social control by *Kaiser* (1996), which tries to explain crime as an event dependent on age or development. Another important theory to be mentioned in this context is the age-graded life-course theory by Sampson and Laub (1995). They emphasize that personal development does not happen continually but that trajectories and transitions can lead to turning points. Typical turning points such as marriage or employment can cause behavioral change.

To review their theoretical concepts Sampson and Laub have reexamined the Gluecks' longitudinal study of 1.000 men. In so doing the hypothesis of turning points has been confirmed. Moreover three types of offenders have been identified: persisters, who continue their criminal careers during adulthood, desisters, who quit, and offenders with zigzag criminal careers. A comparable study in Germany, led by Stelly and Thomas (2001), had similar results.

Farrington et al. (2006) and his colleagues have discovered that criminal careers usually take place between the age of 19 and 28. All other probands, even the persisters, showed decreasing social abnormalities corresponding with general social integration. Moffit[14] figured out that chronic offenders are rare whereas episodic youth delinquency is significantly more frequent.

All these studies curry to the following conclusion: there is no reliable way to identify future chronic offenders.[15] Typical criminal careers do exist but changes and dropouts remain possible at any time.

At this point a special method of producing anamnesis, diagnosis and prognosis, the so-called MIVEA, has to be mentioned. MIVEA – which can be translated as "method of comparing ideal-typical individual cases" – is based on a German longitudinal study with 200 arrested young offenders who have been compared to an equal number of non-offenders.[16] MIVEA intends to provide anamnesis, diagnosis and prognosis by exploring delinquents in three dimensions: a longitudinal (life course) dimension, a cross-section, situational dimension and a dimension of interdependence and value orientation.[17] The explored dimensions are finally compared to typically criminal behavior and non-delinquent behavior.[18] This does not mean that the explored person is *typed* but only that he or she is *compared* to ideal types. Similar procedures are constantly carried out in our brains to organize our – sometimes overwhelming – everyday life. We just do not realize

---

[14] Dunedin Study, most recently 2012, but ongoing.

[15] Haapanen (1990), p. 144; Bliesener (2012), p. 60.

[16] Göppinger (1985); Göppinger and Bock (2008); Bock (2013).

[17] See Schöch (2010), p. 95.

[18] Göppinger (1985).

it. Of course there is nothing wrong about doing so – what simply has to be underlined is this: ideal types open a spectrum where one might find the concrete case. But: they do not automatically fix it.

5 Classifications in other Sciences

Other sciences that are linked to criminology and penal law also work with certain classifications. Just think about the psychopathy checklist (revised) in forensic psychiatry developed by Hare (2003), an important tool to identify people with dissocial disorders. The checklist searches for certain symptoms, equates them with a specific number and adds them to a final score. Other comparable models, like the HCR-20[19] or the SVR 20,[20] focus on violent criminals or sex offenders. All these instruments are also used in Germany when it comes to prognosis-based decisions, for example the release of people from preventive detention that are to some extend non-treatable.

Again: These strategies are certainly a useful first approach. But as the before mentioned ideal types, they do not predefine offenders. Every judge, every decision maker in a penal procedure must recognize that typing an offender means limiting him to typical characteristics that might not be applicable in this individual case.

6 Summary

In sum, the risks of working with categorizations and types of offenders have to be pointed out and the question whether - and under which conditions - they might be useful should be answered.

6.1 Risk of Exclusion

Categorizations are based on the idea of attributing certain people to certain characteristics and vice versa. This gets dangerous as soon as it comes to general characteristics that do not leave any space for individual characters any more. This is because it bears the risk of excluding individuals just by attributing them to a certain category – in the beginning, exclusion might only take place in a linguistic manner, but it is not certain that linguistic exclusion is the end of the road.

---

[19] Webster et al. (1997).

[20] Webster et al. (1997).

6.2 Labeling

Categorizations are also comparable to labeling processes.[21] These processes are reflected by the affected individuals and may lead to what is called self-fulfilling prophecy. Getting back to the described multiple-level-model this means that in this regard labeling would form an additional fourth level at which the offender's reflexion would take place before he reacts in the world outside.

6.3 Type I Errors

As mentioned above, criminal careers cannot be predicted based on what is known so far. In addition the rate of type I errors among offenders who are considered to be extremely dangerous is very high.[22] Persisters do exist. But they are small in numbers and cannot be identified with certainty.[23] As a consequence categorizations such as "persister" or "non treatable offender" have to be left out in terms of law – not only, but especially in cases in which they are supposed to be the base for severe punishments. Otherwise turning points would be impossible.

6.4 Time Dimension

When talking about the pros and cons of classifying offenders the dimension of time has to be kept in mind. All the attributions discussed are static and do not allow any individual development. Life course research indicates that 99 % of all human beings change during their lifetime. This shows the need for a more flexible way of looking at offenders if turning points shall be not impossible.

6.5 Practical Needs

After all these actual or potential risks linked to the use of categorizations, the practical needs and benefits that make classifying approaches important in modern times still have to be highlightened. Penal law does not work without them. Individual treatments of offenders demand an examination of their personal and

[21] See Becker (1973); Lemert (1951, 1972).

[22] Alex (2013b), p. 171; Alex (2013a), p. 358; Höffler and Kaspar (2012), p. 110, p. 131; Walter (2014), p. 103.

[23] Nedopil and Stadtland (2007), p. 548.

behavioral structure.[24] However this must not lead to the fact that individual developments are consequently disregarded.

Another problem is that classifications take place without becoming conscious – which can cause stigmatization. The focus should be instead placed on the function of classifying approaches – resocialization. Recent research in psychology has discovered that appreciation towards detainees can create stronger self-confidence and raise chances of successful reintegration into society. Thus negative attributions have to be avoided.

Applying all this on the above mentioned level means that on an additional level five, generalized attributions to individuals must be brought to mind so that the consequences they might cause for the offenders can be considered. Exclusion is not allowed as this would have counter-productive effects on the process of resocialization. Classifications are *one* way to get closer to appropriate solutions when dealing with offenders and the search for the right treatment. They are not a panacea for the – presumably fortunately – unsolved problem that human behavior is individual, subject to change and hardly predictable.

7 Conclusion

It is important to know that human beings are able to change their habits and characters at any time in their lives. Not only criminology teaches us so. Denying this would also mean violating the human dignity of those who are considered as "non treatable offenders".[25] Even when it comes to dangerous criminals, we have to keep in mind: Change is always possible.

References

Alex M (2013a) Rückfälligkeit und langer Beobachtungszeitraum. NK 25(4): 350–361

Alex M (2013b) Nachträgliche Sicherungsverwahrung – ein rechtsstaatliches und kriminalpolitisches Debakel, 2nd edn. Felix, Holzkirchen/Obb

Becker HS (1973) Außenseiter, Zur Soziologie abweichenden Verhaltens. S. Fischer, Frankfurt a. M

Bliesener T (2012) Persistent juvenile offenders. In: Bliesener T, Beelmann A, Stemmler M (eds) Antisocial behavior and crime: contributions of developmental and evaluation research to prevention and intervention. Hogrefe, Cambridge, MA, pp 53–70

Bock M (2013) Kriminologie, 4th edn. Vahlen, München

Bockelmann P (1957) Strafrechtliche Untersuchungen. Verlag Otto Schwartz & Co, Göttingen

Dahm G (1940) Der Tätertyp im Strafrecht. Weicher, Leipzig

[24] Nedopil (1991), p. 259.

[25] See Margalit (1996), p. 127; Hörnle (2013), p. 102.

Farrington D, Coid JW, Harnett L, Jolliffe D, Soteriou N, Turner R, West DJ (2006) Criminal careers and life success: new findings from the Cambridge study in delinquent development. findings 281, Home Office, UK Gov. http://www.crim.cam.ac.uk/people/academic_research/david_farrington/hofind281.pdf. Accessed 20 Aug 2015
Freisler R (1939) Gedanken zur Verordnung gegen Volksschädlinge. Deutsche Justiz 1939:1450–1452
Göppinger H (1985) Angewandte Kriminologie. Springer, Berlin
Göppinger H, Bock M (eds) (2008) Kriminologie, 6th edn. C.H. Beck, München
Haapanen R (1990) Selective incapacitation and the serious offender. Springer, New York
Hare RD (2003) Manual for the revised psychopathy checklist, 2nd edn. Multi-Health Systems, Toronto
Höffler K, Kaspar J (2012) Warum das Abstandsgebot die Probleme der Sicherungsverwahrung nicht lösen kann. Zeitschrift für die gesamte Strafrechtswissenschaft 124:87–131
Hörnle T (2013) Warum sich das Würdekonzept Margalits zur Präzisierung von "Menschenwürde als geschütztes Rechtsgut" eignet. In: Hilgendorf E (ed) Menschenwürde und Demütigung: die Menschenwürdekonzeption Avishai Margalits. Nomos, Baden-Baden, pp 91–108
Kaiser G (1996) Kriminologie, 3rd edn. C.F. Müller, Heidelberg
Lemert E (1951) Social pathology. McGraw-Hill, New York
Lemert E (1972) Human deviance, social problems, and social control, 2nd edn. Prentice-Hall, Englewood Cliffs
Lombroso C (1876) L'uomo delinquente: studiato in rapporto all'antropologia, alla medicina legale ed alle discipline carcerarie. Hoepli, Milano
Margalit A (1996) The decent society, 1st edn. Harvard University Press, Cambridge, MA
Meier B-D (2007) Kriminologie, 3rd edn. C.H. Beck, München
Moffit T (most recently 2012, ongoing) The Dunedin multidisciplinary health & development study. http://dunedinstudy.otago.ac.nz/studies/assessment-phases. Accessed 20 Aug 2015
Nedopil N (1991) Tätertypen und Tatsituationen bei der Beurteilung von Aggressionsdelikten. In: Schütz H (ed) Medizinrecht – Psychopathologie – Rechtsmedizin: Diesseits und jenseits der Grenzen von Recht und Medizin; Festschrift für Günter Schewe. Springer, Berlin, pp 253–260
Nedopil N, Stadtland C (2007) Das Problem der falsch Positiven: Haben wir unsere prognostische Kompetenz seit 1966 verbessert? In: Lösel F, Bender D, Jehle J-M (eds) Kriminologie und wissensbasierte Kriminalpolitik. Entwicklungs- und Evaluationsforschung. Forum Verlag Bad Godesberg, Mönchengladbach, pp 541–550
Sampson R, Laub J (1995) Crime in the making. Harvard University Press, Cambridge, MA
Schöch H (2010) Schulenstreitfall. In: Kaiser G, Schöch H (eds) Kriminologie, Jugendstrafrecht, Strafvollzug, Juristischer Studienkurs, 7th edn. C.H. Beck, München, pp 1–26
Stelly W, Thomas J (2001) Einmal Verbrecher – Immer Verbrecher? Springer, Wiesbaden
Thornberry T (1987) Toward an interactional theory of delinquency. Criminology 25(4):863–892
Von Liszt F (1883) Der Zweckgedanke im Strafrecht. ZStW 3:1–47
Von Liszt F (1905) Die psychologischen Grundlagen der Kriminalpolitik, Strafrechtliche Aufsätze und Vorträge, Band 2: 1892–1904. Reprint 1970. De Gruyter, Berlin
Walter T (2014) "Beyond Mollath" – Strafrechtliche Unterbringung in der Psychiatrie. Zeitschrift für Rechtspolitik 47:103–106
Webster C, Douglas K, Eaves D, Hart S (1997) HCR-20: assessing the risk for violence (Version 2). Simon Fraser University, Burnaby
Wirtz MA (ed) (2014) Dorsch. Lexikon der Psychologie, 17th edn. Verlag Hans Huber, Bern

International Criminal Law as a Means to Fight the 'Hostes Humani Generis'? On the Dangers of the Concept of Enemy Criminal Law

Andreas Werkmeister

Contents

Abstract The exercise of state power in the form of criminal punishment directly impacts on personal liberty of living individuals. In the criminal law judges can ultimately decide to imprison the offender. Taking into account the severity of the consequences for the individual standard liberal principles require an especially strong justification and limitation.

The certainty of this liberal basis seems to be at question when it comes to International Criminal Law: Recently some scholars do not shape International Criminal Law as liberal criminal law but as an enemy criminal Law – in other words as a means to fight the *hostes humani generis* – the enemies of all mankind.

International Criminal Law is about the core crimes of the international community: war crimes, crimes against humanity, genocide and aggression. It has its modern roots in the war crimes tribunals in Nuremberg and Tokyo after the Second

This article is based on a speech given at the conference "Law and Behavior" hosted by Kyushu University in February 2013. Thanks are given to Professor Petra Wittig for her continuing support and to Professor Toshiyuki Kono and Professor Mark Fenwick of Kyushu University for the fruitful conference.

A. Werkmeister (✉)
Faculty of Law, Munich University, Munich, Germany
e-mail: Andreas.Werkmeister@jura.uni-muenchen.de

M. Fenwick, S. Wrbka (eds.), *Legal Certainty in a Contemporary Context*,
DOI 10.1007/978-981-10-0114-7_11

World War. In the 1990s the UN-Security Council established the International Criminal Tribunal for former Yugoslavia (ICTY) to prosecute core crimes committed on the territory of the former Yugoslavia during the ethnic conflicts, and the International Criminal Tribunal for Rwanda (ICTR) to prosecute the Rwandan Genocide. In 2002, the first permanent, treaty based, International Criminal Court was established. The ICC is based on an international treaty. The ICC generally has jurisdiction only over crimes committed on the territory of a state party or by a citizen of a state party. However if the UN Security Council refers a situation to the Court, it has jurisdiction over crimes regardless of the place of commission or the nationality of the perpetrator.

The following analysis wants to contribute to the theoretical basis of this emerging field of criminal law. It begins with the concept of an enemy criminal law which law professor Günther Jakobs developed in German criminal law. After that the main focus is on the possible dimensions such a conception could have in the context of International Criminal Law. Regarding the critique of enemy criminal law the author highlights the question whether the conception is at odds with the principle of human dignity.

Keywords International criminal law • Enemy criminal law • Purposes of punishment • Human dignity • Criminal law theory

1 Introduction

The International Criminal Court "is fighting impunity". The International Criminal Tribunal for former Yugoslavia described how "the torturer has become, like the pirate and the slave trader before him, *hostis humani generis*, an enemy of all mankind".[1] And also Hannah Arendt, when writing about Eichmann, averred that Israel was capturing an outlaw, a *hostis humani generis*.[2] These quotations indicate that in the political, philosophical and juridical discourse about International Criminal Law, the refrain of a fight against the enemies of all mankind is fairly common.

Vis-à-vis the universal enemy, the question whether and why international institutions have the right to punish individuals seems to be almost obsolete. Taking into account the cruelty of the core crimes – genocide, war crimes, crimes against humanity and aggression – this seems understandable, but is it also acceptable? The exercise of power in the form of criminal punishment directly impacts on the personal liberty of living individuals. In criminal law, judges can ultimately decide

[1] ICTY Judgment of 10 December 1998, Prosecutor vs. Furundzija, IT-95-17/1-T, no. 147 [citing a USA court in *Filartiga v. Pena-Irala*, 630 F. 2d 876, 2d Cir.1980.

[2] Arendt (1985, p. 451, 2011, p. 400).

to imprison the offender. Taking into account the severity of the consequences for the individual standard liberal principles require an especially strong justification and limitation. Recently in (international) criminal law theory some scholars however do not shape criminal law as liberal criminal law in that sense, but as enemy criminal law – in other words as a means to fight the *hostis humani generis* – the enemies of all mankind. It is against this backdrop that I will discuss the dangers of the conception of enemy criminal law in an international context.

My reflections about that topic will be structured in three parts. First, I will analyze and then criticize the implications of the concept of enemy criminal law. I will conclude with some remarks about the framework for an alternative conception of punishment in International Criminal Law.

2 Analysis of Enemy Criminal Law

2.1 Background Information

In German criminal law, law professor Günther Jakobs has made the most significant developments to the concept of an enemy criminal law.[3] The concept, as Jakobs propounded it, drew a distinction between a normal "criminal law for citizens or persons" and a "criminal law for enemies".[4] Whereas citizens or persons are fundamentally geared to the notion of right and wrong, Jakobs defined enemies as those who (presumably) have permanently abandoned the legal order.[5] As concrete examples for the category of enemy criminal law, Jakobs mentioned, *inter alia*, anti-terrorist legislation, the laws to fight organized crime and International Criminal Law.[6] However I do not want to refer especially to Jakobs' concept, it is just offered as one example of theorizing the enemy.

In enemy criminal law punishment has different, extreme purposes – the (deontologically structured) constraints such as the principle of guilt or core procedural rights of the defendant that define a liberal criminal law can be passed over. In the opinion of the theorists of the enemy criminal law the exclusion of the enemy is inevitable to guarantee the rule of law for the rest of the society.[7] In the context of an incompletely developed international society theorists think that International Criminal Law is a sort of enemy criminal law as long as no constituted world community exists.[8] As signs of enemy criminal law, theorists mention *inter alia* the position of International Criminal Law towards the principle of *nullum*

[3] Jakobs (2000, p. 47, 2004a, p. 88, b, p. 47–48, 2006, p. 289).

[4] Jakobs (2006), p. 293.

[5] Jakobs (2000), p. 52.

[6] Jakobs (2000), pp. 52 and 54.

[7] Jakobs (2000, p. 53, 2004a, p. 92); similar Pawlik (2008), p. 40.

[8] Jakobs (2004b), p. 47; Pawlik (2006), p. 291.

crimen, nulla poena sine lege, the conception of defenses and a greater political influence on juridical decisions.[9] Before I go a bit deeper into the discussion about the different conceptions of punishment in an international enemy criminal law, I will analyze the distinction that theorists draw between enemies and persons. This distinction is fundamental as it describes the line between two different legitimating narratives.[10]

2.2 *Persons and Enemies*

2.2.1 Enemies and the State of Nature

The idea is that the enemy has to be regarded as being excluded from any form of social contract or any concept of society. In other words: the enemy is not part of the society judging him.[11] For international criminal law, that means that the enemies (of all mankind) are excluded from world society. Rather, they are often associated with the state of nature as described by many theorists of the social contract.

The (universal) enemy of human rights, so deeply and visible demonstrates his dangerous or amoral capacities that he deprives himself of the condition of being a person. The enemy thus reduces himself to the state of nature, where legal personality supposedly does not exist as a notion of law.[12] In that sense the exclusion of the enemy is self-exclusion.[13] Pawlik describes this as a radicalization of a liberal paradigm.[14]

The idea of self-exclusion gains traction if we think of crimes in ethnic conflicts, where, for example, perpetrators of core crimes continue to deny any sense of community with those whom they have wronged.[15]

2.2.2 Hostis Humani Generis

To make the point that the human rights abuser is not only excluded from national societies there is also reference to the Roman notion of *hostis humani generis* (enemy of all mankind) which can be traced back to Cicero's philosophy: *Nam pirata non est ex preduellium numero definiturs, sed communis hostis omnium.*[16]

---

[9] Pawlik (2006), p. 291.

[10] Pawlik (2008), p. 40.

[11] Jakobs (2004a), p. 95.

[12] Jakobs (2004b), p. 44.

[13] Jakobs (2006), p. 293.

[14] Pawlik (2008), p. 38.

[15] Duff (2009), p. 91.

[16] Cicero (44 BC), III. 107.

This makes clear the global dimension of the exclusion of the perpetrators of core crimes. The *hostes humani generis* are seen as global outlaws: they stand outside every legal order.[17] In that sense, "the withdrawal of social protection from the wrongdoer is universal".[18] The concept was previously only used to describe the legal status of pirates, but theorists have also applied it to human rights abusers.[19]

2.3 *Purposes of Punishment*

2.3.1 Three Models of Enemy Criminal Law

With regards to the purposes of punishment in an international enemy criminal law one has to distinguish three different conceptions. The first one is motivated by preventive reasons, the second is motivated by vengeance and the third one is motivated by symbolism. Equally, one could distinguish three forms of enemies: a dangerous enemy, an amoral enemy and a defeated enemy. That of course exceeds the definition of enemy criminal law by Jakobs who only refers to the dangerous enemy.

2.3.2 Prevention

Regarding the preventive line of thought, the enemy is seen as the origin of a global danger which needs to be controlled.

There are those who argue that punishment in International Criminal Law does not reaffirm an existing legal order, but rather it is about the creation of a new one by use of coercive means.[20] Where international crimes are committed effective norms in reality either do not exist or they are corrupted.[21] The use of force against the enemy however could be justified as long as it helps to create a globally constituted order.[22]

Another line of thought rehearses to the categories of the law of war.[23] As the *hostis humani generis* has declared war against all mankind, all mankind must declare war against him.[24] In the name of all mankind an international court could

[17] Duff (2009), p. 81.

[18] Luban (2004), p. 140.

[19] Luban (2004), p. 140. It should be noted that the conception of "hostis humani generis" can be distinguished from the notion of "homo sacer" which is recently discussed in political philosophy especially by Agamben (2002) (see for an important analysis in the context of criminal law Wittig (2011)).

[20] Jakobs (2004a), p. 94.

[21] Jakobs (2000 p. 54, 2004a, p. 94).

[22] Jakobs (2004a), p. 95.

[23] Pawlik (2008), p. 40 in the context of terrorism.

[24] See Blackstone (1765–1769), p. 71.

punish the enemies as an act of warfare to eliminate the origin of a global danger. Theorists claim that these versions of enemy criminal law are still a somehow limited conception which only pleads for those acts that are necessary to defeat the dangerous enemy,[25] which thereby are also necessary to create a globally constituted order.

2.3.3 Vengeance

In the vengeance orientated line of thought the enemy is seen as an amoral individual against whose amoral deeds mankind must retaliate. "This great crime offends nature, so that the very earth cries out for vengeance".[26] The punitive actions of the international community are driven by a moral lust to punish.[27] Having committed atrocities the perpetrators become anyone's and everyone's legitimate enemies,[28] they were outlawed.[29] In other words, the enemies of all mankind are seen as legitimate objects of vigilante justice. In this context it is interesting to note that it was suggested that it might have been legitimate for a Jew to assassinate Eichmann,[30] or that the young Armenian who executed Talat – the man directly responsible for the Armenian genocide – has remained unpunished.[31] Punishment would be constructed as a final act of exclusion and could be communicated with the following words borrowed by Hannah Arendt: "We find that no one, that is, no member of the human race, can be expected to want to share the earth with you. This is the reason, and the only reason, you must hang".[32] According to some thinkers, institutionalized vengeance could be understood as being part of an evolutionary process possibly leading towards a constituted world order.[33]

2.3.4 Symbolism

The symbolic line of thought regards the perpetrator as defeated enemy who shall now once again be defeated in front of the judges.[34] It seems like the military defeated enemy is regarded as morally defeated "evil".[35] Therefore the perpetrator

---

[25] Pawlik (2008), p. 41.
[26] Yosal Rogat; cited in Arendt (2011), p. 401.
[27] Du Bois-Pedain (2011), p. 211.
[28] Luban (2004), p. 140.
[29] Arendt (1985), p. 451.
[30] Arendt (2011), p. 387; Luban (2004), p. 140.
[31] Zaffaroni (2009), p. 5.
[32] Arendt (2011), p. 404.
[33] Du Bois-Pedain (2011), p. 232.
[34] Fronza (2007), p. 123.
[35] Fiandaca (2009), p. 35; see also in the national context Neumann (2006), p. 305.

has to be punished at any price to give the military and moral defeat a counterpart in the communication system of law. The purpose of this symbolic process is not the determination of individual responsibility but rather is the creation and dissemination of a historical record of mass atrocities[36] or even is the international community recounting its own past "as a progress narrative from 'Nuremberg to The Hague', impunity to the Rule of Law".[37] The international court would not communicate something to the offender but it would communicate to the public via his punishment. In that context punishment is not seen as a medium of law but a medium to execute the political decision to "fight impunity".[38] It has the character of an educational theater in which international criminal justice demonstrates its moral supremacy over the defeated enemy.[39] Symbolic punishment thus could lead to the construction of an elusive and "self-congratulatory" international community out of the tragedy of others.[40]

3 Normative Critique of Enemy Criminal Law

3.1 Basics

Even though it is sometimes disputed the concept has the potential to go beyond a descriptive dimension: It does not only describe elements of enemy criminal law and argues that enemy criminal law is inevitable but it also implies that enemy criminal law is legitimate.[41] Regarding the critique of the enemy criminal law one therefore also has to distinguish between the description of elements of enemy criminal law in the existing International Criminal Law, the question of empirical inevitability and the question of normative legitimacy.

There might be – at least in the past – some evidence that the practice of International Criminal Law included elements of enemy criminal law. A possible example is the symbolic pathos with which a trail chamber of the ICTY delivered its judgment in the case of General Kristic: "In July 1995, General Kristic, you agreed to evil. This is why the Trial Chamber convicts you today and sentences you to 46 years in prison".[42] But of course one would have to analyze in depth whether such elements can also be observed in the practice of the ICC.

In any case one can cast doubt on whether the category of enemy criminal law is inevitable as its advocates think. On a theoretical level however it seems even more

[36] Fronza (2007), p. 123.
[37] Koskenniemi (2002), p. 34.
[38] Fronza (2007), p. 123.
[39] Fronza (2007), p. 123.
[40] Koskenniemi (2002), p. 34.
[41] See, e.g., Pawlik (2006), p. 291.
[42] ICTY press release no. 609 of 2 August 2001, available under www.icty.org/sid/7964.

important that even if enemy criminal law was inevitable there might be normative reasons, why we cannot legitimately accept such a conception as justified.[43] In my evaluation I will therefore focus on the normative legitimacy.

Of course enemy criminal law can be criticized in many other ways. It shifts for example the perspective from a criminal law of the crime ("Tatstrafrecht") towards a criminal law of the perpetrator ("Täterstrafrecht"). It is demonizing the criminal as enemy and thereby it further inflames the rhetoric of war. I want to focus my normative analysis on the question of whether the (international) enemy criminal law is at odds with the principle of human dignity because this principle can be seen as the normative core of liberal constraints of criminal law.

3.2 Violation of the Offenders' Dignity

There are of course many different conceptions of human dignity, emerging from different historical, philosophical or religious roots. In legal philosophy the work of Immanuel Kant is often seen as groundbreaking for any modern conception of dignity. Kant famously says in his Metaphysics of morals: Persons may never be treated simply as means but always at the same time as ends in themselves.[44] Law needs to address the individual not mere as object but as subject with a fundamental claim on his (intrinsic) worth.

From the Kantian perspective the "instrumentalization" of the individual seems to be most problematic with regards to international enemy criminal law. One could therefore argue that international enemy criminal law violates the principle of human dignity because it uses the offender not to reaffirm an existing legal situation but only to establish a "new legal order" or a "constituted world order" or to create an "elusive international community". The Kantian conception of human dignity however has various problematic consequences in this context. It is based on an idealistic conception of human dignity and is focusing on the abstract idea of human being's gift of reason. It is not taking into account the interests and needs of the vulnerable individuals.[45] Jakobs himself makes reference to Kant to support his conception: In his writing on the perpetual peace Kant says that the human being in the "state of nature" could be forced to accept constituted-legal conditions.[46] Of course Kant does not support any violation of human dignity. But Jakobs concludes that punishment to establish a "new legal order" by way of exclusion of the enemy is no violation of human dignity whereas it might not be legitimate to use the enemy as a means to deter others.[47]

[43] Greco (2010), p. 40.

[44] Kant (1797), Rechtslehre § 49 E I.

[45] See Werkmeister (2015), p. 89–117.

[46] Kant (1796).

[47] Jakobs (2004b), pp. 43–44.

However this leaves aside a crucial problem of enemy criminal law: namely the idea that "the withdrawal of social protection is universal",[48] the implication that the individual offenders are excluded from world society. Therefore their hard treatment cannot be part of any legitimating considerations within that community. The individual declared as enemy simply does not matter any longer. Following the logic of the enemy criminal law the excluded enemy especially cannot have any claim on his own behalf that the community should restrict its punitive power.[49] This aspect can directly be determined as a violation of human dignity[50] by integrating concrete communicative elements into the conception of human dignity itself.[51] From this perspective it is elementary to include the individual in an organized community as citizen.[52] The idea of humanity, which is central to international criminal law, commits us, to see each other as members of an inclusive community which is excluding no person.[53]

3.3 *Forfeiture of Human Dignity?*

However the theorists of enemy criminal law could try to argue that the offender reduced himself to the state of nature and therefore has forfeited his dignity.

Even if there was in the context of International Criminal Law no such thing as an entirely constituted world community or a worldwide social contract it does not seem logically imperative and adequate to derive such serious practical consequences as the forfeiture of human dignity with reference to the thinking model of the state of nature.

Furthermore, it can be seen as common core of human dignity that it is an absolute constraint, which cannot be forfeited.[54] This holds true not only for the Kantian tradition which refers to human being's gift of reason but also for newer conceptions which are supported in this analysis. In a communicative conception dignity can be seen as a common promise to refrain from acts that degrade others.[55] As a basis one can furthermore take into account the important work of Margalit.[56] He is rehearsing to men's capacity of reevaluating and changing one's life at any given moment.[57] Therefore dignity does get a future orientated element. If the

---

[48] Luban (2004), p. 140.

[49] Greco (2010), p. 47.

[50] See Margalit (1996), p. 108.

[51] See Habermas (2005), p. 98.

[52] See Habermas (2010), p. 350.

[53] Habermas (2005), p. 98.

[54] Neumann (1998), p. 154.

[55] Neumann (1998), p. 165.

[56] Margalit (1996).

[57] Margalit (1996), p. 70.

individual can change his life at any given moment one cannot forfeit ones dignity only because of crime committed in the past.[58]

It is also as an absolute value that human dignity is reflected as a founding principle or material concept in positive human rights law.[59] The preamble of the Covenant of Civil and Political Rights affirms that the provided rights "derive from the inherent dignity of the human person". Article 1 of the Universal Declaration of Human Rights stipulates that "all human beings are born [. . .] equal in dignity and rights". Although in a debate that goes beyond the existing positive law it is not enough to quote that law. However, these basic provisions form part of a discursive process and cannot be ignored when it comes to practical consequences.[60]

The international community would contradict itself in an (hypothetical) discourse about the justification of punishment if it is communicating to the offender that dignity does not exist in the normative universe of International Criminal Law: Under the ICC Statute "outrages upon personal dignity, in particular humiliating and degrading treatment" are punishable as a war crime.[61] It cannot refer to an inherent human dignity to establish punitive power but not stick to this concept when it comes to the criminal offender. It is therefore, in the interest of coherence, paramount that the established punitive power respects the dignity of the criminals it wants to address.

4 Concluding Thoughts

We can summarize that all versions of enemy criminal law violate the dignity of the offender and are therefore unacceptable as a legitimization of punishment in the international context. If we were limited in our rationalization of the practice of international punishment to rehearsing the semantics of enemies, we would have to abandon that practice. But before abandoning we should think of alternative conceptions. In the following I will only roughly sketch the limits that any such theory of punishment should accept.

If we can agree to take respect for human dignity as a central value for our account of punishment, then our normative theory should in the first place refer to the individual most concerned, that is the individual offender, who is – whatever he has done – worthy of being given adequate reasons for actions that affect him in a substantive way.[62] An individualistic line of thought is recently gaining ground in the field of public international law where a shift from a state-orientated to an individual-orientated international legal order was noticed.[63] The normative core of

[58] Werkmeister (2015), p. 111.

[59] Petersen (2012), para. 9.

[60] Neumann (2006), p. 313.

[61] Articles 8(2)(b)(xxi) and 8(2)(c)(ii) ICC Statute.

[62] Forst (2010), p. 734.

[63] Peters (2011), p. 411.

this approach seems to be expressed in the preamble of the Universal Declaration of Human Rights according to which the "[...] recognition of the inherent dignity and of the equal and inalienable rights of all members of the human family is the foundation of freedom, justice and peace in the world". An important consequence of an individualistic approach is that any legal order stipulating binding duties on individuals and not on states or other entities needs to give subjectivity and subjective rights to the individuals it wants to address.[64] From that perspective punishment could only be justified within an international community that respects basic individual legal positions of the offender as intrinsically justified.[65]

Only if this requirement is met the international community can for the purposes of International Criminal Law be understood as a partly constituted community, which has overcome the state of nature even though it cannot be regarded as a world state. It is at the end, an important function of every constitution to limit public authority by means of constituting principles, which are in particular, the basic rights of the citizens.[66]

In the positive law of the ICC Statute there might be an indication for a constitutional provision which ultimately limits the punitive power of the international community. According to Article 21(3) ICC Statute the application and interpretation of statutory law must be consistent with internationally recognized human rights. Many authors think that this article gives human rights a higher rank compared to other forms of applicable law.[67] And one can also find support to suggest that the motivation for this article was to protect the rights of the accused or sentenced criminal. In that sense one has to shape the argument as the polar opposite to that which underpins the enemy criminal law. Only by accepting that dignity and human rights of each individual, when confronted with supranational power, are not a legal fiction but rather a central value will the international community demonstrate and reaffirm its own status as partly-constituted normative community.

References

Agamben G (2002) Die Souveränität Macht und das nackte Leben, 1st edn. Suhrkamp, Frankfurt
Arendt H (1985) Hannah Arendt/Karl Jaspers: Briefwechsel 1926–1969. Piper, München
Arendt H (2011) Eichmann in Jerusalem: Ein Bericht von der Banalität des Bösen. Piper, München
Blackstone W (1765–1769) Commentaries on the Laws of England. https://www.avalon.law.yale.edu/18th_century/blackstone_bk4ch5.asp. Accessed 31 Aug 2015
Cicero MT (44 BC) De officiis

[64] Peters (2011), p. 411.

[65] See also Werle (2012), para. 143.

[66] Walter (2001), p. 196; see also Zaffaroni (2009), p. 8.

[67] Werle (2012), para. 206.

Du Bois-Pedain A (2011) Von der "moralischen Wollust des Strafens" oder: Strafgewalt ohne Staatsgewalt aus hegelianischer Sicht. In: von Hirsch A, Neumann U, Seelman K (eds) Strafe - Warum? Gegenwärtige Strafbegründungen im Lichte von Hegels Straftheorie. Nomos, Baden-Baden, pp 205–225

Duff A (2009) Can We Punish the Perpetrators of Atrocities? In: Brudholm T, Cushman T (eds) The Religious in Responses to Mass Atrocity: Interdisciplinary Perspectives. Cambridge University Press, New York, pp 79–104

Fiandaca G (2009) Feindstrafrecht, Eine Theorie, die vermieden werden muss, eine Realität, die nicht beseitigt werden kann. In: Vormbaum T (ed) Kritik des Feindstrafrechts. LIT, Berlin, pp 21–41

Forst R (2010) The Justification of Human Rights And The Basic Right to Justification: A Reflexive Approach. Ethics 120:711–740

Fronza E (2007) Feindstrafrecht und Internationale Strafgerichtsbarkeit. Journal der Juristischen Zeitgeschichte 2007:121–128

Greco L (2010) Feindstrafrecht. Nomos, Baden-Baden

Habermas J (2005) Die Zukunft der menschlichen Natur. Auf dem Weg zu einer liberalen Eugenik? Suhrkamp, Frankfurt

Habermas J (2010) Das Konzept der Menschenwürde und die realistische Utopie der Menschenrechte. Deutsche Zeitschrift für Philosophie 58:343–357

Jakobs G (2000) Das Selbstverständnis der Strafrechtswissenschaft vor den Herausforderungen der Gegenwart. In: Eser A, Hassemer W, Burkhardt B (eds) Die deutsche Strafrechtswissenschaft vor der Jahrtausendwende. C. H. Beck, München, pp 47–56

Jakobs G (2004a) Bürgerstrafrecht und Feindstrafrecht. Onlinezeitschrift für Höchstrichterliche Rechtsprechung zum Strafrecht 2004:88–95

Jakobs G (2004b) Staatliche Strafe: Bedeutung und Zweck. Ferdinand Schöningh, Paderborn

Jakobs G (2006) Feindstrafrecht? – Eine Untersuchung zu den Bedingungen von Rechtlichkeit. Onlinezeitschrift für Höchstrichterliche Rechtsprechung zum Strafrecht 2006:289–297

Kant I (1796) Zum ewigen Frieden. Ein philosophischer Entwurf. Friedrich Nicolovius, Königsberg

Kant I (1797) Die Metaphysik der Sitten. Friedrich Nicolovius, Königsberg

Koskenniemi M (2002) Between Impunity and Show Trials. Max Planck Yearb U N Law 6:1–35

Luban D (2004) A Theory of Crimes Against Humanity. Yale J Int Law 29:85–167

Margalit A (1996) The Decent Society. Harvard University Press, Cambridge

Neumann U (1998) Tyrannei der Würde, Argumentationstheoretische Erwägungen zum Menschenwürdeprinzip. Archiv für Rechts- und Sozialphilosophie 84:153–166

Neumann U (2006) Feindstrafrecht. In: Uwer T, Organisationsbüro der Strafverteidigervereinigungen (eds) "Bitte bewahren Sie Ruhe": Leben im Feindrechtsstaat. Schriftenreihe der Strafverteidigervereinigungen, Berlin, pp 299–314

Pawlik M (2006) Strafe oder Gefahrenbekämpfung? – Die Prinzipien des deutschen Internationalen Strafrechts vor dem Forum der Straftheorie. Zeitschrift für International Strafrechtsdogmatik 2006:274–292

Pawlik M (2008) Der Terrorist und sein Recht, Zur rechtstheoretischen Einordnung des modernen Terrorismus. C. H. Beck, München

Peters A (2011) Das subjektive internationale Recht. Jahrbuch des öffentlichen Rechts der Gegenwart 59:411–456

Petersen N (2012) Human Dignity, International Protection. In: Wolfrum R (ed) Max Planck Encyclopedia of Public International Law. Oxford University Press, Oxford, paragraphs 1–37

Walter C (2001) Constitutionalizing (Inter)national governance – possibilities for and limits to the development of an international constitutional law. Gerivian Yearb Int Law 44:170–201

Werkmeister A (2015) Straftheorien im Völkerstrafrecht. Nomos, Baden-Baden

Werle G (2012) Völkerstrafrecht, 3rd edn. Mohr Siebeck, Tübingen

Wittig P (2011) Die Herausforderung des liberalen Strafrechts durch die politische Philosophie Giorgio Agambens. In: Heinrich M, Jäger C, Schünemann B (eds) Festschrift für Claus Roxin zum 80. Geburtstag. Walter de Gruyter, Berlin, pp 113–129

Zaffaroni ER (2009) Can criminal law really contribute to the prevention of crimes against humanity. J Scand Stud Criminol Crime Prev 10:2–25

Index

M. Fenwick, S. Wrbka (eds.), *Legal Certainty in a Contemporary Context*,
DOI 10.1007/978-981-10-0114-7

MIX
Papier aus verantwortungsvollen Quellen
Paper from responsible sources
FSC® C105338

FSC
www.fsc.org

If you have any concerns about our products,
you can contact us on
ProductSafety@springernature.com

In case Publisher is established outside the EU,
the EU authorized representative is:
Springer Nature Customer Service Center GmbH
Europaplatz 3, 69115 Heidelberg, Germany

Printed by Libri Plureos GmbH
in Hamburg, Germany